Commercial Dispute Resolution

An ADR Practice Guide

Commercial Dispute Resolution

An ADR Practice Guide

Karl Mackie
Of Gray's Inn, Barrister
Chief Executive, CEDR
Special Professor in ADR
University of Birmingham

David Miles
Solicitor
Partner, Glovers

William Marsh
Solicitor
Director of Mediations, CEDR

Butterworths
London, Dublin, Edinburgh
1995

United Kingdom	Butterworths, a Division of Reed Elsevier (UK) Ltd, Halsbury House, 35 Chancery Lane, LONDON WC2A 1EL and 4 Hill Street, EDINBURGH EH2 3JZ
Australia	Butterworths, a Division of Reed International Books Australia Pty Ltd, CHATSWOOD, New South Wales
Canada	Butterworths Canada Ltd, MARKHAM, Ontario
Hong Kong	Butterworths Asia (Hong Kong), HONG KONG
India	Butterworths India, NEW DELHI
Ireland	Butterworth (Ireland) Ltd, DUBLIN
Malaysia	Malayan Law Journal Sdn Bhd, KUALA LUMPUR
New Zealand	Butterworths of New Zealand Ltd, WELLINGTON
Singapore	Butterworths Asia, SINGAPORE
South Africa	Butterworths Publishers (Pty) Ltd, DURBAN
USA	Lexis Law Publishing, CHARLOTTESVILLE, Virginia

A CIP Catalogue record for this book is available from the British Library.

Reprinted 1999

ISBN 0 406 02011 6

Typeset by Phoenix Photosetting, Chatham, Kent
Printed and bound in Great Britain by Antony Rowe Ltd, Chippenham, Wiltshire

Visit us at our website: http://www.butterworths.co.uk

Foreword

In recent years the adoption of alternative means of resolving disputes has increasingly been seen as the answer to what is often the slow, cumbersome, and expensive traditional litigation process. The pace of modern business life cannot tolerate the expense which such delay involves.

London has traditionally been pre-eminent in providing professional services, not only for this country but internationally. That this tradition is still flourishing is clear from the publication of this book on commercial dispute resolution. Professor Karl Mackie, David Miles and William Marsh have been pioneers in this field and this book seems set fair to provide an authoritative standard text. It covers the historical background, analyses thoroughly the entire process in all its variations, and gives clear, comprehensive advice on how ADR works, and how professionals and businessmen can use it.

Legal education and training must play an important part in the development of ADR. What lawyers should be engaged in is problem-solving, resolving disputes with the minimum of cost and trauma. As a former President of Columbia University once said: 'The idea that we should spend all our time in law school teaching people how to win instead of how to settle is very damaging.' Whilst I recognise that some welcome changes have been made, we need to shift the balance decisively from teaching litigation to teaching problem-solving. This book will be invaluable in enabling the legal profession to become thoroughly well-versed in dispute resolution and its applications to their clients' needs.

It will also be of great use to those involved in business and commerce, particularly with the growth in cross-border transactions where the potential for disputes is high.

I thoroughly recommend this book to all those who wish to inform themselves about ADR.

Lord Alexander of Weedon QC
November 1995

Preface

ADR or Alternative Dispute Resolution has its roots in the profound dissatisfaction of many litigants with the current litigation and arbitration systems, and the experience of many involved in conflict that 'there must be a better way'. In that sense, ADR is a response to perceived and real failings. It would be wrong, however, to conclude that the appeal of ADR lies solely or even mainly in the absence of better alternatives. In its own right, ADR has staked out new philosophical and practical ground, and challenged many of the traditional assumptions about conflict, not least in finding a structured way to redefine it as opportunity, and in bringing to its resolution a significantly greater degree of creativity. Its success in the commercial and civil arenas, which now seems assured, reflects its inherent strength of fundamental common sense. Whatever objections have been levelled at it, no one has seriously thought to challenge this feature, and it is this which ultimately will propel it into widespread use.

During the search for 'a better way' there have been many differing emphases, individuals and organisations claiming the foreground. This book concentrates on the commercial world and civil litigation, and on the United Kingdom in particular. However, the general background should not be forgotten. There have been important influences from techniques and practitioners in labour relations, family and community disputes, where mediation was in many ways a precursor to the 'discovery' of mediation and ADR in commercial disputes and civil litigation. Equally important is the international dimension, since ADR has established a basis for dispute resolution that crosses frontiers far more readily than traditional law or legal procedures. Finally it is our belief and experience that new approaches to dispute technology do not just 'happen', nor rest on solely intellectual discovery. Their promulgation takes dedication and commitment, and requires the establishment of a dispute resolution 'architecture' – recognised procedures, contract clauses, ADR organisations to act as training and referral bodies – in order to begin to compete with the well-established traditional systems.

The development of ADR merits comparison with the development of equity in the common law system. The potential for ADR to acquire such a level of prominence is already apparent on the international scene, although it has been slower to develop in the United Kingdom and continental Europe. In this book we have tried to avoid the temptation to continue writing in the vein of a marketing text although we have all been closely associated with the work of CEDR to alter the climate of opinion on ADR. Instead we seek to regard the field as sufficiently established to merit a serious practice manual for legal or other professional practitioners working with ADR. More extensive experience with this specialist area will no doubt force us to make many changes should we come to revise this work for a future edition. In particular, whilst we write with extensive experience of mediation, considerably less experience of the other ADR techniques is currently available. However, the fact that we can contemplate such a prospect is itself a sign that ADR is now an integral and established feature of the dispute resolution landscape.

Finally, we should not leave on a theoretical note. One of the joys for lawyers in ADR is the degree to which the process is challenging both at the intellectual and the personal level. We owe a debt of thanks to many people who have shared with us the 'trials' of ADR development, those who helped launch CEDR, the many members and supporters behind CEDR, and last but not least the families and secretaries who have helped us nurse this book into being.

Karl Mackie
David Miles
William Marsh
Fetter Lane
London
1995

Contents

Contents

Contents

Contents

CONTENTS

CHAPTER 1

ADR in Commercial Disputes and Civil Litigation

1.1 THE ROOTS OF ADR

There are many positive reasons for lawyers and other business advisers to adopt Alternative Dispute Resolution ('ADR') as a key technique in disputes. However it is more common (and historically more accurate) to identify enthusiasm for ADR as stemming from a negative source – experience of the delays, costs and inadequacies of the litigation process. UK lawyers initially tended to dismiss ADR as a phenomenon specific to the USA – where companies were more litigious, faced individual plaintiffs whose cases were funded by lawyers paid on contingency fees, or fought out disputes without the prospect of recovering most of their legal costs if they won. However by the late 1980s this approach had been superseded in the industrialised, common law world by a more considered recognition of the part ADR could play in overcoming some of the disadvantages of a highly expensive and often rigid adversarial system. The pace of business life picked up sharply through the 1960s into the 1980s driven by new technology, increasing domestic and global competition, and more active and critical consumers. The legal system had lagged behind these developments, and ADR (together with other attempts to reform the legal system) was one of the key responses which matched business concerns in the new environment. Now ADR is rapidly developing its own national institutions, experience, and theoretical and practical development, and at the same time offering a simpler cross-border dispute resolution approach.

The essential advantage of ADR is to extend the range of options on offer to businesses or litigants who find themselves in deadlocked negotiations with others. ADR offers many of the beneficial features of the legal system without some of its inherent disadvantages. It offers structured, formal third party intervention but without either a requirement to fit into the rigid routines of traditional litigation or the high risks of a legally binding judgment. Thus the 'Alternative' description given to this approach. However the label is frequently criticised as misleading, and with some justification. ADR techniques may have begun outside the system as an alternative to litigation or arbitration, but they can and frequently do complement or accompany such processes – indeed ADR can often be most powerful against the backcloth of existing litigation or arbitration. ADR can also be used for situations where litigation is not really a viable 'alternative' – for example if a family business wishes to develop more consensus on the future shape of the business and is struggling to do so by direct discussions between those concerned. As ADR theory has developed, stress has been laid on choosing techniques to match the needs of the dispute and the joint interests of the parties – thus 'Appropriate' dispute resolution is often canvassed as the alternative to 'Alternative'. 'Amicable' is also sometimes proposed, particularly in the construction industry, to stress the non-adversarial objectives of ADR. However the latter is less useful a term as many 'non-amicable' disputes can also be amenable to ADR.

In this book we seek to provide an introduction to and assessment of the major techniques and practices of ADR in commercial disputes so that professional advisers can recognise where they are appropriate and when and how they can be used.

The problems with litigation are well-recognised and need not be dwelt on for the purposes of this book. Apart from injunctive procedures or other means of rapid relief available in special cases, litigation usually involves parties in delay, costs, distraction from day-to-day management affairs, and loss of control of the conduct of the case once the case is 'handed over to the lawyers'. Systems differ in the degree to which parties may face particular difficulty in one or more of these areas, but they tend to recur for litigants in most jurisdictions. Most business associations can readily quote horror stories about efforts to achieve satisfactory 'justice' in a business dispute, particularly across national frontiers. It is this common international phenomenon that has encouraged ADR to spread around the globe. However the sense that the US system was a special case – more litigious, no rule on losers paying costs, contingency fees to allow for vaguely meritorious claims to be aired with jury verdicts to add to the unpredictability of the system – for a time allowed lawyers in other jurisdictions to classify ADR as a strictly American phenomenon. In fact most countries have evolved elements of ADR systems in order to escape some of the difficulties of litigation, but without labelling them as 'ADR' as such – duties on judges to conciliate, administrative tribunals, Ombudsman systems, family and labour conciliation agencies. However the promotion of the use of alternative remedies for the general class of civil and commercial actions, and the promotion of 'ADR' as a more systematic business and professional dispute discipline and technology, were a novel development.

The legal profession is often held responsible – usually by non-lawyers, although lawyers have been known to cite this as explanation to their clients of some of the delays – for the problems of the litigation system. The more cynical claim that lawyers control the system to generate revenue for themselves in the same way as other businesses seek to generate income from the ventures they control. More often, blame is attributed to the 'system', about which the average litigator or litigant can do little. Either way the result appears to be negative for the client. However the strength of ADR does not need to rest on the classic pastime of 'rubbishing' lawyers. It does seem reasonably universal that systems of 'justice' tend to increase delays and costs. Such systems require the judge to find the truth of the matter – by adversarial or inquisitiorial means, based on the evidence laid before the court. Since the parties have a great deal at stake in the decision reached, there is a natural tendency to produce the best arguments (and therefore advocates) and evidence, while doing the utmost to undermine the other side's arguments and evidence. It does not take much by way of imagination or the pressure of business interests to extend this dynamic by adding an element of gamesmanship where parties or their advisers seek to use procedural manoeuvres or ploys to wear down, undermine, or bankrupt the other side in the case. In turn such ploys confirm hostilites and intensify the stakes and emotions in the dispute and its outcome.

Quite apart from these procedural defects of the litigation process, there are substantive or jurisprudential questions which also need to be considered in estimating the downside of litigation. Outcomes in the common law system are determined by the evidence and arguments put before the court. The court's duty is therefore not to decide on grounds of truth or justice as such, nor on grounds of what makes for commercial sense or improved business relationships, but rather purely on the basis of the evidence and arguments put before it. Further, the question of whether circumstances have changed in the business fortunes of one or more parties is not a key issue. The judge's duty is to decide 'according to law' – principally an exercise of examining the past and allocating fault. Was there a contract? What were its terms? Was it breached? By whom? What damage flowed from breach? And so on.

While in substance the litigation process can be said to work tolerably well because of the good sense of the judges and parties to the system, it is not in itself a system guided by a creative search to establish problem-solving remedies or commercial solutions to difficult issues. Many

5

disputes are not black-and-white in character, yet judges must tend towards such assessment 'on the balance of probabilities'. In some cases this 'balance' may be tipped one way by rather narrow aspects of the case or strict legal principles. It is therefore not surprising that many litigants may feel aggrieved by 'losing'.

In addition to these apparent defects, the system also embodies a way of multiplying the cost, delay, uncertainty of outcome, and potential for gamesmanship through the levels of appeal which may be available depending on the nature of the case.

What about arbitration? Designed initially as a process whereby 'commercial men' determined their own disputes, it boasted some considerable advantages. Parties can agree procedures which simplify the hearing of the case, and which allow for the use of an arbitrator who possesses specific knowledge in a given technical area. In this way arbitration can be held to be 'the' alternative to litigation – the parties achieve a legally binding adjudication in accordance with law but without the full trappings of litigation, and without its publicity or its judges who may have no particular qualifications in the subject matter in dispute.

However many commentators – including many members of the arbitration community – feel that arbitration has been 'hijacked by lawyers', and that its promise has not been fulfilled. Arbitration cases may be equally procedurally complex and lengthy, and deliver a judgment equally (or more) uncertain than that of a court, while the parties are faced with the additional disadvantage of paying for the private arbitrator when the public judge is free. There are also arguments about whether arbitrators have proved to be sufficiently robust in the face of lawyers trained in the adversarial and over-complex procedures of the courts. Whatever the merits of this debate and its historical twists and turns, it must be said that arbitration remains intrinsically susceptible to these problems because it carries the essential character of litigation – a procedure designed to find for or against the parties on the basis of arguments or evidence presented to the judge.

It is important to note however that arbitration does still represent a viable 'alternative' to the full litigation procedure, principally in freeing the parties to determine their own procedure, elect their own judge, ensure the privacy of the proceedings, and avoid appeals to the courts in appropriate circumstances. Arbitration can therefore have significant advantages for some parties and should consequently be located towards one end of the spectrum of dispute resolution techniques, which stretch from negotiation through to litigation, very close to litigation in form and content. Its separate historical development in the United States has led it often to be often described there as an ADR technique. In the United Kingdom and elsewhere, arbitration is usually excluded from the range of ADR techniques. We have followed that convention in this book and arbitration is not discussed in detail.

1.2 WHAT IS ADR?

As a field which has evolved for different motives and with different emphases, there are many ways of defining ADR. The most common classification is to describe ADR as dispute resolution involving a structured process with third party intervention which does not lead to a legally binding outcome imposed on the parties. Mediation is the archetypal ADR process falling within this classification. While a useful rule of thumb, it is not a perfect definition. Some techniques outside litigation and normal arbitration can be useful in resolving disputes although they may be binding in certain forms – for example an Ombudsman may give decisions which can be binding on a commercial party but not on a consumer. Or a Disputes Panel can make an adjudication which is said to be legally binding on the parties if neither chooses to challenge it within a certain period of time. Or a labour arbitration may be treated by the parties as binding 'in honour only'. Are these ADR procedures?

Like many areas of social practice, definitions are not watertight or conclusive. What is more important is to recognise the intent behind the development of ADR; to avoid the rigidity and inflexibility of traditional procedures and institutions for resolving disputes, and focus instead on analysing what is appropriate to the parties in a particular case in order for them to achieve, with the least direct and indirect costs, a similar or better result than they might have achieved from a trial or an arbitration. Rather than classifying ADR as Alternative Dispute Resolution, we can therefore talk of Appropriate, Additional or Complementary dispute resolution. All of these expressions have been suggested as 'alternatives' to 'Alternative' Dispute Resolution, in order to escape the suggestion that alternative means that ADR is not quite 'mainstream'. Rather ADR should be a primary option for parties faced with a dispute.

These suggested substitute terms are also often proposed to emphasise another vital aspect of ADR. Alternative Dispute Resolution may be used as an alternative to litigation or arbitration. However it is equally widely used (perhaps most so in the early stages of its development) alongside arbitration or litigation proceedings to complement and improve settlement negotiations. Most civil litigation ends in out-of-court settlement, but usually late in the day 'at the courthouse door', 'on the steps of the court', or 'in the hall'. ADR can bring forward such settlements to save the parties some time and costs, and possibly to lead to a more satisfactory process for the parties and better, or at least different, outcomes than they might otherwise have achieved. We shall be considering below how this claim can be justified, and the circumstances necessary to achieve these results.

First we shall examine the spectrum of processes which can be classified under ADR.

1.3 THE DISPUTE RESOLUTION SPECTRUM

There are many ways of classifying dispute resolution. For the purposes of ADR it is useful to consider the degree to which the parties have control over the process and the outcome.

1.3.1 Unilateral action

At one end of the spectrum is unilateral action – the decision to escape or avoid the conflict, for example by a consumer not making or following up a complaint, or a company treating a failure to pay as a business loss. Unilateral action in a dispute can also be taken by other routes which are not intended to avoid a situation but to influence it in one's own favour. This could include the use of publicity, or economic leverage, or involving third parties. An extreme version of this would be issuing legal proceedings as a threat or as a way of utilising the state's powers. In all such unilateral action the protagonist has complete control over his actions.

1.3.2 Negotiation

Negotiation is the next most powerful method for a party in terms of their control of process, subject only to the constraints imposed by the other party (or their own constituents). This is the business method that can be said to be used more than any other, and with good cause – it is the most flexible, informal, and party-directed, closest to the parties' circumstances and control, and can be geared to each party's own concerns. Parties choose location, timing, agenda, subject matter, and participants. Further it need not be limited to the initial dispute topic – either party can introduce other items as trade-offs for an acceptable agreement.

The growth of interest in alternative dispute resolution has in turn fuelled and fed from a wider interest in the 'science' of negotiation: particularly because new theories of negotiation have emphasised the more extensive possibilities for joint gains and interest-based negotiations. It is also useful for us to look at negotiation in more detail in order to understand why third party methods may become necessary in disputes to resolve deadlock or even to make negotiations that are not deadlocked more efficient (see Chapter 2). A common first reaction from many lawyers or clients on hearing of the business-directed aims of ADR, is to claim that that is already what they attempt in their own negotiations or – 'I've been mediating all my life'.

1.3.3 Mediation and conciliation

Mediation is the third-party technique that is closest to negotiation. The process is also sometimes described as conciliation (see below for the distinction sometimes drawn between these two terms). Essentially mediation is a process of negotiation, but structured and influenced by the intervention of a neutral third party who seeks to assist the parties to reach an agreement that is acceptable to them. The mediator does not make an award, nor does he or she, in the purest form of mediation, evaluate party claims. However the dynamic of third party involvement can be much more subtle than this bald description suggests. The chapters on mediation articulate in more detail the role of the mediator.

For present purposes we can distinguish between *'facilitative'* mediation – where the mediator facilitates the parties' negotiation towards a settlement, and *'evaluative'* mediation – where the mediator assists the parties to settle their dispute by introducing a third party view of the merits of the case or of some of the issues between the parties. Such evaluation can be informal, or formally built into the process. Mediations conducted in the shadow of the court or arbitration will sometimes of necessity lean towards this style. Indeed in a number of legal systems a duty to mediate is imposed on the judge who will hear the case and the judge will tend to do so by giving the parties an indication of 'which way his mind is moving'.

In some forms, evaluative mediation may involve the third party issuing a recommendation, usually written, to the parties on how they should settle the case. Where evaluative mediation flows out of a less legal context (as in UK industrial relations mediation) recommendations may be based on what the mediator regards as reasonable terms of settlement. In more legalistic contexts, such recommendations will usually reflect a view of the merits. Finally in the most formal contexts (for example under some forms of construction contract or in court-annexed mediation in some US states), these recommendations may be used in further proceedings to bind the parties or to assess costs if a party fails to improve, in court, a level of award set out in the recommendation which they had not accepted.

A distinction between conciliation and mediation is sometimes drawn in terms of one process (usually mediation) leading to written recommendations or to more active intervention by the third party in terms of making settlement proposals, and the other excluding this option. We do not find this a useful distinction to adopt in this textbook and will henceforth refer only to mediation as encompassing both possibilities. The distinction is not only at times somewhat specious, but to complicate matters further, there is not an international consistency – sometimes mediation refers to the process where recommendations are made, sometimes conciliation. While we do not dwell on these distinctions in terminology, however, it is important to remember the substantive distinction in terms of process possibilities, and the need to check in unfamiliar contexts exactly which definitions a party or their advisors have in mind.

1.3.4 Evaluative processes

Mention of recommendations or opinion moves us on to third party processes where the parties have less control over the outcome than in facilitative mediation. Rather than involving a third party directly in the negotiation process parties may seek some form of neutral and independent evaluation – an expert opinion on the case or one of the issues, or a third party review of the case in terms of the likely outcome. This is sometimes described as 'early neutral evaluation' – a preliminary assessment of facts, evidence or legal merits designed to assist parties in avoiding unnecessary further stages in litigation, or at the very least to serve as a basis for further and fuller negotiations. Processes such as judicial appraisal also come within this definition.

Again, the categorisation is not watertight, since clearly a process such as evaluative mediation spans this divide between mediation and evaluative processes. It is however a useful starting point from which to assess various processes.

1.3.5 Adjudicative processes

Finally we enter the adjudicative range of the spectrum – ie where the processes culminate in some form of decision or judgment being delivered. Within this range there are many variations. For example, parties can contract for an expert to determine all the issues between them; or to determine certain facts, leaving the parties to negotiate the financial implications of those findings; or can invite an adjudication which does not have the exact features of arbitration (usually to avoid the finality of arbitration). The parties may agree to a 'non-binding' arbitration, or to an adjudication which will only become effective as an arbitral award if one party does not seek to challenge or appeal it within a certain specified time period or until completion of, say, a construction contract.

Also within the range of adjudicative processes lie the various Ombudsman or grievance resolution schemes, which have evolved as cost-effective and readily-identifiable systems of redress in many consumer sectors. Typically the industry involved (or government or public bodies under consumer pressure) adopts the approach as a collective solution to a gathering cloud of individual consumer grievances that threaten the reputation of the industry as a whole or add to pressure for statutory regulation of the industry. The detailed mechanisms of Ombudsman schemes vary, but often they combine the processes of neutral fact-finding, mediation and adjudication in various tiers through which consumers may pursue their complaints.

Finally, arbitration and litigation also lie within the range of adjudicative processes. At this end of the spectrum, party control of the process is very limited, although clearly more is available in arbitration than in litigation. Even in litigation, however, there may be elements of process choice – for example choice of forum, or whether to use a small claims procedure or the full court process.

1.3.6 Hybrid processes

It is important to note that because most ADR procedures are a function of contract and practical utility at the parties' choice, there is not the same rigidity as is imposed in litigation or arbitration. There is no *'White Book'* on mediation procedure nor indeed should there be, since much of its potency is derived from its inherent flexibility and freedom from regulations. Also, the categories mentioned above are merely the more common ADR choices. Since the whole thrust of ADR is to adopt the process most suited to the particular problem, it follows that numerous hybrid versions of the basic procedures exist. For example the mini-trial – a more formal evaluative mediation; or med-arb – mediation which switches to arbitration to resolve any outstanding issues from the mediation. Party control of ADR opens up these, and many more, possibilities.

1.4 WHY ADR WORKS

Despite the fact that the most common ADR techniques do not guarantee resolution of the dispute, most such techniques do in practice lead to a binding settlement. Further, ADR works where previous negotiations have failed – indeed it is usually not resorted to until negotiations reach deadlock. How does ADR achieve this result? It is important to understand the dynamic underlying ADR to understand why and when it is appropriate.

1.4.1 Creating a focus on settlement and a forum for settlement

ADR procedures tend to involve the parties coming together, lawyers and clients, with a view to achieving a settlement. This factor alone probably contributes 30-50% of mediation's success. When direct negotiations appear unproductive with parties locked into entrenched positions or into a serial litigation 'dance', it can be hard to achieve even the right context or environment for a negotiated outcome. ADR procedures create a *formal setting* to bring advisors and clients together for a serious attempt at resolving a problem.

In many cases this may be the first occasion in months (or even years) that the parties have jointly addressed the question of settlement. ADR intensifies, therefore, the *objective* of settlement.

Further, if negotiations have broken down or been conducted at arms-length between advisors or hostile parties, the ADR procedure may be the first occasion for some time, pre-trial, when the parties have a credible and serious forum in which to address issues and concerns as a *joint effort*. The credibility of the process is linked to the scale of acceptance of ADR, recognition of it by lawyers and clients and the extent to which courts, governments or private organisations attempt to integrate ADR into their mainstream practice (see below).

1.4.2 The neutral role

It is almost impossible properly to define the affect of a 'third party neutral' on the negotiating process. We look at the mediator's role in more detail in Chapter 7. Suffice it to say that the presence of a third party adds to the sense of forum, of 'objective' debate, of seriousness. Quite apart from the competences and quality of the neutral, the very presence of a third party creates a feeling of a 'hearing' rather than occasion for argument and unmoderated venting by each party and imposes a form of discipline or structure on the proceedings.

1.4.3 The structure of the process

ADR procedures have evolved over time to optimise the opportunities to achieve resolution. In mediation for instance, the structure of a joint meeting followed by private shuttle diplomacy helps contribute to the chance that the parties can make real progress on the case – first by 'hearing' each other, secondly by having a procedure in which they can communicate more fully and frankly through the third party neutral. In the mini-trial there is a formal setting, in which senior executives can take a more detached view of their subordinate manager's (and lawyer's) previous actions.

1.4.4 The qualities of the neutral

The parties are usually most sensitive to this aspect of ADR, neglecting the other elements that contribute to the dynamic underlying ADR. However the quality and competence of the neutral of course add an important element to the success of ADR. The effective neutral uses the other factors to achieve maximum impact in the process. Knowledge of the ADR process is of course vital, alongside abilities to generate trust and respect, to facilitate communications, to defuse emotions, and to evolve an effective 'neutral negotiator' strategy and tactics towards resolution.

1.5 'INSTITUTIONALISING' OR 'MAINSTREAMING' ADR

As awareness has developed of how ADR can complement arbitration and litigation and can help filter cases out of log-jammed court lists, there has been an increasing tendency to bring ADR 'into the mainstream'. This has been evident not only in the increasing use of ADR by lawyers and clients on an ad hoc basis, but also by its increasing inclusion in contracts or organisational policy guidelines, and most importantly in the integration of ADR into court practice.

The trend towards 'court-annexed' or 'court-referred' ADR has taken a number of forms. In the UK, to date the major development has been Practice Directions in the Commercial Court and High Court requiring pre-trial consideration of ADR by legal advisers. ACAS also has a statutory duty to seek to conciliate in industrial tribunal cases.

Globally, interesting variations are evident with most variety being found across the many US state courts. Amongst the key options being used are:

1. Early neutral evaluation

Case appraisal at an early stage of proceedings by a judge, master or senior attorney. This is designed to help the parties settle and may be combined with attempts at mediation, arbitration or litigation case management.

2. Case settlement conferences

Requirements for trial lawyers (possibly with clients) to meet formally in order to review the case and attempt to negotiate settlement.

3. Court-annexed mediation

A mediator is appointed by or at the instigation of the court to help the parties achieve a settlement.

4. Advisory arbitration

A court-appointed arbitrator makes an award which becomes binding if one party does not appeal it. There may be costs awards against parties who appeal from arbitration but fail to improve on the amount awarded.

5. Settlement weeks

Certain weeks are designated as weeks within which parties with cases filed can seek to mediate settlement. The courts write to litigants to give notice of the procedure.

6. Multi-door courthouse

The court may encourage litigants to have an initial meeting with an information office(r) which may guide the potential litigant into the most appropriate process – mediation, arbitration, small claims, case appraisal, case management or full trial.

7. *Judge-conciliators*

In certain parts of Europe and Asia judges themselves may be charged with a duty to settle cases where possible as part of standard litigation procedure.

All these attempts to make ADR 'mainstream' generate their own practical and theoretical issues that are worth bearing in mind but do not merit extensive discussion (yet) in a practitioner's guide aimed at the European professional. These issues are best left for debate in relation to the details of a particular scheme. Their existence and growth however confirm the trend internationally for ADR to become a successful and legitimate professional tool by which lawyers and other advisors can extend the services they offer their clients.

CONTENTS

CHAPTER 2

From Negotiation to ADR

2.1 ADR AND NEGOTIATION

Interest in ADR as a structured form of third party assistance to settlement has contributed to a growth in understanding of negotiation skills and practice. Why do direct negotiations often fail where third party mediation can succeed? What does mediation or ADR add to direct negotiations to make them more effective? Does ADR understanding improve negotiating performance?

Lawyers often latch on to the emphasis in ADR on achieving 'commercial settlements', in order to claim they have been practising ADR throughout their professional life, since their objective has always been to achieve a good settlement for their client. However this underestimates the differences between direct negotiations and third party assisted negotiations, even though good ADR builds on good negotiating practices.

To understand ADR's contribution, we therefore need to review how negotiation works and particularly how negotiations (and sometimes ADR) can fail. Indeed the starting point of ADR may be 'dispute diagnosis' – if we know why direct discussions are not making progress, we can develop ideas of what 'cure' to bring to the ailing negotiation. Equally, understanding what ADR adds and why it works may in turn help professionals rethink core negotiating strategies so that they can improve results from direct negotiations.

2.1.1 Disputes, negotiations, consensus-building

Before reviewing negotiating practice and ADR's curative role, we should not forget the broader context of disputes. Some 'disputes' can be said to follow a breakdown of existing commercial relations or an existing negotiation relationship – for example an argument over payment for goods or services that the purchaser claims were defective. Other disputes arise where the parties have not had a previous relationship, say a claim for breach of intellectual property rights. There may be attempts at negotiation in the latter type of case or an immediate initiation of legal proceedings. In either case, litigation is only one of the options open to the aggrieved party. They may attempt to exert pressure on the other side through the use of economic pressures (non-payment, boycotting purchases of other products by the offending company) or business contacts (an individual or business association that is a contact common to them both), or finally they may accept a business loss and walk away from the situation rather than choose the time, trouble and expense of legal proceedings.

ADR has been most developed for use in disputes which have entered or are likely to enter legal proceedings, having developed further as part of lawyers' litigation practice than it has in business management practices. However the other sectors should not be ignored as ADR can and does make a significant contribution in business disputes which have not entered litigation. Indeed these areas can represent major potential for 'practice development' amongst ADR practitioners, whether as neutrals or partisan advisors.

Finally, there are settings where negotiations may not be part of the standard practice or culture, albeit that behaviour by one party may cause grievance to others. Typical of these would be the development of consumer action groups protesting against world labour exploitation, environmental side-effects of business operations, or the inequity of a business practice in an industry in terms of its impact on small business suppliers or consumers. Another common example would be the impact on interest groups of decisions taken by public authorities or regulators, where there may even have been 'consultation' before a decision but where 'negotiation' seems an inappropriate term for a 'consult-decide-defend' sequence of public decision-making.

These approaches to decision-making, which frequently generate grievances rather than disputes or overt negotiations, have also begun to be influenced by ADR theory and practice. Consensual decision-making, involving all interest groups in the relevant community, may be more effective for long-term stability than unilateral decisions which lead to campaigns by disaffected interest groups attacking the source of the grievance and lobbying public bodies to amend what they regard as 'bad laws'.

The application of ADR to these fields tends to introduce negotiation practice or at least problem-solving committee approaches to decision-making practice. The approach in environmental and public policy contexts has become a growing field of ADR practice in the US in particular, although the field has grown under the label '*consensus building*' rather than ADR (since there may be no clear initial dispute). The most advanced legal recognition of this has occurred in the US where statute now enables regulatory agencies to draft regulations by negotiating processes and not only by traditional consultation methods. (To add to the terminological complexity, this branch of consensus-building is often described as 'reg-neg', regulatory negotiation.)

Normally, therefore, ADR intervention either builds on existing negotiations or generates a forum in which negotiations take place. For that reason it is important for ADR specialists to understand negotiating practices.

2.1.2 Bargaining in the shadow of the court

The issuing of legal proceedings has a significant impact on all negotiations, and in turn ADR, for three reasons.

First it sets *deadlines* to 'end' or 'process' the dispute. This may increase the pressure on parties to enter negotiations and certainly to conclude them before the risk of an adverse judgment, or significant cost if the case is allowed to proceed towards trial. There will often be a pressure on both parties to negotiate just before the stages of procedure which heighten costs or risks. The clearest of these stages is immediately pre-trial when most civil actions settle even without ADR.

Second it may alter the *agenda* of the negotiations, adding arguments over likely trial outcomes, costs of preparation, principles of law applicable, and perhaps publicity issues, to what may have been a dispute framed in other ways by the business parties. Indeed the fact that one party enters litigation at all may provide a justification to another party for breaking off negotiations or for raising the stakes by issuing a counter-claim or making a payment into court.

Finally, litigation usually introduces for most business parties a new '*principal-agent*' relationship. Negotiations become to some extent taken over by litigation specialists who bring to the case their own judgments and professional agendas of how to manage settlement opportunities or discussions in the phases leading up to trial. While professional theory suggests that the client takes all decisions, in practice many business users of litigation will defer to the advice of the professionals unless they are 'repeat players' such as insurance companies, used to dealing with a stream of litigation.

Litigation therefore is double-edged in its impact. It can speed up settlements or it can prolong the dispute. Overall however most forms of civil litigation at some stage induce settlement by negotiation between parties or their legal advisors.

2.1.3 ADR as 'alternative'

We see therefore that the concept of ADR in the context of an overview of 'disputes' is a more complex issue than normally considered. Equally its potential is richer if used effectively. We can summarise ADR's links to negotiating practice, as drawing on four strands.

1. ADR is often not an 'alternative' to court proceedings but an alternative to traditional settlement practice within those proceedings. For ADR to be justified, it should prove faster, cheaper or more 'effective' in its outcomes than those that can be achieved by the parties and their advisers working within a litigation system without ADR.

2. For disputes which have not entered litigation, ADR should provide an effective alternative to negotiations which would otherwise break down, or to disputes which would otherwise enter litigation without the adoption of ADR.

3. In some situations where negotiating practice is not a standard response, ADR approaches may assist in the development of negotiating structures and processes to help parties generate consensus on an issue.

4. In its most refined form, ADR may be promoted where it can be suggested that in some sense parties might achieve a 'better' or more efficient outcome through its use, even if they might anyway achieve some form of negotiated settlement without it.

In all these contexts negotiation practice is a central question.

To assist us to understand why ADR works where negotiations fail in the above senses, we outline below three core negotiating strategies and the problems they raise. The strategies are a little caricatured to emphasise their features, but still broadly accurate. We can then consider how to design and implement ADR to meet some of these problems.

2.2 NEGOTIATIONS: WHY THEY WORK, WHY THEY FAIL

2.2.1 Positional negotiating

The classic negotiating strategy, taught to managers and lawyers alike, can be described as '*positional*' negotiating. The assumption behind this in its elementary version is that negotiations are a competitive game in which you need to distrust or at least be wary of the other side and to outsmart them by following well-known tactics which strengthen your likelihood of coming away with a greater slice of the 'pie'. 'Positions' need to be carved out in advance or adhered to during negotiations in order to strengthen your hand.

The aim in positional negotiation is to maximise your outcome. Of course the other side will (unless naive negotiators) have their own positional framework worked out too. In negotiations the key is to be able to test how far up your claim ladder they will go, or even whether there is in the first place a possible overlap of negotiating positions – their bottom line is above your top line.

If there is an overlap in the bargaining range, the negotiators effectively compete to assert the strengths of their case and to undermine the other side's in order to come out 'higher' in the range towards their ideal. If it appears that there is a mismatch of expectations, deadlock may ensue and the parties are forced back to litigation or other means of bringing the other party back towards a 'realistic' position.

Typical tactics associated with positional negotiations are:

1. Preparation of the bargaining range chart

Good preparation of his own positions, as well as a good idea of the likely stance of the other party, helps a negotiator establish his own aspirations and provides a means of assessing the other side's likely expectations.

2. Aiming high

There is evidence that negotiators who start with high aspirations, tend to do better. So think through your best case and work from that. Strongly positional negotiators find ways of starting from 'extreme' positions.

3. Planning and pacing of concessions

In positional negotiating, you know movement from your high opening position is likely. But how much movement? When? How often? And how will this be presented? Positional negotiating theory has a number of maxims to help negotiators strengthen their outcomes. 'Move small, move slow', 'never give without getting', 'look for concessions of high value to them but low value to you'.

4. Concealing information

In a situation where negotiators are looking for means to exploit their advantages, giving the other side fuller information may expose your weak points. Therefore positional negotiators often withhold information which may make their side vulnerable to exploitation. A statement by an injured plaintiff's solicitor that 'my client does not want to have the stress of a trial' will only assist the insurance company defendant.

5. Making threats or bluffing

Threats and bluff are often associated with positional negotiating because of its competitive nature and the need to find means to dislodge other negotiators from the firm positions they have taken (as recommended in classic negotiating training).

6. Haggling

When a deal becomes more visible after the initial opening phases of positional negotiation, the challenge in the final phase of sewing up the deal is how to score the last few points within the negotiating range by haggling. 'Never give without getting' and 'move small, move slow' become intense features of the process as each side tries to raise/lower the final offer/demand.

7. Agreement somewhere near the middle of the bargaining range

The ritual dance of concession-giving in positional negotiating, means that parties often work inwards from opening positions and end up (in an evenly matched contest) somewhere near the middle between the real opening positions adopted. Both may come away feeling they have had a tough contest and extracted less than their ideal but perhaps above their worst-case 'bottom line' position.

2.2.2 Principled negotiating

The classic world of positional bargaining was turned upside down by the work of the Harvard Negotiating Project, crystallised in the international negotiating best-seller *Getting to Yes* by Roger Fisher and William

Ury (2nd edn, 1991), Penguin. Their theory of principled negotiating (sometimes referred to by other writers as problem-solving negotiating) suggests that one can avoid the gamesmanship and competitiveness inherent in positional bargaining. The key is to look for the settlement that will satisfy both sides' interests by keeping a clear sight on one's best alternative to a negotiated agreement (BATNA) and on options for mutual gain. While the goal of positional negotiating is 'victory', the goal of principled negotiating is 'a wise outcome reached efficiently'. Whereas negotiations become more difficult if both parties are trained in positional bargaining, negotiations become easier if both sides approach a negotiation with a principled negotiating style. There are four key principles which underlie this approach.

1. Separate the people from the problem

It is easy in competitive negotiations to mix up aggression over the issues with attacks on the people on the other side. Principled negotiating stresses the need to be 'hard on the problem, soft on the people', in other words to be firm in searching for ways of meeting one's interests while simultaneously working towards good relations with the other party. Good relations make it easier to solve problems.

2. Focus on interest, not positions

This is one of the essential differences between principled bargaining and positional bargaining. In the latter, the negotiator sets demands based on apparent interests, for example 'we need to claim £½m for this loss'. As a result negotiations become a process of digging in and justifying this position, with the other side countering it with rejection or a lower offer, making it difficult to move from these stated needs. In principled negotiation, the key question is 'Why – what are the interests that underlie such a demand?' By focusing on these instead, the way is opened to problem-solving, to more fluid discussions and opportunities to generate other options such as staggered payments, new contract arrangements, offers of free publicity or whatever else might be appropriate to meet the real needs of a party. The classic example quoted on this by Fisher and Ury is of the mother discovering two sisters arguing over an orange. When she asks each of them why they want the orange, one says she needs the peel to bake a cake at school, the other wants to eat the flesh. Both needs can be met when interests are discovered. With a purely positional approach, the assumption is that each should have half – in fact not fully meeting the interests of either. (Structured settle-

23

ments in personal injury litigation are a good example of the evolution of a legal remedy that often better meets both parties' interests than the traditional one-off lump sum.)

3. Invent options for mutual gain

By focusing on interests, it becomes easier to explore a range of ways of meeting the real needs of each party. However, the need to problem-solve, brainstorm, look for ways of 'expanding the pie' is also an explicit requirement of principled negotiating. Out of this can come 'Win-Win' opportunities, rather than the 'Win-Lose' or 'Lose-Lose' outcomes typical of positional bargaining. Negotiators are encouraged to search for a variety of options before deciding which option best meets the interests of the parties.

4. Insist on objective criteria

Part of the principled aspect of this approach to negotiating is a search for rational standards by which settlement terms can be judged, rather than the subjective demands made by negotiators. Is there an objective criterion against which to match an offer? (eg price paid by other customers, market rent, level set by legal precedents). 'Objective criteria' can be applied to *process* as well as *substantive factors*, as in the traditional ploy to prevent arguments between children cutting a cake – 'you slice, he chooses'.

2.2.3 Pragmatic negotiating

Principled negotiating theory has provided a very powerful counter-weight to the classic instruction manuals of the positional negotiator, and has helped reshape practice in many negotiation settings. However many experienced negotiators believe the real world of negotiating remains more complex and requires often a mix of positional and principled approaches. Even in those settings where it is possible to 'expand the pie' and search for 'Win-Win' options, at some stage it is necessary to slice any pie and allocate rewards. 'Claiming' then takes precedence over 'creating'.

Similarly, being open about one's interests and preferences may in some situations leave one vulnerable to exploitation by a competitive negotiator. The '*negotiator's dilemma*' is therefore inherent in the tension of balancing the openness needed for effective problem-solving in any situation, with the avoidance of misuse by the other side of information they have been given. Even a matter as basic as telling the other side how much you are really willing to settle for, will tend to preclude them from offering you more.

Skilful negotiating therefore requires a sense of balance in the approach adopted and an ability to lean towards one direction or another in any negotiation or stage of negotiation. Typically, principled negotiating practice is easier to adopt when the negotiations are with parties with whom there is a longer-term relationship or greater trust, whereas positional negotiating may come to the fore in one-off deals such as in claims for damages from a party with whom there is no intention of working again, or in a one-off sale of a house. Similarly certain types of negotiator are more inclined to competitive, positional practice and it can be risky or simply too difficult to try to change their approach towards a preferred practice of principled negotiating.

It is important however to stress caution to hardened positional negotiators who are inclined to dismiss principled approaches. Principled negotiating can be applied to one-off deals or with parties one distrusts, and can yield better, perhaps unexpected, results in many cases. Would-be mediators should in particular work hard at learning this approach as it underlies good mediation practice.

2.3 DESIGNING ADR TO OVERCOME BARRIERS TO SETTLEMENT

Having reviewed the negotiating and dispute contexts in which ADR can play a part we are now in better position to understand how and why ADR can add value to current negotiating practice. ADR interventions, whatever their exact design, always change in some way the dynamics of a negotiation or dispute. Bringing in a neutral third party itself adds a new figure to the equation, at least temporarily shifting the attention of the parties from their conflict and the personalities in it towards the contributions of the neutral and the third party procedure. Good ADR design is about using intelligent analysis or intuition to determine exactly when, how and why such neutral intervention should be applied, whether formulated in initial ADR contract clauses or as an ad hoc intervention in an existing conflict.

ADR design is not an exact science nor a universally-applicable fixed procedural remedy such as litigation. Rather it is often as much a question of people judgment and process analysis as of issue analysis. Hence the justified prevalence amongst ADR techniques of the flexible approach of mediation, which leaves individual mediators free to choose from a range of tactics and techniques to assist settlement in any particular case. However mediators also must assess within a mediation why previous negotiations have 'failed' and therefore decide which approaches will best help the parties reach a settlement that they can accept. We need therefore, to consider the underlying causes of settlement failures or 'inefficient' negotiations, and the implications of these for the design of ADR techniques or approaches.

2.3.1 Problems inherent in implementation of negotiating strategies

2.3.1.1 Positional negotiating

Of the three core approaches described in the last section, the one with perhaps the greatest inherent chance of breakdown is competitive or positional negotiating (borne out in an empirical study of US litigators by Gerald Williams). The essence of the 'game' is to hold out for maximum gain whatever the cost to the other side. Delay, insistence on positions, minimal concession-giving, refusal to acknowledge weaknesses or uncertainties in their case – all may work to their advantage in a certain percentage of cases. However in others, particularly where matched with competitive negotiators on the other side, this approach will grind negotiations to a halt as neither side will budge.

In litigation proceedings, this gamesmanship will take parties 'up to the tape' as they engage in bluff to force the other party to 'chicken out' before the next phase of risks and costs imposed by the adjudication system. Indeed one might argue that the strict theory behind 'adversarial' litigation procedure is premised on competitive negotiating – the object is to 'win' by presenting one's best case rather than for the adjudicator to investigate the truth or justice of the dispute, as more typically occurs in an inquisitorial approach. (This is to some extent a caricature of the systems but does reflect inherent tendencies found in them.)

At the extreme, competitive negotiators will be unable even to open up negotiations. A mere request to negotiate may be perceived by them as a sign of weakness. The result may be that no real negotiations take place until immediately before the threat of an imposed decision by the adjudicator, generating a settlement on the steps of the court which may force one side suddenly to offer a large concession. The problems of this approach are self-evident. Costs, delays and lack of trust are driven up to high levels. These tend to epitomise 'Lose-Lose' approaches where ultimately parties will martyr themselves (literally or to professional fees) rather than give way.

At its broadest level, the encouragement to use ADR represents a challenge to the ethos of adversarial negotiating practice by litigators and businesses. However even within the traditional culture, positional negotiators have some sense of a need to consider the costs of total intransigence.

Designing an ADR approach for this circumstance means finding ways to assist the parties to explore the bargaining range without loss of face. A contract clause requiring an ADR stage early in any dispute will help parties overcome a feeling that the suggestion of negotiations may undermine their claims. The absence of such a clause often makes it much more difficult for such negotiators to agree to ADR in the early stages of a case. ADR intervention becomes a delicate matter of indicating to all parties that an ADR procedure is a neutral effort to save all parties' costs rather than an indication of any side's unwillingness to fight on.

Mediators faced by parties locked in a competitive strategy are usually able to take some, but by no means all, of the gamesmanship out of the negotiation. To begin with they can channel communications and offers or counter-offers in a less competitive or confrontational way than the parties may have done. As shuttle diplomats, they can extend and defuse the 'haggling' stage, making it easier for parties to review offers without the antagonism or face-saving requirements generated in direct, face-to-face negotiations. For example parties will often reveal to a mediator that they are willing to move their position if the other side will move, or they may tell a mediator what they say they will *really* settle for, if the other side will also indicate their position. (Usually such offers will be given initially to the mediator in confidence so that the potential for useful further bargaining can be assessed – in other words, have the parties come close enough in their offers? Stating such an offer publicly to the other side would appear to compromise their overt claims.)

Most commercial mediations may go through a stage like this where a financial settlement is involved. Mediators therefore need to know how to work with positional bargainers and to know how to detect whether there might be further movement possible that has not yet been revealed to the mediator (competitive negotiators may use gamesmanship in mediation as well as elsewhere). Good mediators however should also explore the potential for principled negotiation, and for more creative options than positional negotiators would normally have reviewed.

2.3.1.2 Principled negotiating

Impasse between principled negotiators is likely to reflect inability to agree on the standards to apply as criteria for settlement terms, or failure to find adequate means of solving a problem in a way that meets their interests. In these circumstances, mediation is again the most likely ADR route to breaking a deadlock although in some cases a technical expert in a facilitative role may also help the parties towards a deal. Amongst the tactics a neutral could adopt would be to help the parties re-evaluate their commitment to standards for decision-making, to help the parties identify and collect information on the case relevant to sensible decision-making, to assist them with further efforts at brainstorming solutions, or to rework earlier options canvassed in negotiations to see if a new formula might be prompted to emerge to overcome the deadlock.

2.3.1.3 Pragmatic negotiating

In the real world mediators are rarely dealing with one of the pure models of positional or principled negotiating. Mediators will find they are working in most cases partly in the mode of problem-solvers, helping the parties search for options or appropriate standards to justify settlement terms, but also partly working with positions and attempts to secure the best slice of cake that the parties perceive to be available.

In each negotiating strategy, mediators also provide an independent review of the case, which may not be an expert or formal evaluation but rather a broad-brush or commonsense appraisal, with each party, of the strengths and weaknesses of their case. Mediators not only work through the issues relating to possible terms of settlement, but also consider with each party how they see their BATNA (Best Alternative to a Negotiated Agreement) as well as their WATNA (Worst Alternative to a Negotiated Agreement) as an aid to encouraging realism.

2.3.1.4 Unskilled negotiators and strategy mismatch

Negotiations can break down not only because of difficulties inherent in negotiating style but merely because negotiators lack basic skills or training in effective negotiating. Many professionals and managers learn their negotiating tactics by trial-and-error or by sitting beside the senior partner in a negotiating team. This may not equip them effectively for certain types of negotiations or for more complex or multi-party cases. Thus one can meet ineffective competitive negotiators who are all threats and bluster and unable to cope with subtler shades of bargaining; or with principled negotiators who have learned the value of 'reasonableness' but who interpret it to mean only the way they see the case.

A particular form of this occurs where there is a mismatch of strategies adopted by the parties to the negotiation. Neither side may be sufficiently flexible or perceptive to understand why they seem to be failing to communicate. This difficulty may be further exacerbated by difference of style and effectiveness between a party and its professional advisers. Mediation intervention can again work if the mediator creates a safer environment through which each side can explore their case more thoroughly and communicate more effectively. To achieve this a mediator needs to bring communication skills and mental flexibility to the negotiation.

2.3.2 Problems inherent in the structure of negotiations

2.3.2.1 Principal-agent tensions

Negotiations are not always conducted directly by the principals. They may have effectively handed the negotiating over to their professional advisors or may have left negotiations to someone lower down the corporate hierarchy. In some negotiations this can create a further likelihood of impasse or delayed settlement – the middle manager who does not want a realistic settlement as it may expose his own failings on a project; the litigation lawyer who is following a blinkered legal agenda. Incentives can also be different – there may be little direct financial incentive for opposing lawyers to settle a case early when they are on an hourly-billing system.

Mediation can assist in these cases by ensuring that those with decision-making authority are required to be present during a mediation and hence focusing on settlement options and the real costs of alternatives. Also during a mediation, a good mediator may identify the need to involve a more senior manager in discussions, or to review commercial settlement options as well as strict legal principles.

Similarly a mini-trial format explicitly creates a more formal mediation approach which calls on more senior managers to review and negotiate a case.

2.3.2.2 Litigation – bargaining context

The timing and nature of settlement discussions may be profoundly affected by the way the court system works in a particular jurisdiction – for example whether judges have a duty to conciliate or not; whether discovery is a formal part of procedure; how information is collected and assessed; the extent of delays in the courts, and so forth. Such variations are likely to impact on the timing of settlement discussions and on pressures to settle. The development of court-annexed ADR schemes are a result of the recognition that parties left to their own devices may not work up sufficient enthusiasm for ADR without court prompting.

2.3.2.3 Resistance to negotiations

Related to the above, the balance of power between parties may induce one party to delay settlement, for example to avoid immediate cash payments. ADR clauses, summary judgment procedures, more efficient litigation systems, interim payment requirements and other procedural features may also be necessary to generate movement towards negotiation or ADR by parties adopting such strategies.

Also, as discussed in the last chapter, there are occasions such as consumer and environment disputes or public policy-making procedures, where there has been no previous culture or practice of negotiated consensus. In these settings ADR specialists may perform a lobbying role, encouraging parties to adopt consensus-building approaches. Mediation or faciliation in this area can require more complex and protracted tactics and process judgments – how to identify interest groups who should be represented in negotiations, managing spokespersons and their constituency relations, the role of expert evidence and procedures for reaching consensus, the provision of neutral funding resources to assist groups without special funding, identifying effectively neutral 'host' organisations who can sponsor the process, and so on.

2.3.3 Problems inherent in the psychology of conflict

It is well established in common sense and in the psychological research on conflict that once parties begin to slide into conflict they act, perceive and think about their situation in ways that make it harder to settle the dispute. Ethnic, national and religious conflicts exemplify this phenomenon over centuries. Lawyers too, faced at a first interview by an angry client, may find it awkward to engage such clients in immediate discussions on the weaknesses of their case or on the advantage of settlement discussions with or without ADR.

The impact of conflict on parties is to reduce their interest in communicating openly with the other side. Communications that do take place are interpreted in ways that devalue offers made or actions taken to fit the hostile perception and judgments brought into the situation. A maxim of positional negotiation that reflects this is the phrase 'Always make them work hard for a concession' – concessions easily won are immediately devalued by the recipient. Thinking grows more rigid about the situation and team members who suggest concessions or the need to re-evaluate the situation can become outcasts and be regarded as betraying the true interests of the group.

Bringing such disputes to lawyers or litigation does not necessarily incorporate reason into the situation. The litigation itself, and the lawyers involved, may be used as an extension of the parties' search for weapons to defeat the other side rather than to resolve a dispute wisely – thus in part the criticism of lawyers' role in divorce proceedings.

Mediators have a particularly challenging task resolving such cases. A primary concern is to conduct themselves in a way that ensures that all sides continue to see them as truly neutral rather than partisan. In this way they can cautiously open up lines of communication, or can help a party move beyond recriminations into thoughts for the future, or can serve as a lightning rod on which each side can finally vent their long-held grievances and hostility with regard to the other party. Mediation thus provides emotionally a form of 'day in court' for such cases and can help release the pressure. Mediations in more complex versions of these cases will very often lead the parties towards new institutions, policies, practices, dispute resolution procedures or other approaches which help establish new structures for the future that can begin to turn party energies towards a more constructive future.

At a simpler level a concession offered via a mediation may appear to have been given more reluctantly (and hence appear more worth winning) than if a party offered it directly.

2.3.4 Judgments of risk

In addition to the psychology of conflict, the psychology of judgments made under risk or uncertainty is relevant to negotiation or mediation. Apparently, faced with a loss, more people will prefer to take a risk and gamble to recover their losses even if the predicted loss will be even higher, instead of cutting their losses. One form of this is the attitude to 'wasted costs' or the phenomenon of 'throwing good money after bad'. If I have spent £50,000 so far on litigation, I may prefer to spend another £100,000 to pursue the chance of succeeding at trial rather than waste the first £50,000 by withdrawing from the action – even though the fact that I have spent £50,000 has no real impact on the probability of success. Combined with a sense of anger at the other side this is a powerful cocktail to encourage continuation of the conflict rather than a realistic resolution.

Mediators may help parties and their advisors think through the risks more carefully. Or a party may be willing to accept a non-binding judgment from a credible third party as a way of finding a more tangible justification for cutting their losses earlier.

2.3.5 Genuine and good faith disagreements

Finally, barriers to settlement may arise from a genuine clash of judgments on the facts of a case or on the principles which should determine terms of settlement or the outcome, or other legal rights which apply. The psychology of conflict, however, suggests that all parties will justify their positions in such terms. Parties and their lawyers inevitably find ways to justify their reasoning as they grow involved in the clash of positions.

Mediation may help strip away some of the other barriers to settlement that are not at the core of the dispute, such as poor negotiating skills, communications, team member problems. However most mediators also have to deal with good faith disagreements. To some extent these can again be tackled by the mediator reviewing the case with each side, exploring strengths and weaknesses, and probing for settlement opportunities. Mediators can informally challenge existing stances and help parties re-assess their case.

However where there is a defined and critical issue that divides the parties, other ADR options may have to be considered. For instance the mediator may have to allow witnesses to be called and to question them so that the parties can reach a considered view on their credibility; or the mediator may have to give a formal evaluation of the merits of the issues dividing the parties (if qualified to do so) or call in an expert to give such a neutral appraisal. If it is clear from the start that there is a core disagreement along these lines, a mini-trial or neutral evaluation format may need to be adopted in preference, or supplementary, to mediation.

2.4 ADR ORGANISATIONS AND DISPUTE SYSTEMS DESIGN

In overcoming the various barriers to negotiated settlements it may be necessary to work to more than one design. While parties themselves or an appointed neutral may be quite capable of doing this, there are many disputes where an ADR organisation's input may be more powerful. For instance there may be an informal 'mediation' required even to get all parties to consider going to an ADR process, then a further phase refining and agreeing the details of procedure or the neutral(s) to be appointed. Involving the individual neutral from the beginning of this whole process has the advantage of allowing the parties to develop a relationship with, and trust in, the neutral. However it has the major disadvantage that in the sensitive early stages, a mediator's preference for certain aspects of procedure may sow seeds of distrust regarding the mediator's neutrality or effectiveness. Also early discussions on the design of the process may reveal the need for a different kind of neutral (in terms of skill, credibility or expertise) than first considered. Finally it is common experience amongst ADR organisations that parties locked in antagonistic conflicts find it initially difficult to agree on anything, least of all the name of a neutral. The fact that one side puts forward a name confirms the other side's presumption of bias!

The essential thrust in ADR design is to take gradual steps towards procedural agreements while retaining maximum flexibility. Attempts to impose too rigid a set of rules or dispute terms of reference can often merely serve in difficult cases to provide further grounds for argument amongst parties already deadlocked on the key substantive issues. Furthermore, too great an enthusiasm for design may end up with parties reinventing a litigation system.

It follows, then, that there is a substantial and critical process of diagnosis required of the dispute professional, at many stages during the life-cycle of a dispute. Only by identifying the barriers to settlement in a case can serious attempts then be made to overcome or circumvent them. In the absence of such a diagnosis the dispute must inevitably become harder to resolve.

It also follows that each different diagnosis will imply the need for a different remedy – or in procedural terms, that the different processes of negotiation, ADR, arbitration and litigation can all prove effective if applied at the right time. The key to the successful understanding and use of ADR techniques is to recognise what they contribute to a dispute, and then to be able to apply the right technique at the right time. Many of the problems of litigation arise not just from its inherent procedural flaws, but from the fact that it is treated as a universal procedural remedy and applied to cases for which it is sometimes highly appropriate and sometimes highly inappropriate. Or, to quote the old adage, 'if all you have is a hammer, everything will look like a nail.'

The diagnostic process is illustrated in the diagram on p35, showing some of the main barriers to settlement and suggesting ADR techniques which might be appropriate to handle them.

For many dispute professionals, the availability of such a wide range of dispute resolution techniques will be entirely new. Thus any previous diagnosis they have conducted will have been limited to making the choice between starting or continuing proceedings, and attempting direct

2.4 *From Negotiation to ADR*

settlement discussions. The extension of choice provided by ADR puts an onus on dispute professionals to approach all disputes with much closer diagnostic scrutiny, and a much more creative range of procedural options. Understanding these options and how best to implement them, are increasingly important for professionals who work in the context of negotiations and disputes management.

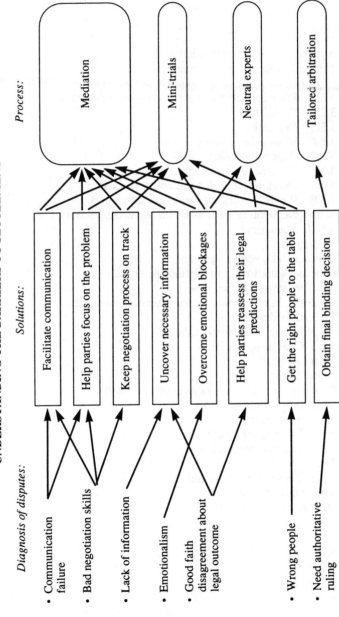

UNDERSTANDING THE BARRIERS TO SETTLEMENT[1]

Diagnosis of disputes: *Solutions:*   *Process:*

Solutions:
- Facilitate communication
- Help parties focus on the problem
- Keep negotiation process on track
- Uncover necessary information
- Overcome emotional blockages
- Help parties reassess their legal predictions
- Get the right people to the table
- Obtain final binding decision

Process:
- Mediation
- Mini-trials
- Neutral experts
- Tailored arbitration

Diagnosis of disputes:
- Communication failure
- Bad negotiation skills
- Lack of information
- Emotionalism
- Good faith disagreement about legal outcome
- Wrong people
- Need authoritative ruling

[1] This chart is derived from a chart developed by Professor Eric D Green, Boston University School of Law and J.A.M.S/ENDISPUTE, © 1993.

CONTENTS

CHAPTER 3

An Overview of the Dispute Resolution Landscape

3.1 APPROPRIATE DISPUTE RESOLUTION

As we suggested in Chapter 2, there are distinctive categories of ADR approach, each having different features and with something to offer to different cases, personalities and circumstances. The diagram at the end of Chapter 2 is a useful guide but only a very broad measure of how to select procedures appropriate to cases.

ADR processes are classified in broad terms only and can vary in their details and emphases according to the cultural or professional background of the neutral. Also many ADR specialists hold to the view that ADR processes should remain flexible to avoid the descent into the rules and rigidity that undermine the reputation and effectiveness of traditional litigation or arbitration. Finally many of these techniques have only been systematised in the last 10-15 years and their variations, strengths, terminology and procedures are still evolving with experience.

All that said, there is nevertheless a surprising unanimity of practice that has grown up around the globe. ADR has therefore become an especially useful technique for cross-border disputes when there is at least a minimum level of ADR awareness and training. Advisors should however check that terms and processes are being used in comparable ways if they are advising clients.

The ADR field offers an important array of options for selecting or crafting a dispute resolution forum that will be especially appropriate in overcoming barriers to settlement in any particular case.

To assist advisors we set out in this chapter the main techniques and features to be found in the landscape of dispute resolution, summarise the main practice points associated with these techniques and identify some of the variations commonly associated with the main techniques.

3.2   THE THREE PILLARS OF DISPUTE RESOLUTION

The major features in the dispute resolution landscape can be described, according to the central driving force of the method, as:

NEGOTIATION   MEDIATION   ADJUDICATION

3.3   NEGOTIATION

Interest in commercial ADR has emerged from, and fed back into, a growing literature on negotiating 'science' in the last 25 years. In particular theories of 'principled negotiating' – allied with a growing sense of the interdependence of business, consumer and public relationships – have stimulated the search for third-party ADR mechanisms which reduce the adversarialism and impasse-tendencies of many commercial or litigation negotiation practices.

While not strictly an ADR technique itself (as there is no third party intervention) negotiation underlies much ADR practice and negotiated outcomes are seen as the objective of the main ADR techniques. Many professionals who have been trained in ADR methods, report that the principles can often be used to improve their direct negotiating practice.

3.3.1   Principal variations on negotiation approaches

Some third party interventions occur at a much 'lower level' of intervention than formal mediation or adjudication, merely attempting to facilitate the parties' activity of formal direct negotiations.

3.3.2   Facilitation

Interventions by ADR organisations to suggest mediation frequently stimulate parties to re-open discussions and to reach their own directly negotiated settlements. Such techniques may be described as 'facilitation', 'good offices' (in diplomatic settings), or 'conciliation', although there tends to be little systematic theory in this sector of dispute resolution.

3.3.3   Evaluation

Parties may seek a third party view of aspects of their case which helps them to address their differences of understanding of the case.

A number of terms are used to cover this type of use of third parties which contributes to the parties' negotiating material but does not seek directly to influence negotiations as in mediation, nor to offer a binding judgment.

3.3.4 Neutral fact finding

This involves an investigation and report of what the facts of a case must have been in the view of a independent third party.

3.3.5 Expert appraisal

Where there is an issue of quality or professional assessment, an expert assessment can give a stronger foundation or 'objective criteria' for subsequent negotiations.

3.3.6 Early neutral evaluation

This is a technique used in certain US state courts where senior lawyers evaluate the likely outcomes of a case: this is expected to lead to more 'realistic' negotiations between the parties.

3.3.7 Executive amicable settlement procedure

Many commercial dispute clauses attempt to deal with the 'wrong people' problem in negotiation by moving the required negotiation stage to senior executive or director level before external dispute resolution. Not only is there then a broader corporate view taken of the problem, but in theory senior executives will be less personally involved in the personal antagonisms or career or budget sensitivities that may have afflicted middle managers dealing directly with the dispute.

3.3.8 Preventive dispute resolution techniques

Many of the ADR third party processes can be said to help settle disputes earlier and more informally and thereby prevent dispute 'escalation'. However thought should be given also to many of the 'better management' approaches which can either reduce conflict or handle it more constructively to prevent a formal 'dispute' emerging. Amongst such systems could be included:

- Training in *principled negotiation* (positional negotiating training may increase the rate of conflicts over time!).

- *Team working* education/consultancy (how to collaborate better, solve problems in group working, etc).

- Application of *quality management systems* to customer or supplier relations ('Total Quality Management' or ISO9000).

- *Partnering* (a term used in the construction industry to refer to team working arrangements between the various parties to a construction project, with early joint education, regular meetings, fund for contingencies and other mutual support systems).

- *Reg–Neg* (a term used in the USA to refer to an approach used by administrative agencies of negotiating new regulations with interest groups rather than the traditional public administration approach of 'consult-publish-defend-amend').

A number of these efforts at improving direct negotiations also involve third parties as educators or consultants. More formal third party approaches to the same end might include:

- *Dispute resolution advisor* (a process involving the presence of a disputes assessor and facilitator with a standing role on a major construction contract).

- *Advisory mediation* (a term used by the industrial relations agency ACAS, in the UK, to refer to the appointment of a facilitator-mediator to work with an employer and employees to devise agreed negotiating or employment procedures that will enhance relations between the parties).

3.3.9 Negotiating skills and third party intervention

Advisors or neutrals working at the level of more formal third party resolution approaches should at least be aware of the range of techniques to facilitate better direct negotiations, even if not themselves skilled in them. In their role as, say, mediators, not only must they have a thorough sense of how negotiations succeed or fail, but they may also wish to draw on some of these techniques during mediation (for example, expert appraisal) in order to overcome obstacles or to propose methods of future working relations between the parties.

3.3.10 Managers

Equally managers should be better informed of the dispute landscape to enhance their own toolbox of techniques. In particular managers and advisors should have an ability to recognise when to initiate third party intervention before conflicts escalate. Mediation and other approaches are often only employed 'in extremis' or once arbitration and litigation also become options.

In fact many public and private sector negotiations will have dragged on or festered for months or years before this stage. Alert managers should be able to trigger constructive intervention before this level of aggravation and inefficiency is reached.

3.4 MEDIATION

Mediation is the central, most frequently adopted ADR technique around the globe. We therefore outline mediation practice in some detail later in this book and merely summarise it here with the major procedural variations found in mediation practice.

3.5 COMMERCIAL MEDIATION PRACTICE

Mediation involves the appointment or intervention of a neutral third party who seeks to help the parties in dispute reach a negotiated agreement. The mediator has no power to adjudicate or impose an award. Typically mediations in commercial disputes or civil litigation are conducted on a confidential basis and 'without prejudice' to other legal rights or remedies of the parties unless they reach an agreement to settle their differences.

A typical commercial mediation goes through four basic stages:

(i) Preparation

This includes agreement to mediate, appointment of mediator, and submission of documents to the mediator and other party(ies).

(ii) Opening joint session

Introduction by mediator, brief presentations on their case by each party.

41

(iii) Private meetings or 'caucuses'

'Shuttle diplomacy' process by mediator seeking to clarify privately with each side the nature of the case and their settlement interests, and to attempt to help the parties design an acceptable settlement between them.

(iv) Termination

Joint meeting to agree or sign terms of agreement (usually legally binding) or to terminate mediation process.

3.6 PRINCIPAL VARIATIONS IN MEDIATION PROCEDURE

3.6.1 Joint/private meetings

Mediators often differ in how much they rely on joint meetings or on private meetings or on how flexible they are in mixing the two. In UK family mediation for instance private meetings are rare. In public policy or environmental mediation, meetings are sometimes held in public. Confidentiality is the norm in commercial mediation. This refers both to confidentiality as between all parties in the mediation and third parties outside the mediation: and confidentiality of communication between mediator and a party in a caucus session unless the mediator is authorised by that party to disclose information to the other party(ies).

3.6.2 Facilitative mediation vs evaluative mediation

Mediators also differ in how they see their role as facilitating negotiations. The 'classic' view of mediation was that mediators avoided opinions or judgments and merely assisted parties to clarify their communications, interests and priorities. To do otherwise was to compromise their role. There has however been increasing recognition in commercial work that mediators may also assist the momentum to settlement by going beyond this into a more evaluative or activist approach. This may involve mediators challenging the parties' assessments by way of common-sense 'reality-testing' of parties' perceptions or acting as 'devil's advocate' or even by way of expert appraisal of the parties' cases. Some mediation agreements formally specify that the mediator may give some form of appraisal during or at the end of a mediation.

As we shall see in our later discussion of mediation practice, the above distinction is often too simplistic to catch the richness of mediation practice. However it can be a useful framework for parties in terms of choosing an appropriate mediator (known to be facilitative or evaluative in style) or deciding what they need from mediation to overcome obstacles to settlement between them and the other party (or between them and their own advisors).

3.6.3 Conciliation

This term has traditionally been used to refer to a process similar to mediation but distinguished from it by virtue of the fact that in one of the processes the third party is more activist in putting forward terms of settlement or an opinion on the case (for example the UK's statutory industrial relations agency, ACAS, distinguishes conciliation from mediation, where third parties issue a written recommendation). Unfortunately there is no international unanimity on which term is regarded as the more activist. Increasingly the term 'mediation' has been adopted as the generic term for third party facilitation in commercial disputes whether or not the third party is activist. We therefore do not use the term conciliation again in this book.

3.6.4 Mini-trial/executive tribunal

This is a more formal type of mediation practice and associated clearly with an evaluative approach. Formal, but abbreviated, presentations of their best legal case are made by each party to a panel of senior directors from each company with (usually) a neutral chairman to manage proceedings. After the presentations the executives adjourn and attempt to negotiate a settlement on the basis of the overview of the case they have heard. The neutral adviser is there to facilitate negotiations or to mediate, if the parties' negotiations stall. The neutral adviser may give a view on the likely outcome if the case went to trial or arbitration in order to facilitate settlement.

The Executive Tribunal is a powerful approach for major corporate disputes and is therefore reviewed more extensively in Chapter 9. It is not used as frequently as mediation however.

3.6.5 Consensus-building

This expression is often used as a substitute for mediation (or facilitation) in environmental or public policy dispute resolution approaches –

for example over planning the location of a new chemicals factory in a community or setting new environmental standards.

It refers usually to a more protracted process where a third party consultant seeks to identify the various interest groups connected with a development, and to facilitate consultation, discussions or negotiation between them. The aim is thereby to achieve a 'wiser' and more consensual outcome than in the normal public policy approach of either lack of adequate consultation or consultation without full participative decision-making. It helps to combat the NIMBY phenomenon ('not in my back yard') on the one hand and on the other hand the defective political process of decision-making that can be summed up as 'Consult–Announce Decision–Defend Decision–Amend Decision' (as those consulted realise the decision does not meet their interests and battle politically or through the courts to amend it). Consensus-building approaches have been most widely used in the USA and Australia and fall within variations on assisted negotiation as well as mediation.

3.6.6 Med-arb

Sometimes parties wish, for reasons of cost or time, to avoid the possibility that a mediation may not achieve final determination of a dispute if the parties fail to agree. They therefore contract to give the mediator power to 'convert' to an arbitrator and make a legally binding award, in the event that mediated negotiations do not lead to settlement of all issues. (A variation on this promoted by the American Arbitration Association is MEDALOA, mediation followed by 'last-offer arbitration' – see below for a description of this form of arbitration.)

This technique, called med-arb, is not widely used but interest in it is growing, for example in the US construction industry, and some jurisdictions have legislated to deal with the potential legal problems for arbitrations conducted under these circumstances.

The main theoretical arguments against med-arb are two-fold. First, the process appears to run counter to traditional rules of natural justice that a party should hear the evidence and arguments put forward against it and have a chance of reply. Mediation caucus meetings undermine this principle unless the mediator is allowed to reveal everything said in private caucus or alternatively can be held to have excluded any unilateral information from his mind in handing down an arbitral award.

On the other hand, med-arb also theoretically undermines the power of the mediation process because each party may feel reluctant to be as open with the mediator on their offers or vulnerabilities, if there is a chance that the mediator will become an arbitrator of their case.

Despite these major theoretical drawbacks, there appears to be growing support internationally for med-arb practice. Parties are said to value the more 'robust' commercial approach involved, and there are many cases where little really sensitive information is revealed in caucus sessions. However it is as yet not common in the UK and parties should be warned of the theoretical disadvantages and perhaps if they do use it should afford themselves a contractual opportunity to opt out of the arbitration phase at the end of the mediation (although this again undermines the robustness of the process).

3.7 ADJUDICATION

In determining the appropriate dispute resolution method to adopt, consideration must of course be given to the option where a third party hands down a judgment. Some of these techniques are associated with the discipline of ADR, although the traditional alternatives of litigation or arbitration are commonly held to be outside ADR, indeed partly the reason for ADR's development (in the USA it has been more common to regard arbitration as one of the new 'alternatives').

It is also important to stress the difference between adjudication (as a conceptual category of techniques involving imposed decisions, as used in this paragraph) and adjudication (as a specific ADR process, dealt with in paragraph 3.8.5 and Chapter 10 below).

Adjudications by definition imply non-negotiated outcomes, decisions handed down by a third party, on a Win-Lose basis. However aspects of these assumptions may be modified by party control of parts of the procedure, or by way of substantive legal principles (for example as the concept of 'contributory negligence' reduces the damages awarded to a plaintiff).

3.8 PRINCIPAL VARIATIONS IN ADJUDICATION PROCEDURE

3.8.1 Litigation and court trial

In common law systems, the civil litigation system has increasingly become a settlement system. Typically over 90% of writs issued do not proceed to trial, and even more cases fail to proceed to judgment. However ADR has been perceived as a valuable complement to this system not just because it helps prevent some cases going to trial, but more widely because it is said to speed up the process of settlement and thereby reduce the cost and management time allotted to litigation. Finally, the litigation system is geared to a specific range of legal principles, legal remedies and historical analysis of cases. ADR techniques offer potentially more flexible, creative and future-oriented outcomes.

It will of course frequently be necessary to decide that litigation is the appropriate route to take either in general or as an initial step to:

- establish a legal precedent

- make a public statement on the importance of an industry practice

- achieve summary judgment

- enforce judgments/awards/agreements

- compel and examine documents/witnesses

- obtain rapid injunctive relief

- force another party into settlement discussions or into judgment

Also relevant to the choice of litigation as a primary approach would be questions which can vary substantially according to the case and jurisdiction involved:

- speed of getting to trial

- costs involved

- likely recovery of costs

- likely recovery on judgment

- quality of judgment

- management time and energy used

- publicity value/damage

Four other major aspects of litigation practice should be noted in considering dispute resolution options:

(i) common law jurisdictions (and civil law perhaps to a lesser extent) are increasingly seeking ways to improve the efficiency, speed and price of access to the courts. This will have some impact on the use of alternatives;

(ii) as part of these attempts at reform, courts and legal systems are increasingly adopting active case management systems;

(iii) also as part of these reforms, courts are increasingly attempting to integrate ADR methods into court procedures by way of 'court-annexed ADR' or 'multi-door courthouse' concepts. Thus lawyers and parties may be advised to consider ADR, or informed of the options, or directed to use it subject to rights of opt-out or costs sanctions;

(iv) in several civil law countries and other jurisdictions (for example Japan) judges have a duty to seek to bring the parties to a pre-trial settlement. The nature and thoroughness of this 'conciliation' duty varies but will often involve the judge giving the parties a preliminary view of the case rather than employing facilitative mediation.

3.8.2 Arbitration

Arbitration has been the traditional private alternative to court, with parties contracting to be bound by a third party private award that is normally legally enforceable as a court judgment.

As a dispute resolution approach, the advantages claimed for arbitration are that it is private, that parties can tailor procedures and timescales to their needs rather than be bound by fixed court systems, and finally that the parties can choose their 'judge' who may have specialist background knowledge to bring to bear on the case.

Over the years however arbitration's reputation has suffered, mainly because it has become increasingly costly and proceedings have extended as much as court timetables. Also parties are not always as free to choose their arbitrator as they would wish, and often become upset on 'losing' their case 'unjustifiably' due to what they consider a poor-quality arbitrator, as compared with judicial standards.

A vigorous debate has taken place in the arbitration world on how to address such issues. We do not consider these further as we take arbitration to be outside our discussion of ADR.

3.8.3 Tailored arbitration

A number of variations of arbitration are worth noting in terms of the landscape of dispute resolution.

3.8.3.1 'Documents only'

A simplified arbitration based solely on documentary, and not oral, evidence or argument, used in a number of consumer arbitration schemes.

3.8.3 An Overview of the Dispute Resolution Landscape

3.8.3.2 'Amiable Compositeur' or 'ex aequo et bono'

An additional arbitration approach found in civil law systems where awards can be guided by equitable or 'fairness' considerations and not according to strict legal rules, used more often in consumer cases, not recognised by common law.

3.8.3.3 'Hi-lo' arbitration

A process where parties agree a limited range of figures within which they will accept an award ie with a minimum and maximum. The arbitrator may or may not be informed of the agreed range. Not widely used as approach.

3.8.3.4 Final-offer/last offer/pendulum/baseball arbitration

A process where parties agree that their last offers will be placed before an arbitrator who can only choose one side's offer or other side's claim figure. Mainly used in industrial relations contexts with the rationale that it will help parties decide to put forward only 'reasonable' figures.

3.8.4 Expert determination

In some instances the parties may be divided only by a 'technical' question, for example the valuation of a company. In such cases a common approach is a contractual agreement to appoint an expert to adjudicate. As a 'valuation', this approach has been treated by the courts as having different legal characteristics and remedies than an arbitral award although the distinction between the two is not always clear.

3.8.5 Adjudication

This expression is often used in a technical sense in construction contracts. It is intended as a procedure that will bind parties to a decision soon after a dispute notice is given. Parties usually have an option to reject the decision and initiate arbitration proceedings within a certain time period and/or after substantial completion of the construction contract.

3.8.6 Dispute Review Board

This is a 'standing' adjudication panel system used in major construction contracts. The board is generally appointed at the outset of the project and stays in close touch with it, adjudicating disputes as they arise. A well-known example of this was the Dispute Review Board appointed to resolve disputes arising out of the Channel Tunnel construction project.

3.8.7 Ombudsman

The Ombudsman system has evolved as a successful approach to citizen or consumer complaints to protect public sector or industry reputations. The Ombudsman office is established as an independent agency to review and adjudicate on complaints. Usually fact finding and adjudication are involved, and sometimes also efforts at mediation during the inquiry stage.

3.9 DISPUTE SYSTEMS DESIGN

The range of dispute resolution approaches continues to grow apace with the evolution of society and the rethinking of the field of dispute resolution of which ADR is a creative part.

For companies, public sector organisations or sectors faced with recurring disputes, the landscape of dispute resolution offers the opportunity to apply some 'systems management' thinking to their problems. Can a dispute procedure be devised which delivers greater benefits? – eg reduction of cost or delay, improved relations, minimum management diversion, or other criteria.

One of the major pillars – negotiation, mediation or adjudication – may in itself suffice, but perhaps more often there is likely to be a need to adopt a multi-step procedure (negotiation–mediation–adjudication–arbitration or litigation) or a multiple-choice system (as in the 'multidoor courthouse' approach) with adequate means of guidance for parties. These approaches can be embodied in contractual agreements.

However most commercial disputants or parties in 'one-off' cases of civil litigation will undoubtedly find that they are still faced with a choice between one or more of the three major pillars of the field. We have already reviewed negotiation and turn now to consider more of the practical steps in advising clients on ADR use and in the detailed workings of the major approaches.

3.9 *An Overview of the Dispute Resolution Landscape*

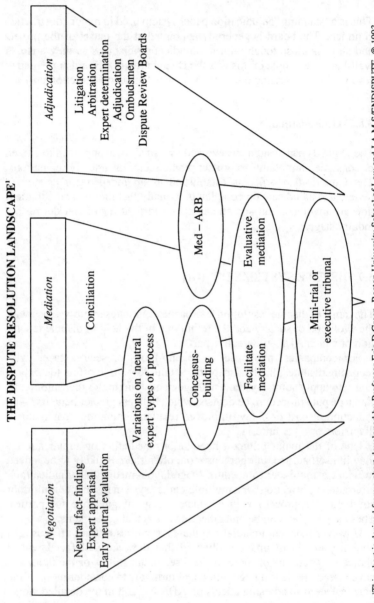

THE DISPUTE RESOLUTION LANDSCAPE[1]

Adjudication

Litigation
Arbitration
Expert determination
Adjudication
Ombudsmen
Dispute Review Boards

Mediation

Conciliation

Med – ARB

Evaluative mediation

Variations on 'neutral expert' types of process

Concensus-building

Facilitate mediation

Mini-trial or executive tribunal

Negotiation

Neutral fact-finding
Expert appraisal
Early neutral evaluation

[1]This chart is derived from a chart developed by Professor Eric D Green, Boston University School of Law and J.A.M.S/ENDISPUTE, © 1993.

CONTENTS

CHAPTER 4

Advising the Client on ADR

4.1 THE DUTY TO ADVISE THE CLIENT

4.1.1 Is there such a duty?

A client approaches his lawyer with the expectation that he will receive advice on the best method of achieving what he, the client, wishes. On most occasions the client wants the resolution of his dispute by the quickest and most effective means available and on the best terms available. In many cases this will be achieved by his lawyer through correspondence and, not infrequently, by negotiation with the other side. In such circumstances, there is no need to resort to the more formal means of the dispute resolution process, ie through the courts, tribunals or by arbitration. Normal negotiation and settlement procedures work perfectly well.

What happens, however, if the settlement process does not work or breaks down? Perhaps the client becomes impatient with the rate of progress and feels that the issue of proceedings will concentrate the opponent's mind.

At this stage another set of choices faces the client and his lawyer. If he has not done so before, the lawyer will address with his client the implications of starting litigation – the risk, the costs, different tactical approaches, the forum, etc. Indeed, the Law Society rules now require certain pieces of information relating to cost and risk to be given to the client before embarking on litigation.

Once the prospect of litigation or arbitration has loomed large, it is not uncommon for differing perceptions to arise in the mind of the lawyer and client. The lawyer may tend to view the litigation in terms of the process itself, as a series of procedural steps and timetables to be adhered to. By contrast, the client still has his initial aims and priorities – to

4.1.1 *Advising the Client on ADR*

resolve the matter as quickly and cheaply as possible and on the best available terms. While those two views will often coincide, most lawyers (and clients) will be no stranger to court actions which 'take on a life of their own'. They acquire an inherent momentum focused on the next procedural step, and often losing sight of the wider commercial or personal picture.

The lawyer's duty is always to safeguard and pursue the client's own priorities and aims. Litigation, or indeed any other process the lawyer can offer, is justified to the extent that it seeks to achieve that. Thus, at all stages during litigation, procedural and tactical choices should be exercised in the light of the client's overriding goals. The process, be it litigation or anything else, is the means but never the end.

Translated into the ADR field, this principle has important implications. The choice of methods to resolve a dispute is extensive – from direct negotiations, at one end of the spectrum, through mediation, mini-trial, and other ADR processes, and on to litigation and arbitration at the other end. Furthermore, the choice is not solely made at the start of an action, but is continually being remade – for example, when new information comes to light following discovery, there may be increased desire to settle or, alternatively, to move away from settlement. Each time a choice of tactic has to be made, ADR is one of the options to be considered. It should therefore be addressed with the client prior to the issue of proceedings and at regular stages during the process of litigation. There is nothing new or 'alternative' about the principle – it is simply an inherent feature of the relationship between lawyer and client. What is new is the range of techniques available.

Other sources of the duty

Recent developments in the UK have begun to create a more express duty on the lawyer to advise fully on ADR. Most recently, the Commercial Court and High Court have issued Practice Directions (see Appendix 6) requiring advisors to bring ADR to their client's attention in all Commercial Court and High Court cases.

The Commercial Court Direction requires legal advisors, in all cases, to:

(i) 'consider with their clients and the other parties concerned the possibility of attempting to resolve the particular dispute or particular issues by mediation, conciliation or otherwise'; and

(ii) 'ensure that parties are fully informed as to the most cost-effective means of resolving the particular dispute'.

54

Whilst this stops short of making ADR a mandatory step in the court process, it is however mandatory to consider it with clients and the court clearly expects compliance with that.

The High Court Practice Direction adopts a slightly different approach. Legal advisors conducting cases are required to lodge with the court, at least two months before trial, a check-list containing the answers to various questions. These include questions as to whether the advisors have discussed the possibility of using ADR with their own client, and with the other side, and whether it is considered that some form of ADR might assist in resolving or narrowing the issues.

Again, ADR is not mandatory. It is, however, realistic to expect that advisors may be called to account for and justify the answers given, for example in post-trial applications for costs.

It is a small step to conclude that non-compliance with (or mere lip-service paid to) either of the Directions might leave the lawyer open to valid criticism whether from the court or the client.

4.1.2 What is the scope of the duty?

Whether the duty is inherent or express, it clearly extends to giving full advice on ADR to one's own client. This advice should include the range of ADR methods available, the legal and financial implications of each, whether the case in question is suitable for ADR, how best to approach the other side, and when the best time might be to attempt it.

The Commercial Court's Practice Direction also appears to require ADR to be discussed, as an option, with the other side. This suggests that compliance with it will require some form of communication between the parties regarding ADR. If that seems draconian to some, it is also a very useful way of circumventing the fear that discussing ADR will be perceived as a sign of weakness, since the party raising it can simply cite compliance with the Direction.

4.1.3 Implications of the duty

It is fair to say that the existence of the duty has not been tested in the English courts. However, suppose that a case takes the traditional course of at least 90% of those following the issue of a writ in the High Court and settles prior to trial, often at the doors of the court. Even if the losing party has agreed to pay costs to be taxed if not agreed, it is well known that the taxation system only permits recovery of between two-thirds and three-quarters of the amount expended on costs. It is difficult, if not impossible, to recover management time to say nothing of the stress, strain and uncertainty of the case hanging over the parties' heads. If, following such a settlement on the steps of the court, a client learns for the first time of ADR, would he succeed in an action for negligence against his lawyer for failure to advise him of the option (subject to demonstrating causation, loss, etc)?

There must be the chance that he would, the more so if his lawyer's conduct was in breach of the Commercial Court's Practice Statement, or the High Court Practice Direction. At the very least, the lawyer would be exposed to substantial and valid criticism.

Furthermore, an action in negligence in these circumstances has succeeded in the US. The UK may follow suit.

In one sense, it is disappointing even to have to address the issue of a duty. ADR is a process inherently in the client's interests (in appropriate cases) and should, and increasingly will, come naturally to many lawyers. However, for those not disposed to use it, the pressure is understandably growing. As ADR becomes more widely accepted in UK commercial and legal life, it will only increase further.

4.2 WHEN TO ADVISE ON ADR

It will be apparent from paragraph 4.1 above that the ADR options can and should be considered at all stages of a dispute, from before proceedings are issued right through to immediately before trial. The most effective use of ADR will often depend on the client receiving advice on it as early as possible, ideally before the dispute has even arisen.

4.2.1 Dispute system design

Bitter and costly experience of disputes has caused parties to give serious thought to putting into place a system designed to cope with and manage the breakdown in a relationship so as to avoid subsequent unnecessary and time-consuming confrontations. The particular strength of this is that the parties address the whole issue of disputes before one arises, and thus at a time when they are able to approach the subject more dispassionately and indeed together. If an effective mechanism is put in place at that stage, much of the acrimony and defensive posturing so characteristic of disputes can be avoided. The growth of this area is reflected in the increased number of attempts to design dispute systems.

For example, in the early 1980s a major contract for the construction of the El Cahon dam in South America introduced what was called a Disputes Review Panel. This consisted of two independent nominees, one chosen by the Owner and one by the Contractor, who together then chose a third neutral chairman. Members of the panel were sent the site minutes and all relevant contract documentation and viewed the construction site on a regular basis. Disputes arising under the contract were put to the panel who gave an interim adjudication. At the conclusion of the contract there were no outstanding claims.

Building on this experience the American Society of Engineers introduced such a panel on a number of its underground sewage works projects. It was also used on some harbour projects, particularly in Boston. In this country the most high profile use has been on the Channel Tunnel. Decisions by the panel have been binding on the parties unless they give notice of arbitration within a certain period. The matter then becomes subject to arbitration in the normal way.

Not only on construction contracts but also in other contexts, one of the problems with disputes is allowing them to fester until the conclusion of the commercial venture. With the passage of time attitudes harden, positions become more entrenched and there is a general reluctance to back down from a position for fear of it being taken as a sign of weakness or considered as a loss of face. The introduction of an intermediate panel allows for an early determination of the dispute thereby nipping any potential problems in the bud. The nature of such a panel can be flexible. In its simplest form it can consist of a nominated executive from each of the contracting parties, indeed such a version is commonly found in joint ventures and commercial shareholders' agreements.

4.2.2 At the contract stage

There is a temptation, amongst non-contentious lawyers, to assume that ADR solely concerns litigation and is therefore not within their concern or province. It must be remembered that it is the non-contentious lawyers who are responsible for drawing up the commercial agreement. Often one of the few clauses that is not argued over is the disputes resolution clause. Many non-contentious lawyers put in such a clause, often choosing arbitration, without proper consultation with their litigation colleagues as to what would be the preferred method of dispute resolution. These days, a standard-form arbitration clause is not always in the parties' best interests.

The introduction of an ADR clause into the contract at a time when the parties' relationships are at their best, with the hopes and aspirations of both sides looking towards a beneficial commercial agreement, is an effective way to introduce the concept of ADR. Most such clauses provide that in the event of any dispute the parties will attempt to resolve their differences through mutual discussion, failing which, the parties will attempt to resolve their dispute through mediation or some other ADR means. A more detailed discussion of such clauses, together with some sample clauses, can be found in Chapter 12 and Appendix 2.

It is difficult to overstate the value of an ADR clause. Its introduction into a contract overcomes one of the fundamental difficulties that one party faces when attempting to suggest ADR to the other – the fear that the suggestion of ADR will be regarded as indicating lack of confidence in their own case. If ADR arises contractually, no such fear need exist.

4.2.3 Post contract

It has to be remembered that many disputes do not even get to the stage where a writ is issued. The majority of disagreements are settled amicably between the contracting parties. Lawyers must keep reminding themselves that they only see the 'tip of the iceberg'. Even then, of the disputes that are referred to lawyers, a large proportion of those are settled through negotiation. Most solicitors and barristers find themselves negotiating at some stage in their careers and many spend the majority of their time carrying out that function, be it discussing the terms of a conveyancing transaction, a commercial agreement or the settlement of a piece of litigation. Before formal legal proceedings are embarked upon, it may well be that the introduction of a third party mediator could break what is otherwise a negotiating impasse. One of the recurrent themes behind the ADR process is that the earlier it is introduced the better, and the greater the saving in time and costs. Whilst traditional litigators are reluctant to embark upon a full negotiation without many of what they perceive are the essential facts at their fingertips, nevertheless it must be remembered that the majority of commercial disputes do settle prior to litigation. Executives take decisions to settle matters often with only the information available from their side. The introduction of a mediator may cause the parties to re-assess the position and possibly widen the scope of the negotiations.

4.2.4 The litigation/arbitration stage

The parties have failed to reach an agreement through negotiations. There seems to be no other alternative but to issue proceedings. In circumstances where the lawyer has not been involved in the contract negotiations, at this stage more than any other, the range of options open to the client should be explored thoroughly. Few lawyers will ever advise their clients to issue proceedings solely in the hope that it will bring the opponents to the negotiating table. Litigation should rarely be embarked upon unless there is a willingness and preparedness to carry the matter through to its ultimate conclusion. One final attempt to conclude matters should be made before embarking upon the long and expensive litigation trail. The introduction of a third party into the negotiating dynamics must be worth contemplating. Even if the matter has not been raised before, it should be discussed with the client at this stage.

Once the litigation process unfurls, it is extremely difficult to stop the machinery from grinding remorselessly on. There is always a temptation to want to go to the next stage, be it seeing the opponent's defence, discovery, exchange of experts' reports or having sight of witness statements before deciding that the moment is right to resume negotiations. All these processes cost time and money. The sooner the suggestion of ADR can be introduced, the better. The likening of litigation to dancing with a gorilla, whilst well-aired amongst the advocates of ADR, nevertheless is a neat illustration of the experience – you only stop when the gorilla wants to stop.

4.3 WHEN TO USE ADR

It is often assumed that a case can either go to ADR or to litigation/arbitration. This is quite incorrect. Many, if not most, commercial mediations concern disputes in which proceedings have already been issued and in some cases trial is due very shortly. In other cases the disputing parties may not even have consulted their lawyer and may regard the use of ADR as a way of avoiding that altogether. It follows that there is no universally applicable 'right time' to take a case to ADR. However, the following general principles should be borne in mind at least as a starting point (see also paragraph 4.3.6 below).

4.3.1 The earlier the better

This is true not just because the cost and time savings are at their greatest, but also because parties tend to become more entrenched the longer the dispute lasts. The scope for a genuinely constructive settlement may decrease as time goes by, and the recovery of professional costs will increasingly distort the substantive issues.

4.3.1 Advising the Client on ADR

In relation to the use of mediation prior to the issue of proceedings, it is of course important to remember the operation of any statutory time periods under the Limitation Acts. The use of mediation (or any other ADR procedure) will not prevent these running. In circumstances where the period is about to expire, it would be prudent to issue proceedings (as a protective measure) even if attempts are then made to mediate the dispute.

4.3.2 Some disputes may have to run for a certain time before parties will agree to ADR

It is not unusual for some parties not to countenance ADR until they have 'fought' for a period of time. This may stem from tactical considerations, perceptions of relative merits, or even pride or the desire for revenge, but in terms of using ADR to resolve a case, it needs to be borne in mind. Refusal to use ADR early in a case may well not equate with unwillingness to use it at all. Indeed, as a case progresses, perceptions of merits and risks change, new information emerges, costs and delays increase and the parties may have vented their initial spleen, all of which can increase the desire for settlement.

4.3.3 Enough information needs to be available to permit a realistic assessment of the case

This is dealt with in more detail in paragraph 4.3.6. Suffice it to say that unless sufficient information is available to the parties to enable them to establish in their own minds the parameters of settlement, it may well be difficult, and even imprudent, for them to settle the case. This may be their 'own' information (counsel's opinion, medical or experts' reports, etc) or the other side's (that which is available in discovery or exchange of reports, witness statements, etc).
That said, two qualifications should be borne in mind:

1. Many disputes are in fact settled by the parties even before the lawyers are consulted. The benefits of an early settlement are weighed against the risks of doing so without (perhaps) all the information which litigation might produce, and a commercial judgment is made. Neither option is objectively 'right'. An early settlement may ultimately prove to be on less advantageous terms then would have subsequently been available, but with savings in costs and time and with relationships preserved. Conversely, liti-

gation may provide an ultimate victory, but with the loss of other commercial opportunities for the client as the consequence. It falls to the lawyer and client in each case to make this judgment.

2. The question of available information usually centres on discovery. The argument is sometimes made that ADR should not be attempted before that, because settlement discussions may be ill-founded. Sometimes, this will be true. Often, however, the discovery process does not reveal anything of sufficient importance materially to change the nature of a case. The desire to complete discovery may reflect the lawyer's very understandable desire to be immune from criticism (and negligence actions) in relation to the terms of settlement. In many actions the issues and relevant information are clear long before discovery. Discovery is not, therefore, a formal prerequisite of ADR, but merely a feature of the process of assessing available information.

4.3.4 Assessing case value

Assessing case value, from a risk management point of view, is clearly a key element of dispute handling, and the assessments reached will necessarily affect the choice of dispute resolution process. Whereas the structure of litigation and arbitration tends to defer a detailed consideration of the case until much nearer to trial (and indeed many clients do not want to face the uncomfortable realities of their positions), ADR necessitates a disciplined focus on the case whenever it takes place – often long before trial. Thus an assessment of case value is both a part of the decision about whether to take a case to ADR, and also a likely product of doing so.

The Heilbron Report (produced in 1993) criticised the lack of early assessment of issues in litigation (paragraph 4.1(ii)):

'Often insufficient time is spent in preparing cases. The result is that lawyers do not get fully to grips with the issues in a case. Thus, they cannot give their clients realistic advice until nearer to the trial itself. This protracts litigation and delays the chance of compromise. Although initially reducing costs, it more often has the reverse effect and increases the costs of the resolution of the dispute. To counter these disadvantages, more thorough preparation at an early stage with consequent "front loading" of costs is required. The actual or imminent risk of having to pay costs as opposed to the distant prospect of having to do so, coupled with realistic legal advice, is as good a recipe as any to make litigants focus on the matters in issue, rather than to postpone decision making.'

4.3.4 Advising the Client on ADR

4.3.4.1 Aim

In litigation terms risk management breaks down into two elements:

(i) A *claims/recovery analysis:* an assessment of one's own likely recovery and that of the other side.

(ii) A *costs/risk analysis:* An assessment of the cost of pursuing the various options, and the attendant risks of each.

4.3.4.2 Claims/recovery analysis

It should be possible though a systematic and methodical approach to carry out a detailed analysis of each item of claim assessed against a degree of possibility and probability of success. The need for a high/low bracket is to allow for the uncertainties of litigation such as the ultimate performance of the witness in the box, the quality of the case presentation and the judge's reaction to it. Having assessed each and every claim in percentage terms, they can then collectively be averaged out.

Obviously, such an analysis would not be complete without carrying out a similar exercise upon any counterclaim. In addition, if a broader view is required, the exercise can be repeated based upon differing 'what if' scenarios.

4.3.4.3 Costs/risk recovery analysis

A similar detailed and methodical approach, coupled with a litigator's experience and a great deal of realism, can produce a reasonably accurate forecast of the likely costs of an action. Each stage (issue of writ, statement of claim, defence, discovery, experts, witnesses, etc) needs to be analysed. A calculation of the cost of each stage in terms of the minimum and maximum number of hours/days can then be produced. Included in these figures needs to be an allowance for counsel, experts and disbursements. The figure can then be worked through to the conclusion of the trial. This figure will be of great use both to the party (from a cash flow point of view) and his advisor. It should always be remembered when considering the expenditure of costs, that the taxation system is only likely to allow for a costs recovery (always assuming an award of costs in the litigant's favour) of between two-thirds and three-quarters of the total bill.

4.3.4.4 *Updating*

For such a piece of management information to be fully accurate and useful, this exercise and evaluation needs to be carried out on a regular basis throughout the course of the litigation as the 'input' factors will change and vary in the light of the experience gained during the conduct of the litigation. In view of the common criticism of lawyers' inability or reluctance to give their clients accurate quotations for the cost of litigation, this can also be a useful marketing tool for professional advisors, quite apart from assisting the client in evaluating the most cost effective time to attempt to settle the case.

Clients in any complex action should ensure they receive a regular update on cost levels, predictions of success in the action and review of appropriateness of ADR including potential cost-saving benefits.

4.3.5 Direct negotiations between the parties/their advisors are not succeeding

Direct negotiation between parties/their advisors is clearly the most efficient and effective method of resolving a dispute. Generally, parties should have attempted these before attempting ADR, not least because it is cheaper. The negotiations may take the form of direct talks or (usually less effective) an exchange of correspondence, perhaps including 'without prejudice' offers. However, it is important to remember that:

1. Some direct talks may in fact drive the parties further apart, particularly if there is personal animosity between the protagonists.

2. Some direct negotiations are obviously 'not succeeding' after a couple of hours, whereas others may prove very effective if left to continue for several days, or even over a period of weeks or months. It is not always easy to assess when talks are not in fact producing results.

3. Since most litigation cases settle before trial, on the basis of direct negotiations, it is tempting to assume that most settlement negotiations 'work'. However, the crucial question is not whether they 'work' (in the sense of ultimately producing a negotiated settlement), but whether they 'work well'. It is not the hallmark of an efficient process if to generate settlement the negotiations have to take place over a number of years, whether or not against the backcloth of expensive litigation, if in fact a mediation might produce settlement in a few days. ADR will usually 'concertina' the

negotiation process into a much tighter time frame, because of the inherent nature of the ADR processes (see especially Chapter 7 on mediation).

4.3.6 Selecting cases

1. A 'Rule-of-Thumb'

Although it is unwise to be too proscriptive, it is nevertheless possible to draw on the above principles to produce a 'rule-of-thumb' for selecting cases suitable for ADR. This can at least act as a starting-point for consideration of a given case. We draw the 'rule' as follows. A case is prima facie suitable for ADR if:

(a) each party has sufficient information regarding the case to enable it to make a reasonable assessment of its position; and

(b) direct negotiations are not proving (or are not likely to prove) effective in generating settlement; and

(c) none of the reasons *not* to use ADR, set out in paragraph 4.4 below, applies.

It will be apparent from this that large numbers of disputes (many more than currently go to ADR) may well be suitable for resolution by ADR at some stage during their life-cycle. This counters a common perception that only the occasional dispute will be suitable. The onus is very much on legal advisers to be recommending ADR where possible.

2. Ad hoc vs systematic case selection

The majority of current ADR use in the UK is on an essentially ad hoc basis. Parties and advisors discuss ADR in relation to a given case, and in due course agreement is reached (or not) with the other side to use it.

From the point of view of a client with a large throughput of litigation (eg typically insurance companies, banks, and some other large corporations), however, the real benefit of ADR can be obtained through a much more systematic approach. For example, an insurance company might opt to use ADR in a consistent and planned way, in an attempt to reduce its overall claims-handling costs. This would begin with the case selection process. Rather than assuming that the question of ADR will be discussed at an appropriate juncture, it might implement:

(a) a formal requirement that the intial, and regular subsequent, reports on each case from its lawyers contain an assessment of the ADR possibilities; and

(b) a presumption that all cases within certain pre-selected criteria are suitable for ADR (usually mediation), unless specific justification is given to the contrary. These criteria might include, for example:

  (i) all claims over X years old/all new claims;

  (ii) all claims within a certain category of cover (eg personal injury, professional negligence, construction, etc);

  (iii) all claims that were not either dormant, fraudulent or required to go to trial;

  (iv) other criteria that fit the insurer's own claims policy and approach.

The use of a more systematic approach to case selection, whilst not removing the need for individual consideration of each case, has a number of benefits:

(a) it is likely to generate a much higher level of ADR use;

(b) it is therefore likely to maximise the benefit delivered to the client;

(c) it removes some of the onus of responsibility for selecting suitable cases from the individual claims handler; and

(d) it can be effectively used to provide an empirical basis by which to measure the benefit that ADR is delivering to the company.

A number of such schemes are already in operation in the UK.

4.4 WHEN NOT TO USE ADR

It should be clear from the above that ADR is not a universally applicable procedural remedy, nor is it intended to replace the litigation and arbitration systems in their entirety. The key to the successful use of ADR is to know when, and when not, to use it. Again, it is unwise to be too proscriptive, but the following general principles should be borne in mind in relation to when ADR is not suitable:

4.4.1 Negotiations proving effective

If the negotiation process is already working there is no need to introduce the agency of a third party. It should be remembered that even taking into account the vast number of litigated cases that settle prior to trial, the majority of disputes do not even reach the stage where proceedings are issued. Countless commercial disputes are settled perfectly adequately without recourse to the courts.

4.4.2 Need for court assistance/protection

If there is a need for an injunction or some other form of relief available only through the court procedure (such as a declaration) then ADR will not be appropriate. Clearly, the need to protect or seize assets will require a court-based approach. However, it may well be that once such protection or seizure is obtained, the underlying issues can be resolved through ADR.

4.4.3 Need to set a precedent

ADR cannot deliver a precedent decision and in circumstances where that is required it is clearly inappropriate. For example, an insurance company might litigate over the interpretation of a policy condition, and require the finality of a court decision in order to substantiate its stance towards all policy-holders. Similarly, a commercial precedent might be required for reasons of corporate policy or image. For example, a company might wish to assert the primacy of a form of conduct – eg a firm commitment to dismissals for theft – or send a particular message to its market-place competitors. In these circumstances, ADR is unlikely to be used, except perhaps as an aid to streamlining the issues for trial.

It is important to remember, however, that a precedent can be a 'two-edged sword'. If the insurance company litigating over a policy-term is unsuccessful, it not only loses that action, but also publicly declares to other holders of a similar policy that they too have a right of redress against the company. Where such concerns exist, the privacy afforded by ADR can be attractive.

4.4.4 Publicity

Sometimes a party may perceive that one of the major benefits (perhaps the only benefit) of litigation is the publicity that it can attract. This can be used to apply commercial pressure, or the pressure of public opinion, which can be a very powerful weapon. The privacy and confidentiality of most ADR processes does not generally permit such publicity.

Interestingly, however, ADR techniques (primarily consensus-building) have been used to great effect in environmental disputes, where the publicity element is often regarded as very important, and provision for it can be made in the design of the process itself. This is a useful reminder that the flexibility of ADR techniques permits a matching of the chosen process with the priorities and aims of the parties.

4.4.5 Economic power

Litigation can often be used by the commercially stronger party in an oppressive way. A party which is perceived to have limitless resources to pursue or resist litigation often can exploit its advantage thereby forcing the weaker party into a compromise at a figure below that which they could reasonably expect in litigation. The weaker party either cannot wait or simply does not have the resources to take the matter right the way through to a conclusion. The risks involved are too great. Often, in addition, merely to sue invites a cessation of commercial relations. This is one reason why many large oil companies appear to have a relatively litigation-free existence. Some of their smaller suppliers simply do not dare issue proceedings. Economic power may therefore be used to prevent, inhibit or determine litigation outcomes. Whether this is an appropriate strategy is a wider issue than the question of ADR use, but when it is pursued, ADR is less likely to be a favoured route.

4.4.6 Summary judgment available

Where summary judgment is available, there is an argument for obtaining it either as an end in itself or so that should there be any subsequent negotiations (eg over enforcement), one can operate from a position of strength. Thus in a straightforward debt recovery action (with no substantive defence) ADR is not often used.

However, even in that situation there are still valid arguments for using ADR, for example the desire to maintain good commercial relations with customers or suppliers. In this context ADR has to be viewed in the light of wider corporate policy or image, and not solely as a strategy question for that particular dispute.

In any event, there are many actions in which summary judgment is not obtainable. If a plaintiff applies for it and fails, that may well be an appropriate juncture to adopt ADR.

4.4.7   *Advising the Client on ADR*

4.4.7 No genuine interest in settlement

ADR processes are consensual, and to that extent require all parties to be interested at least in exploring settlement opportunities (though that is by no means tantamount to a willingness to settle on any terms). If one or more parties to a dispute can genuinely be said to have no interest in settlement, then manifestly ADR is unlikely to work, except to the degree that such an attitude may itself change as a result of an ADR process.

However, it would be unwise to assume too readily that any party is genuinely uninterested in settlement. Very few parties litigate for the sake of the process, unless perhaps motivated by a desire for vindication or revenge. Most parties are interested in the substantive outcome, not the process. If terms can be found that satisfy their demand (in the light of the strengths and weaknesses of their position) then settlement can be achieved. The question is simply which process will be more likely to generate such terms.

Therefore, great caution should be applied in interpreting the inevitable posturing of both the other side and indeed one's own client. Such behaviour is by no means necessarily inconsistent with a willingness to settle.

4.5 BENEFITS OF ADR

Any advice to clients on whether or not to use ADR will need to contain an assessment of the benefits and risks of doing so. Although these are touched on in other parts of this book, it is useful to draw those strands together and summarise them. Clients for whom ADR is new will almost certainly want to address these at some length.

4.5.1 Cost

It is self-evident from the informal and fast nature of ADR processes that the costs are likely to be significantly less than commencing or continuing with litigation or arbitration. The costs element is dealt with in more detail in paragraphs 4.6.3 and 4.6.4 below.

4.5.2 Speed

The speed with which ADR can achieve solutions is in marked contrast to litigation or arbitration. A typical mediation lasts one, sometimes two, days. An exceptionally lengthy one might last five. Moreover, a mediation can be set up as quickly as the parties require, the only constraining factor being the availability of those who will attend. Typically, a mediation might take place some four to eight weeks after the parties have agreed to proceed, but if the situation demands, there is no substantive reason why it cannot take place almost immediately.

The importance of speed cannot be underestimated. Commercial disputes take place in a commercial context, not a vacuum. The inability of business managers to plan for the future due to the uncertain outcome of a dispute, which in litigation may remain uncertain for many years, can be a major business problem, touching not only on cash-flow, but often on much wider issues of corporate planning and strategy. Similarly, lay plaintiffs often find the slow nature of litigation incomprehensible and deeply frustrating.

4.5.3 Control

Businessmen (and many lay people) are used to the negotiation process, in which they retain a large measure of control over both the process and the outcome. In litigation they find they have very little, if any, control, and that in itself is immensely frustrating. The process is largely dictated by pre-determined court procedures, and the outcome is dependent on the presentation of their case, the performance of their witnesses, and the opinions of the judge – all of which are largely beyond their control.

ADR returns the element of control to the parties (in conjunction with their advisors). The process is not pre-determined, but open to the parties to decide. Thus a process can be chosen or even designed to reflect their intentions and priorities, as well as the nature of the problem. The similarity of mediation (in particular) to the normal methods of direct negotiation means that many clients are instinctively familiar and at ease with the process. The outcome, too, remains entirely within their control, in the sense that terms cannot be imposed upon them, but only arrived at through negotiations. Furthermore, the informality of the process, and its similarity to direct negotiations, makes their active and confident participation far more likely, and compares very favourably to the experience of being in the witness box!

4.5.4 Relationship

The adversarial nature of litigation and arbitration forces parties into confrontation. Not only does confrontation not always generate results efficiently or effectively, it may drive the protagonists further apart. In some cases this may not matter, since the parties have no ongoing relationship to consider. In a commercial context, however, the effect on business relations can be a major disincentive to, or detrimental by-product of, litigation or arbitration.

By contrast, ADR is an approach far more likely to minimise the deterioration in relationships, and in some cases may even provide a forum for new and more creative future working relationships to be established. That is not to say that the atmosphere of a mediation is not a tough and often aggressive one, but rather that the process itself is contributing to, rather than destroying, the parties' relationship.

This can also have implications for a company's image or reputation. Consistent and fair use of ADR (where appropriate) may be used to send a significant message to business suppliers, customers, and others. The use of ADR should, at best, go far beyond consideration of individual cases, and inform a company's approach to its corporate image. A good example of this is the 'corporate ADR pledge', used to good effect by leading companies in the US. This involves a public commitment to the use of ADR in appropriate cases. In reality, the discretion over ADR use is left entirely to the company, on a case-by-case basis, but the message sent to the market-place is an important one. Furthermore, it is much easier for a party in dispute with such a company to suggest ADR in the light of such a pledge.

4.5.5 Creative and forward-looking solutions

Litigation and arbitration are historical exercises, based on an analysis of rights and obligations. The focus of any search for a solution, or the final judgment, tends to be based solely on what happened (historical facts) and what rights and obligations attach to the parties as a result (law).

These elements certainly feature in ADR, but other elements are also involved – in particular, the parties' interests and needs. Necessarily, therefore, the scope for settlement is wider, generating more possibilities and making settlement more likely. Settlements reached in ADR will often reflect much more than a straightforward payment of damages. A typical example is terms of settlement including an agreement for A to supply B with certain products at discounted rates (say, cost price). B will then receive something with a value of, say, 100 units, which only costs A 50 units to supply.

Furthermore, it is entirely logical that a settlement should reflect not only the strict legal position (or rather the parties' perceptions of it), but where possible their personal or commercial interests and needs as well. There are often situations where the payment of damages, whilst always welcome, does not in itself address the underlying commercial problem. Such interests and needs are simply not relevant as far as a judge or arbitrator is concerned, in arriving at a decision, but are highly relevant in ADR.

4.5.6 Confidentiality

There will often be situations where, for example, commercial considerations demand confidentiality. Litigation is almost always a public forum, and arbitration can become public on appeal. ADR is a private process, and this is frequently cited by parties as a reason for using it. For example, a company may wish to settle with a certain litigant without that information becoming known to other litigants with similar claims. A charity might fear the effect on its donation income if it is seen to be involved in a bitter and costly dispute. A professional partnership may wish to deal with a negligence claim against it without any public knowledge that the claim was made, not least for reasons of professional reputation.

4.5.7 Discipline and focus

The structure of the litigation and arbitration processes permit, and perhaps even encourage, many disputes to 'drift'. It is often not until relatively late in the process that the case begins to be analysed in full. To some extent this is a by-product of the need to extract more information (discovery, experts' reports, witness statements, etc), before analysing the case in the light of it. Equally, however, it can often reflect an unwillingness, perhaps on the part of clients, properly to focus on the case, address the issues and take decisions.

Ultimately, the only procedural step (in litigation or arbitration) which forces them to do so is the final hearing or trial – hence the tendency for such focused analyses to happen late. ADR engenders the same effect, 'forcing' rigorous analysis, debate and decision-making, but can do so at any stage. It operates as an 'artificial court-room door', creating much of the atmosphere and focus associated with an imminent trial, but doing so much earlier.

4.5.8 Satisfaction and compliance

ADR processes are often more satisfying to the parties than a trial or hearing, for many reasons. The fact and relief of reaching settlement, and

71

of doing so by consensus, coupled with all the other attendant benefits referred to in this paragraph, tend to generate very high levels of satisfaction. Inevitably, some of this will reflect well on their advisors, and furthermore, the parties are much more likely to return to those advisors with future disputes if the whole experience has been a positive one. Secondly, ADR is likely to provide a much more satisfying 'day in court' than a real day in court. The informality means that parties can participate fully, rather than solely through their advocate, and there is none of the stress of cross-examination by the other side. They can, and often do, speak their minds, and indeed some element of 'venting of spleen' may be vital in generating settlement.

Finally, since any settlement is reached by consensus, it follows that implementation or enforcement is much less likely to be a problem than it is where judgment is imposed.

4.5.9 Effectiveness

Finally, ADR processes do have a remarkable track-record in generating settlements. Whatever the arguments, this fact alone suggests that the use of ADR should always be considered.

4.6 RISKS OF ADR

It is generally accepted that ADR is not, on the whole, a risky process. The fact that it is voluntary, confidential and 'without prejudice' leaves little real scope for parties to be exposed or prejudiced as a result.

However, such concerns as there are, do need to be addressed, not least because clients may well wish to discuss them.

4.6.1 'I will disclose my hand'

The current underlying trend in the litigation process is a movement towards a 'cards on the table' approach. This has developed throughout the court process (often led by practices adopted either in arbitration or the more specialised courts, such as the Construction and Commercial Courts) whereby experts' reports are exchanged, 'without prejudice' meetings of experts take place prior to trial, and written skeleton arguments are lodged with the court, culminating in the most recent procedure (universally adopted by the courts) of requiring parties to prepare and exchange witness statements before trial. The underlying philosophy behind these developments is that neither party should be taken by surprise or caught unaware by their opponent. That being the case, it is likely that parties to litigation are going to be in a position to judge the strengths and weaknesses of their opponent's case much earlier than has hitherto been the practice. In such circumstances, it is unlikely that resort to an ADR process will have what is perceived to be the adverse effect of giving the other side early notice of one's 'clever' points. Furthermore, the reluctance to disclose one's hand contains an underlying logical flaw. The only way to make no disclosure at all is to have no contact with the other side, and make no attempt at all to settle, thereby virtually guaranteeing that the case will have to be tried. Very few cases are fought on that basis.

Once it is accepted that some degree of communication and discussion, and therefore disclosure, is necessary, the argument is simply one of degree. All potential disclosures will be subjected to a cost/benefit analysis. What is the perceived or likely benefit of making this disclosure, in terms of generating movement towards settlement? What is the potential risk if settlement is not achieved? Those familiar with mediation will be aware that parties frequently conduct such an analysis during the mediation itself.

Furthermore, mediation contains a structural feature which enables, in effect, a 'partial disclosure' – that is, a matter can be disclosed to the mediator, but without giving the mediator permission to disclose it to the other side. This enables hitherto highly secretive points or concerns to be raised for discussion, and exposed to neutral third party input, without the risk of raising them directly with the other side. In addition, the mediator may well be in a position to assist that party in assessing the value of extending the disclosure to the other side, and is more likely to know how such a point would be received.

Finally, three further points are worth noting:

1. If a party has a strong case what is the point in keeping all those strengths hidden? If the intention is to encourage or force the other side to change its position, early disclosure is likely to assist.

2. If a party has a weak case, how much advantage is there in 'prolonging the agony'? Of course there will always be instances where, for tactical, financial or commercial reasons, one party perceives it necessary to prolong the litigation process for as long as possible. However, that has to be offset against the ultimate and far greater exposure of losing at trial. Furthermore, discounted settlement terms may be available in exchange for a quick settlement.

3. In practice the majority of cases are not sufficiently strong or weak to guarantee an outcome. If they are, summary judgment is always available. If a plaintiff fails to obtain summary judgment, there is almost by definition enough doubt about the outcome of the case to justify consideration of ADR.

4.6.2 'ADR is merely a delaying tactic'

Another perceived risk is that ADR can be used merely as a delaying tactic by the other side. ADR should not delay the overall prosecution of the case. A vigorous plaintiff need not allow a stay in the litigation timetable while ADR is considered and takes place. Whilst some orders given by some judges may allow a breathing space of days, weeks or months, nevertheless there is perfectly adequate scope for the two processes to run in parallel. The defendant (as it is often perceived that it will be the defendant who is raising objections to the ADR process) can be made aware that the plaintiff has every intention of vigorously pursuing his timetable and adhering to the programme throughout. Indeed, the prospect of having to prepare for discovery, draw up experts' reports or take proofs of evidence can usefully serve as a constant reminder to the reluctant party that the clock is still ticking and the costs rising – a useful means of concentrating the minds on endeavouring to reach a solution to the argument.

4.6.3 'There are no real cost-savings'

Another objection to mediation is that it can only usefully be carried out once the whole panoply of the various litigation steps have been completed (ie after discovery, experts' reports and even exchange of witness proofs), and therefore the cost and time savings will be minimal. It is often said that one of the factors which contributes to the high proportion of settlement 'at the steps of the court' (certainly in English procedure) is that it is only shortly before trial that the barrister who is to conduct the case is fully briefed with all the relevant information to hand and is thus in a position (some say for the first time) to make a detailed and fully-informed assessment of the case.

The question of what stage a case needs to reach before it can be referred to ADR is dealt with in para 4.3 above. At this stage a number of observations can be made.

1. Even where a case is referred to ADR shortly before trial, the cost of doing so can compare very favourably to the cost of the trial itself.

2. Where a case does not settle in ADR, on the face of it increased costs have been incurred. However, most cases do settle in ADR. Of those that do not, many settle shortly afterwards, as a result of input in the ADR process. In the remainder, much of the preparatory work for ADR can be used at later stages. Finally, it may well be that following unsuccessful ADR, the resultant litigation is on narrower or more clearly-defined issues than before, thus making it cheaper to conduct.

3. Finally, a company whose policy is to use ADR where possible will almost inevitably find overall cost-savings. Even if one particular case fails to settle in ADR, and thereby generates increased costs, others will settle and the overall result is likely to be a net saving, rather than a loss.

4.6.4 'There is pressure to settle'

Those who experience mediation for the first time often reflect that they had not appreciated how much the process builds up a 'pressure to settle'. The combined effects of parties thinking about settlement objectives and the structure of mediation in a skilled mediator's hands mean that a considerable momentum builds up towards settling the case. This is seen in the high percentage of cases which settle in mediation, which is normally regarded as a virtue of the process.

However, there may be cases where clients need to be advised that they can achieve better settlement terms than those finally on offer in a mediation (assuming that the advice is sustainable, and that 'better' takes into account the wider considerations of uncertainty, commercial risk, the stress of continued litigation, and so on). Alternatively, a period of reflection might be more appropriate than signing up to a late-night agreement.

The pressure or momentum built up during mediation is not so much a risk of the process, but rather a warning to parties to ensure that they are properly advised in relation to settlement proposals.

4.6.5 'I will give the impression of weakness or liability'

It is a common problem in many disputes that, each party having taken up its position, neither wishes to suggest any form of settlement discussion (including ADR) for fear of appearing weak or exposed in its case. The problem has to be addressed at some stage, however, otherwise both parties will find themselves committed to a trial they may not want. It is therefore important that ways are found to break this deadlock, and to the degree that ADR is to be used, this issue is addressed in more detail in Chapter 5.

4.7 THE LEGAL FRAMEWORK

Although ADR techniques offer a very flexible and informal approach, they are couched within a well-defined legal framework. Indeed, much of the success of ADR is derived from the 'no risk' environment created by this framework.

For the purposes of this book, we will deal mainly with the legal framework of mediation, since that is undoubtedly the primary and most popular ADR process.

4.7.1 The mediation agreement

The terms on which a mediation is conducted are usually set out in a short agreement between the parties and the mediator. This will establish:

1. The practical arrangements for the mediation, such as date, time, venue, identity of mediator, costs, etc.

2. The legal framework governing the mediation.

A typical mediation agreement is set out at Appendix 3. The brevity of the document is immediately apparent, particularly to lawyers. This is partly because there are not many issues to include, but also because the document needs to be one which the parties, already locked in dispute, will be prepared to sign. The straightforward and relatively innocuous nature of the agreement can act as an encouragement to parties to enter into the process. Some parties may wish to extend the agreement with additional clauses which they feel will protect their position or give them some advantage, but frequently this can create suspicion and a further dispute and even jeopardise the mediation itself. A simple document may well be the most effective.

4.7.2 Main legal features of mediation

Certain legal features are vital to a mediation.

1. *Without prejudice*

Clause 10.1 of the mediation agreement at Appendix 3 states that 'The entire process of mediation shall be treated as privileged and will be conducted on the same basis as without prejudice negotiations in an action in the courts (or similar proceedings)'. This is critical to the success of any mediation. It is an environment in which arguments, issues and suggestions can be aired with relative freedom, and clearly that will only take place on a 'without prejudice' basis.

It is worth remembering, however, that the 'without prejudice' rule will not 'sterilise' or protect an admission of fact which can be proved other than by reliance on that admission. This came to light notoriously in the Australian (NSW) case of *AWA Ltd v Daniels* (24 February 1992, unreported), Supreme Court NSW. During the course of a mediation, Party A disclosed to Party B expressly on a 'without prejudice' basis, the existence of a certain document. The case was not settled in mediation and subsequently Party B sought, on an interlocutory application, an order forcing Party A to disclose a copy of the document, which was germane to the case. Party A responded that, in making the application, Party B was relying on a 'without prejudice' admission as to the existence of the document made to it, which it was not entitled to do. Andrew Rogers CJ (now a respected mediator!) heard the application and ordered disclosure of the document on the ground that the document itself was within the scope of the discovery process, and that the applicant was therefore not seeking to rely on the 'without prejudice' admission as a basis for requesting the document, but on the fact that it ought properly to be disclosed on discovery.

2. *Confidentiality*

The confidentiality of a mediation is also vital to its success. Many parties do not want their dispute aired in public, particularly where confidential commercial information is involved. Even the mere existence of a dispute can compromise some parties.

The confidentiality aspect should operate on two levels. First, the mediation should be confidential as between the participants, protecting them from third party knowledge. This should extend not just to matters disclosed in the mediation, but also to the fact of its existence. Secondly, matters discussed between one party and the mediator in private sessions or caucuses (see Chapter 7) should be confidential between them, and may not be disclosed to any other party without express consent. It is this feature, perhaps more than any other, which generates a frank and open discussion, in private, between the mediator and each party, and enables progress to be made towards settlement.

3. Mediator immunity

The agreement should provide that the mediator will not be called as a witness by either party in any hearing pertaining to the dispute and that his notes are not discoverable by either party. Again this is vital in generating a level of trust between the parties and the mediator which will permit frank, private discussion. Some mediators, such as those operating on behalf of ACAS, are granted statutory immunity. That is not yet available for commercial mediators in the UK and the issue therefore has to be dealt with by contract.

4. Authority to settle

Each party should be represented at the mediation by someone with full authority to settle the dispute. It is helpful, not least to emphasise this to those representatives themselves, if this feature is an express term of the mediation agreement.

Sometimes, for a variety of reasons, a party may send a representative with limited or fettered authority. The authority may extend up or down to a certain financial limit, or may require the representative to discuss the matter with others before concluding a settlement. This situation is by no means ideal. If a deal is struck after 12 hours of mediation, and final agreement is subject to a phone call to someone who has not been present, the latter may object to some of the terms. Not having been present to hear all the debate and watch the deal slowly emerge, he is not well placed to judge its terms properly – ie, within the context of the mediation. If, however, this situation is genuinely unavoidable, then the parties and the mediator will simply have to work within that constraint.

Three particular situations are worth bearing in mind. First, where the liability of one or more parties is insured, the insurer's consent may be required to any settlement. Frequently, insurers themselves will attend the mediation in such circumstances, and this is obviously the optimum solution. If they are unable or unwilling to attend, the lines of settlement authority should be cleared in advance.

Secondly, where a party is one of a group of companies, care should be taken to ensure that authority to settle is present on behalf of all those companies in the group who are likely to be involved in the settlement (which may be a wider group than those who are party to the dispute). The same principle applies to appropriate channels of authority and consent in respect of a partnership.

Thirdly, complications may well arise with public bodies. It is unlikely, given the decision-making structures of government bodies, that any individual(s) will be able to attend a mediation with unfettered authority to settle. More likely, those who attend will be authorised to agree settlement terms subject to obtaining final approval from the appropriate committee – typically a finance committee. Although not ideal, for the reasons given above, mediation can and does still operate effectively in these circumstances. It may be helpful, however, to obtain a commitment in advance that the appropriate committee will meet within a specified and short period following the mediation, so that the matter is not left unresolved for too long. Additionally, the mediator may even be asked to attend that meeting to assist in explaining (and if necessary justifying) the settlement terms.

CONTENTS

CHAPTER 5

Approaching the Other Parties

5.1 OBTAINING AGREEMENT FROM OTHER PARTIES

Perhaps the most difficult stage of all in the mediation process is persuading the other side to agree to mediation. It may be that by this stage the relationships between the parties are extremely mistrustful, not to say acrimonious. A dispute has arisen, relationships have broken down, and feelings are running high. In such circumstances, the suggestion of any process by one of the parties is often viewed with the utmost suspicion by the other. Even where relations are relatively good, the common reaction in litigation is that if one party is suggesting something, in all probability it is to their advantage and, therefore, to your disadvantage. Why should the suggestion of mediation be any different? The problem is exacerbated at present since knowledge of ADR is still relatively limited in some circles. Why should either party, or lawyer, risk a process about which he knows so little? Further, the apparent absence of 'rules' provokes suspicion. In litigation some certainty, and therefore comfort, can be derived from the *White Book*. The suggestion of a differently structured process can cause deep unease to a person used to operating with the familiar rules and practices of litigation and using them to his advantage.

As ADR, and in particular mediation, has become more familiar to lawyers and their clients, these problems have eased. Nevertheless, persuading the other side to agree to mediation remains one of the most common problems for those wanting to use it, and considerable thought needs to be given to developing the right approach. It is certainly true that there is no 'right' method; each case will depend on its particular facts, circumstances and personalities.

5.2 METHODS

There is a variety of methods available for raising the ADR option with the other side. The choice of method will turn on the lawyer's and client's analysis of which is the most likely to succeed.

5.2.1 ADR contract clauses

The problem is largely eradicated if there is a contract between the parties containing a clause referring the dispute to ADR. The importance of such clauses in promoting an effective dispute resolution avenue, and therefore in helping to ensure the smooth performance of the contract, cannot be overemphasised. These clauses are dealt with in detail in Chapter 12 below. For the present, it is important only to note:

1. It is largely irrelevant whether, as a matter of law, the clause is enforceable or not. (The debate about enforceability is set out in Chapter 12.) The primary value of the clause does not lie in giving either party the right to mandate the other to attend a mediation. Indeed, one might readily conclude that a mediation taking place in such circumstances would have lost much of its potential for successful resolution. Rather the value of the clause is first that it enables the subject of ADR to be raised without any fear of indicating a concern about the strength of one's own case. Secondly, it reminds the parties that, at the time the contract was signed and relations were better, ADR was generally perceived to be a sensible route to take.

2. The responsibility for the inclusion of these clauses rests with the non-contentious lawyers, being those charged with drafting the agreement in the first place. ADR is not only for the litigators.

5.2.2 Court-related ADR

As with contract-derived ADR, the suggestion by a judge or arbitrator that ADR be attempted makes the process of persuading the other side to engage in it considerably easier. To date there is no such thing as mandatory ADR (in the commercial field) in the UK. However, there has been a growing involvement by the courts (in England and Wales) in the ADR field, expressed most clearly through two Practice Directions (set out in detail in Appendix 6). Neither Direction imposes an obligation on the parties to use ADR. However, the mere fact that the Directions exist lends a significant degree of 'institutionalisation' and credibility to ADR processes, and presents an entirely valid pretext for ADR to be raised and discussed with the other party and their advisors. Indeed, the Commercial Courts' Practice Direction actually requires consideration and discussion of ADR both with one's own client and with the other side.

By contrast, the High Court Practice Direction merely requires the lawyer to indicate (amongst other things) whether or not ADR has been discussed. Furthermore, compliance with it is only required some two months before trial. Although ADR can serve a valuable role at any stage prior to (or even during) trial, it may well be that some of the attendant benefits are lost by leaving it so late.

Thus, as with ADR contract clauses, the value of the court's intervention is not so much in creating an obligation (whether legally enforceable or not) to use ADR, but more in enabling the issue to be raised in a relatively neutral way. In a sense it permits continued aggressive posturing, while at the same time providing for an ADR route to be discussed.

Mandatory ADR, as a feature of the court process, does exist in some US and Australian jurisdictions. Contrary to some expectations, surprisingly high settlement rates are achieved in such circumstances. For the present, however, the UK has not chosen this route.

5.2.3 Persuasion

Assuming that there is no contractual or court-derived obligation to use ADR, the only route to the mediation table is through persuasion. This is a skill in itself, requiring considerable thought and diplomacy. There is almost certainly very little to be gained from a demanding or heavy-handed approach, the subtler approach is more likely to bear fruit.

The opening approach can take place at various levels.

1. Party to party

If parties to a dispute have not yet consulted lawyers, any suggestion of ADR will be made directly between them. If lawyers are already involved there may still be good reasons for introducing the subject party to party rather than lawyer to lawyer.

Lawyers often discourage direct client to client contacts when a case is in litigation so that rights are not prejudiced. However, a direct contact between clients may be one of the primary ways to help people restore negotiating momentum. It is the clients who can really take decisions to progress the dispute. One of the reasons third party ADR methods are often successful is that the resultant meeting produces client contact, often for the first time in many months or even years.

Furthermore, where, for example, talks between lawyers have failed to produce agreement to go to ADR, a subsequent dialogue between chairmen of the disputing companies, or their managing directors, may offer a second chance. Indeed, disputes are not infrequently disposed of in their entirety at this level, after previous settlement negotiations have failed.

2. Lawyer to lawyer

If litigation or arbitration is underway, the majority of formal contact between the parties (whether concerning settlement or not) will be directly between each side's lawyer. Thus if the suggestion is to be made that ADR be used, it can very properly be made through the lawyers. This has the advantage of introducing ADR within the context of the litigation or arbitration process, and thus avoiding the (false) impression that it is not part of the mainstream. Furthermore, it enables the lawyer to whom the approach is made to feel that the process is not one which will exclude him, a common fear amongst some practitioners.

3. Good offices

This expression is commonly used in international diplomacy where a third party country intervenes to act as a channel for making contacts and re-opening discussions between parties. The same role in commercial disputes can be performed by contacts which are common to the parties involved, such as a business associate, an acquaintance, an industry association or other interested third party. A good example of this was in the dispute between Euro Tunnel and TML over claims towards the end of construction of the Channel Tunnel. There was pressure from the governments of Britain and France and shareholders for the two parties to negotiate a settlement which they had failed to do. The Bank of England stepped in to 'hold the ring' while the parties met and ultimately achieved a settlement that at least allowed for completion of the Tunnel, although it did not resolve every disputed claim.

4. *Formal ADR approach*

One of the benefits of ADR organisations is that they can take over the task of reopening bridges or making contacts to facilitate further negotiations. If one party approaches an ADR organisation, most such organisations will offer to contact the other side. In some disputes they may even initiate contact with both parties in order to encourage a more beneficial settlement. Where neither party has invited this approach, it has the added advantage that neither loses face by agreeing to further discussions under the auspices of the organisation.

In the right circumstances, an indirect approach to the other side, through an ADR organisation, can succeed where a direct approach has failed, or is likely to. It is often perceived as more independent or neutral. The party receiving the approach has the opportunity to discuss its misgivings or anxieties about ADR more openly, as well as to inform itself about the process in more detail. In short, some of the inherent strengths of the mediation process can be used even before the mediation itself formally takes place, in winning the consent of all parties to participate.

5.3 CHOICE OF APPROACH

Given the difficulties often experienced in getting other parties to the table, the choice of approach should be informed by the likelihood of success. A certain amount of forethought may be important and the following considerations may assist:

1. Is there any objective information to refer to? For example, does the other side have any form of corporate pledge or public statement on its use of ADR? Is the other law firm a member of an ADR organisation and/or has it a track record of using ADR? In particular, it is worth noting that if a government department is involved in the dispute, the guidance note at Appendix 5 can be referred to. It contains 'best practice' guidelines for all disputes involving government departments and encourages the use of ADR where possible.

2. Is the suggestion most likely to be well received by the party/their lawyers/other advisors? Are the lawyers likely to have to persuade their clients, or the reverse?

3. Will the use of a third party approach make the suggestion seem more independent, and is that particularly important in this case?

4. Do the other side/their lawyers understand what ADR is about? At all costs, avoid putting the other side/their lawyer in a position where they have to respond to the suggestion of ADR without having time to inform themselves. Ideally, once the suggestion has been made, they should be encouraged to discuss the matter with an ADR organisation, before giving a response.

5. What factors would make ADR unattractive to you if you were advising the other side, and can they be met/addressed in any way?

6. Offer 'talks about talks'. These can be very effective in obtaining unanimous consent to mediation. They will often consist of a meeting of all parties/advisors together with the ADR organisation which has been engaged, often on a 'without prejudice' basis. Views can be canvassed as to the most appropriate ADR process (mediation, executive tribunal, expert or judicial appraisal, etc), the ground rules that would be acceptable, a proposed timetable, and so on. A standard form of mediation agreement makes a useful focal point for discussion. The mediation process can be explained and discussed with reference to each clause of the agreement. It soon becomes apparent that the nature of the obligations that the parties are being asked to accept under the agreement are not particularly onerous. The process then becomes much less intimidating. Furthermore, the mere fact of bringing parties together for discussions (albeit not of the substantive claim) creates a constructive momentum and opportunity to re-open settlement discussions which may lead to an agreement without further third party intervention.

7. Emphasise that the likelihood of both parties gaining from the outcome is greater than in litigation, or at least that an effective review of both parties' case will result.

8. Emphasise that the offer of ADR should not be taken as a sign of weakness. Contrary to much expectation, the offer of ADR can in fact indicate, and be read as, a position of strength. What need is there to 'camouflage' the factual and legal issues of the case behind the procedural technicalities of litigation? Surely the confident party will be willing to discuss the issues fully and frankly?

9. Emphasise too a genuine willingness to hear the other side's arguments.

10. Indicate, if your mind is not made up, that the approach does not

prejudge the nature of the ADR process to be used, nor does it commit to the selection of a particular mediator or neutral – these can all be the subject of genuine dialogue.

11. Recognise in particular that parties reluctant to use ADR at first may agree to it months or even years later. Many disputes have their own momentum, and will only come to ADR (if at all) once that 'force' has been 'spent'.

12. Be thick-skinned! If you want to use ADR, accept the fact that not all the offers you make will be accepted. This is not a flaw in the process, but simply a fact of life. Your position after a refusal is unlikely to be materially worse than if no offer was made.

CONTENTS

CHAPTER 6

Setting up a Mediation

6.1 INTRODUCTION

Once all parties have agreed to participate in a mediation, there are a number of issues to be dealt with and in most cases agreed with the other side.

However, as with all approaches to ADR, flexibility is critical. It may be, for example, that many of these points need to be discussed and agreed before a party will give final consent to participating in the mediation. A rigid procedural approach should therefore be avoided. Whilst the various points below do need to be addressed, they can easily be done so conditionally upon final consent to mediate being given. Indeed, satisfactory answers to these points may be what finally brings a reluctant party to the mediation table.

6.2 CHOOSING A MEDIATOR

6.2.1 Sources of mediators

A mediator may be selected either through an ADR organisation or independently. In the latter case it may be, for example, that an obvious candidate suggests himself to one or both sides, perhaps someone they have worked with in the past, or whose role is in any event inherently 'in the middle'. Obviously if it is someone whom the parties already trust and respect, his role as a mediator will be enhanced to that degree before the mediation even begins.

An ADR organisation provides a useful source of mediators. Most will have available a range of individuals trained as mediators who mediate for the organisation as and when required. The advantage of this approach is that the organisation takes responsibility for ensuring the quality and ability of its mediators and ideally should have been involved in their initial mediation training. They therefore come with a certain (unofficial) 'seal of approval' which can be comforting to the parties. Furthermore, it helps to ensure that matters such as mediator's professional indemnity insurance cover are addressed. Also the organisation's staff can help deal with general administrative arrangements, preliminary issues or with sensitive issues concerning the mediator's handling of the case, in a neutral capacity.

6.2.2 What qualities are you looking for?

The role and therefore the required qualities of a mediator are set out in some detail in Chapter 7.

6.2.3 Subject matter expertise vs mediation skills expertise

It is perhaps inevitable, given the relative inexperience in mediation of many parties and advisors, that the request for a mediator should sometimes be accompanied by lengthy and detailed requirements as to his expertise in the subject matter of the dispute. One organisation reports having received a request for a mediator with eight different specialist qualifications, and the likelihood of finding any individual who combined them all was negligible! This approach tends to reflect a preoccupation with an essentially arbitral (or at least very heavily evaluative) approach, where (albeit under the guise of mediation) the mediator is expected to 'give a view' on the merits of the case – hence the importance of someone with expertise in the given area. Indeed, if the parties in fact want an essentially evaluative, as opposed to facilitative, mediation (see Chapter 7), then the requirement may be more justified.

The heart of mediation, however, tends to lie in a more facilitative approach. In that case, the priority for a mediator should be strong 'mediation process' skills. These are addressed in more detail in Chapter 7, although in reality entire books could be devoted to discussing and analysing them. To a great extent, too, these skills are partly innate (in terms of personality of the individual) and partly acquired by knowledge and experience. They are certainly not a product of mere book knowledge.

So in selecting a mediator, some useful questions to ask may be:

1. What kind of mediation, primarily facilitative or evaluative, do I want?

2. How vital will the subject matter expertise of the mediator be? ie, am I looking primarily for an 'answer' or a 'negotiating opportunity'?

3. What other factors might suggest the importance of strong process skills? For example are there strong or difficult personalities involved which need to be well 'handled'?

As professionals and parties become more experienced in mediation, the choice will seem less daunting. Although it is difficult to generalise, it is likely that most people currently underestimate the importance of process skills and overestimate the importance of subject matter expertise. This is partly due to immersion in the arbitral/litigious processes, with their preoccupation in finding a factual/legal answer to a specific question, and partly because the nature of the mediation process is widely misunderstood. Much, if not all, of the subject matter expertise required in a mediation is provided by the parties themselves, together with their respective advisors and experts. The mediator's role is much more concerned with working with their input, than with providing his own. In reality, of course, many good mediators will have some combination of the two skills, albeit in differing proportions.

6.2.4 Other ways of balancing the skills

A number of options are available where a combination of mediation process skills and subject matter expertise is insisted upon.

1. The use of experts

A good 'process' mediator can be selected to lead the mediation, assisted by a subject matter expert in whom all the parties have confidence, who will provide specific expert input. This method has been used to great effect in a number of mediations we have been involved in. It has similarities with the process of early neutral evaluation, or expert appraisal, referred to in Chapter 3, but with the additional benefit of a mediator present to negotiate with the input provided by the parties and the neutral expert.

However, there are obvious cost implications of having an additional professional on the mediation team.

6.2.4 *Setting up a Mediation*

2. The use of co-mediators

Two mediators may be able to work together effectively on a dispute, by bringing to it a combination of differing skills and personalities. This can be a useful way of resolving a dispute between the parties as to the kind of mediator each wants, although great care has to be taken to ensure that the co-mediators can establish a realistic joint modus operandus in advance of mediation itself. That is particularly the case in mediation where each mediator tends to have his own style and approach, which may not be shared by the other, and of course their ability to work together is central to their effectiveness. Again there are cost implications too.

3. The use of 'pupil' mediators

As part of its training programme for would-be mediators, CEDR pioneered the approach of using 'pupil' mediators, ie, trained but inexperienced mediators who work alongside experienced mediators for a number of cases. Apart from its value to the individual, it can also be a useful way of combining different professional expertise in the mediation, in all probability without the cost implications of formal co-mediators.

6.3 ESTABLISHING THE GROUND RULES

Whilst the flexibility of mediation is rightly emphasised, there are nevertheless some fundamental ground rules which should govern the process. These are designed to provide a necessary level of protection for the parties, in terms of confidentiality and the 'without prejudice' nature of the process, so as to give the parties confidence in it and generate an environment for frank discussion.

6.3.1 The mediation agreement

For the sake of clarity, the terms on which the mediation is to take place should be agreed in writing between the parties and the mediator. A short mediation agreement is the most common format. CEDR's standard form mediation agreement is set out at Appendix 3, and is discussed in detail in Chapter 4.

6.3.2 Codes of conduct

In addition to the mediation agreement, some mediators operate under written codes of conduct. These govern the ethical position of the mediator in various situations. Examples of some codes are set out in Appendix 4. The neutral and confidential position of the mediator is one which may create difficult ethical scenarios for him and it is as well to have thought those through and be able to rely on a written code of conduct should the need arise. Indeed, some mediation agreements incorporate an ethical code of conduct into their terms by reference. It is also important that the parties have the opportunity to consider the terms of any code prior to appointment of the mediator, so that their consent to its terms is obtained.

An example of the kind of ethical problem which might arise is the situation where one party discloses to the mediator, in a confidential private session, that the bridge which it has built (the final account for which is the subject of the mediation), may have a design fault. Although the chances are very slim, it is conceivable that the bridge may collapse in certain circumstances. The mediator is instructed not to divulge this information to the other side. What does he do? Clearly he has a contractual and tortious duty of confidentiality to the disclosing party. But what kind of duties does he have to the other party and to third parties and members of the public? At what point, if at all, is he released from his duty of confidentiality? Should he merely resign from the mediation and inform no-one?

Another important issue would be in relation to conflicts of interest. In view of the importance of the mediator's neutrality, mediators should also operate under a duty not to act in circumstances where any conflict might arise. For example, if in the past a mediator has acted as an advisor to one party, is he prevented from ever mediating a case in which they are involved? Or merely for a period of time, and if so for how long? And at what point should he be influenced if his firm has acted for one of the parties in a related matter?

These are all issues which a code of conduct might cover.

6.4 COSTS OF THE MEDIATION

6.4.1 Who pays?

The costs of a mediation can be divided into two elements – the costs of the mediation itself (ie, mediator's fees and expenses, neutral venue hire, etc) and the associated costs for each party (ie, of preparing for, and having legal or other representation during, the mediation etc).

The most common position is for the former to be split equally between the parties while each party bears its own costs in relation to the latter. This reflects the fact that parties to a mediation are, in essence, buying a 'negotiating opportunity', and that opportunity applies equally to both/all parties.

There is value too in each party investing financially, as well as in time and effort, in the mediation. Experience and common sense tends to show that those who have invested their own money in the process will approach it with a greater commitment to making it work than those who have not.

6.4.2 Variations on who pays

(a) Typically for ADR, flexibility is the key. If one party simply cannot afford the cost of a mediation, or is unwilling to because it is not convinced of the likelihood of success, it may be worth the other party paying all the fees. This is a relatively common practice, usually where the paying party has previous experience of mediation and therefore of its value, and the non-paying party does not. It is an indication too of the perceived value of the process that one party is prepared to pay both sides' fees simply to get them 'to the table' to talk. A variation of this is for one party to pay the other side's fees (as well as its own), but with the proviso for reimbursement in the event that settlement terms are (or alternatively are not) reached in the mediation. If the settlement terms involve any payment being made, the reimbursement can easily be built into it.

(b) Those steeped in litigation will often instinctively want to apply a 'costs in the cause' approach to ADR. This is very unlikely to prove workable, since it presumes that one party will be the designated 'winner' in the mediation and the other the 'loser'. This can very rarely be said to be the case in any negotiated settlement, whether in ADR or in direct settlement negotiations between the parties.

(c) The relative informality of ADR means that the negotiations can include a wide range of matters, including costs. Thus although the starting point for setting up a mediation may have been that each party has paid its own share of the mediation fees, there is no reason why the terms of settlement reached should not include, for example, reimbursement by one party of the other's mediation fees (and indeed of their legal costs of preparation for and representation during the mediation). This is purely a matter of negotiation.

(d) In certain cases the mediator may agree to accept payment (or higher payment) only if the process achieves a settlement during the mediation (or within a defined period after the mediation). This is however not a common practice and any financial involvement of the mediator in the fact or terms of settlement may entail an unacceptable compromise of his position.

6.4.3 Costs of the litigation/arbitration

If a dispute has been in litigation or arbitration for some time, each party may have incurred very substantial legal and other professional fees, and the question of who eventually pays for these will usually be a substantive part of the terms of any settlement negotiated through mediation.

6.4.4 How much?

Most mediation fees are charged on a similar basis to any other professional fees, that is an amount per hour, per day, or whatever. However, the very short time periods required for a mediation (often only one day) mean that the costs are never likely to be that high.

The advantage of a daily, as opposed to hourly, rate is that it frees parties from the pressure of watching costs rise as each hour of the mediation passes. Some take the view, however, that such pressure is effective in terms of making the parties, and therefore the whole mediation process, more focused on their priorities and negotiating stances and preventing it from 'dragging on'.

Whatever the amount and basis of charging, fees will usually be agreed (and often settled) in advance of the mediation.

6.4.5 Legal aid

At the time of writing, the Legal Aid Board has not to our knowledge been prepared to grant legal aid to cover the full cost of a legally-aided party taking part in a mediation. This is obviously a political as much as a legal issue, although it seems odd to many, since it appears highly likely that the strategic and appropriate use of mediation in disputes where one or more parties are legally-aided would have the effect, by settling the dispute earlier, of reducing the costs eventually paid out under the legal aid certificate. This is further borne out by the various settlement statistics of ADR, showing that between 70% and 90% of cases in ADR settle.

The Government Green Paper on Legal Aid (1995) has signalled an intention to reform the Legal Aid Scheme to extend legal aid to mediation services in family and civil cases.

However, the current absence of legal aid cover need not prevent a mediation taking place with a legally-aided party, since it is always open to the non-legally-aided party to agree to cover both parties' costs of the mediation. This is a relatively common practice, and again points to the perceived value of the mediation process.

6.5 WHO WILL BE INVOLVED?

It may sound a simplistic question to ask, but the effectiveness of a mediation can be enhanced or reduced by the choice of who attends, and careful thought should be given to it. This applies to which parties attend, as well as to which of their representatives and advisors.

6.5.1 Which parties should attend?

(a) Two-party disputes

Clearly in a two-party dispute both parties need to be present at the mediation. They will be signatories to the mediation agreement and should play an active role in the process. This is of immense importance. Mediation provides the parties with an opportunity to take control of, and 'own', their dispute and any solutions reached. It is these elements of control and ownership that are so often squeezed out by the formal litigation process. The temptation to think that the legal advisors alone can attend the mediation, and then report back to the clients by phone for final approval of the terms of settlement, should be resisted. Settlement terms 'emerge' during a mediation, and in order to be acceptable to parties, they will often need to have seen them emerge, and to understand them in the context of all the discussions in the mediation. Full participation by the parties is integral to successful mediation.

(b) Multi-party disputes

Similarly, in a multi-party dispute, it is important for all parties to take part in the mediation. Indeed, resolution of the dispute may only be possible if all do, for example, because the terms on which A settles with B may depend on the terms which B can agree with C, and so on. Similarly, a first defendant may only agree to pay the Plaintiff £X if the second and third defendants also accept a proportion of the liability. In fact, mediation can often be particularly effective in multi-party disputes because the process is one in which all the various permutations of settlement can be explored with all the parties present.

However, if some, but not all, parties in a multi-party dispute want to mediate, and the remaining one(s) cannot be persuaded to take part, the willing parties can still use the mediation process to great effect. This feature is often overlooked. For example, three defendants to an action might easily mediate as between themselves on the question of how any settlement with the plaintiff will be apportioned amongst them. This may then put each of them in a much stronger position viz-à-viz the plaintiff, focusing all their attention on defending or negotiating the question of liability to the plaintiff, rather than defending their positions viz-à-viz each other as well.

The same logic applies to the issues which parties wish to address in mediation. Most mediations aim to achieve permanent and binding settlement of all the issues in dispute between the parties. However, many disputes contain an array of different issues. If agreement cannot be reached to attempt mediation in respect of all of them, it is entirely valid to agree to attempt resolution of only some.

Similarly, mediation can be used to address procedural questions, as well as substantive ones. An example of this was a recent mediation in which the parties sought to address not the substantive claims and counterclaims, but disagreement between them over the extent of discovery of documents which should take place. Rather than argue their respective cases at an interlocutory hearing, they chose to bring the matter to mediation (in fact, once the mediation was under way they chose to address the substantive issues as well and were able to settle the matter in its entirety).

(c) Group or associated companies

Mediated settlements can be wide-ranging in nature, sometimes touching on new commercial arrangements in their terms. Where a subsidiary company in a group is involved in a mediation, it is worth bearing in mind the possibility that another group company might ultimately be involved in any terms of settlement, and that representation of that company at the mediation (with appropriate settlement authority) might therefore be useful. However, that may be difficult to predict.

(d) Insurers

Much easier to judge is the involvement of any insurers in a mediation. If, for example, the defendant in a dispute is indemnified by insurers in respect of any liability to the plaintiff, the insurers will no doubt be playing a key role in the litigation. Any settlement terms may well require their approval. Thus their presence in the mediation would be very important and indeed in such situations it is fairly typical for insurers to attend.

6.5.2 Who will attend for each party?

(a) From the party itself

One of the most important elements of a successful mediation is the presence at the mediation of those with full authority to settle the matter, on behalf of all the parties to the dispute. (It is interesting how often a mediation is the first occasion on which all those with such authority have met with a view to settling the case.) For individuals and sole traders, that should not present any problems. For companies, partnerships and other bodies or legal entities, the appropriate delegation of authority may need to be considered (eg, board minutes, etc). Many mediation agreements contain express provisions confirming that those attending have full authority to settle (see Clause 3 of CEDR Standard Form Mediation Agreement, at Appendix 3). Other questions relating to authority to settle are addressed in Chapter 4.

The other aspect to consider is whether anyone attending may be in a difficult personal position in relation to the matters being discussed. For example, a middle-manager allegedly responsible for the error which gave rise to the dispute may have a degree of personal involvement which will colour his views and position in the discussions and may make any acceptance of liability difficult. On the other hand, his first-hand knowledge of the issues may also be important and informative. If the middle-manager were to attend with a more senior colleague, the former might be excessively defensive for fear of being reprimanded by the latter for the original error.

Mediation often claims to 'separate the people from the problem'. There are no rigid answers to these kinds of questions, but each party should give careful thought to whom they will send to the mediation.

(b) Legal advisers

Opinion is divided on whether lawyers should attend mediations of their clients' disputes. Some regard mediation as essentially a form of business negotiation with a purely 'commercial' interest-based objective. The process should be essentially 'non-legal' in nature and the presence of lawyers will only serve to over-formalise it. Others regard it as no different, in principle, to any other form of settlement negotiation and if their lawyers are already integrally involved in the case, they would expect them to be fully involved in any settlement of it.

The need to have lawyers present may depend on the nature of the dispute and the sophistication of the executives or others attending from each party. Thus, a dispute may be relatively simple in legal terms, but with complex commercial implications for the parties. A sophisticated senior manager may be much better suited to dealing with the negotiations, without legal representation.

In general, however, we feel that lawyers have an important role to play in the mediation process in many civil or commercial disputes, assuming they approach it with appropriate knowledge of the process.

(c) Other experts

The value of each party's independent experts at a mediation again turns on the nature of the dispute and the approach/personality of the individual. A complex software dispute, with technical issues dividing the parties, may well benefit from the presence of each party's expert and this approach is relatively common. The only qualification to that is whether the experts themselves adopt a constructive and open approach to the discussions, or whether they are part of the problem in being too partisan or losing sight of their clients' broader commercial agenda. Clients and mediators should be alert to the potential obstacles that professional advisors may place in the path of favourable negotiations.

(d) Unrepresented and unsophisticated parties

This situation can present particular difficulties for a mediator, and great care should be taken before embarking on a mediation where one or more parties is unrepresented and not sufficiently sophisticated to make a sensible appraisal of their rights/obligations/negotiating position. The mediator may feel under great pressure to give informal advice to such a person and to attempt in that way to influence the outcome. Furthermore, the settlement reached may be extremely 'unfair' to such a party, in terms of how it reflects their actual rights and obligations in the situation.

Although it is not the mediator's responsibility to determine or impose fairness, a significant imbalance of power between parties creates a situation in which a manifestly 'unfair' outcome is possible, and/or the mediator compromises his role by becoming an informal adviser to the weaker party. The situation should therefore generally be avoided. At the very least unrepresented parties should be encouraged to bring a 'friend' to the mediation, so that they have someone to share concerns with, and/or be given a 'cooling off' period to consider the terms of agreement reached.

6.6 DOCUMENTATION

In most disputes, there will be some relevant documentation which it will be important for the mediator to see prior to the mediation itself. In addition, it is common practice for each of the parties to submit to the mediator a brief written summary of the dispute and its position. This helps to inform the mediator in advance. Furthermore, in a complex case, drafting such a summary may be a valuable exercise in itself for those concerned, since it requires reducing extensive pleadings, etc, to a brief format.

The emphasis in preparing documentation should be on brevity, in keeping with the whole thrust of mediation towards ascertaining key and fundamental issues (additional documentation can always be produced during the mediation if necessary, since there are no rules governing the inclusion or exclusion of documents). Give thought to what the mediator *really* needs to see in order to be informed about the dispute, and to what documents reflect the *key* issues and arguments that you want to see addressed. Equally, however, in cases of extreme complexity, it may be that more extensive paperwork is necessary, not least so that the mediator can understand the situation in advance of the mediation. Even here, though, it should be remembered that the purpose of the mediation is not to generate a binding decision, and therefore the documentation is likely to play a less important role than in litigation/arbitration.

Once the parties' case summaries have been prepared, with relevant documents appended to them, they are exchanged between the parties and copied to the mediator. This is normally done expressly on a 'without prejudice' basis.

Various options are available in relation to documentation:

1. Each party can produce its own case summary and related documentation.

2. The parties can agree a joint bundle of relevant documents, and even a joint case summary or list of key issues.

3. The parties can have joint or separate summaries and documention which they are prepared for the other side to see (as in 1. and 2. above, and further private summaries, position papers or documentation which they will bring to the mediation for the mediator only to see (eg counsel's opinion, experts' reports not yet exchanged, etc).

Again, the flexibility of the procedure permits these and other options.

CONTENTS

CHAPTER 7

The Mediation Process

Unless incorporated in court procedures, there are no strict legal requirements on the procedure by which a mediation or other ADR process is to be conducted. The management of mediation procedure is therefore very much a matter for the mediator's discretion, subject to appropriate consultation with the parties and any preliminary agreements on procedure between the parties. However in commercial mediations a 'typical' structure has evolved of an initial joint meeting for opening presentations, followed by a series of private or 'caucus' meetings between the mediator and each party and a final 'wrap-up' meeting. A preliminary meeting or contacts with the mediator or an ADR organisation, as described in the last chapter, will normally have established the legal framework or ground rules for the conduct of the mediation itself, particularly the confidential and 'without prejudice' nature of the process.

This chapter reviews the mediation process itself as a guide both for mediators and for professional advisors. It outlines some of the strategies and tactics necessary to make a mediation effective, and addresses some of the pros and cons of choice of tactics by mediators and advisors.

7.1 ORIENTATION TO MEDIATION

The mediator: manager of the process, facilitator of the result

- In general mediators should aim for a balance, being robust and firm in managing the mediation *process*, without being domineering or autocratic. The mediator after all is supposed to be the skilled process manager.

- More careful handling and explanation of procedural decisions may be required where parties are unfamiliar with mediation practice or where the case is novel or has complex aspects, for example in a multi-party case, or where issues of public accountability are involved.

- A mediator should not in general bring the same style to the *issues* in the case (as distinct from the *process*), since it is for the parties to determine on what terms the case should settle.

- At all times the mediator should have in mind the objective of the process – a *negotiated* outcome that both parties can live with.

- Mediators should therefore avoid arguments with parties/advisors or giving opinion or approval to one party on facts and merits, but rather aim to establish a working atmosphere where the parties sense that the mediator is on a joint problem-solving venture with each of them, to ferret out a solution to their problem. The mediator should be 'challenging', but not 'confrontational' or 'judgmental'. This distinction is vital. The key is to be able to address the issues raised by each party in an analytical way which will help that party to a better understanding of the strengths and weaknesses of their position, without leaving them feeling that the mediator has 'judged' them or 'come down in favour of the other side'.

- Search for 'interests' (what they are really looking for from this situation), not just 'rights' (what they are claiming). In most mediations a settlement outcome is achieved without any 'decision' as such being made on details of the case or on the technical/legal principles at issue.

- While the ultimate objective is a settlement that meets the parties' interests, in most cases the parties will need to 'air' the legal issues, claims or grievances they bring to mediation in joint and private sessions. It is a matter of experience and judgment as to how much time to spend on such issues and conflicts of view, although mediators with legalistic or adjudicatory backgrounds tend to spend overlong on them. Judge by (a) how much these issues themselves are really responsible for the negotiation deadlock (rather than lack of information about the other's case etc) and (b) by the strength of feeling the parties have about them – if strong, spend more time reviewing them to ensure parties or advisors feel they have been adequately addressed before turning to the issue of what would be sensible settlement offers in the light of the issues aired and reviewed.

- The mediator's primary duty is to ensure a fair, unbiased *process*, not to ensure what he considers a just *result*. It is for the parties to decide what is fair for them.

- Mediator 'intervention' to influence the substantive outcome should be limited to exceptional cases where the integrity and reputation of the process may be at stake such as:

  (a) *Need for a workable agreement:* Where the terms of agreement emerging seem to be acceptable but the mediator has a strong sense that the agreement will break down soon afterwards. (Test this concern out carefully in caucus sessions first – for example it may be that one party does not expect workability but is using mediation to achieve a simple agreement on which they can sue for summary judgment.)

  (b) *Unrepresented parties:* There is a need to prevent undue or unfair influence on an unrepresented party. (Raise concerns about the mediation going ahead in caucus first with the party exerting apparently unfair influence, or even before the mediation begins – this issue is addressed above in Chapter 6.)

  (c) *Unethical conduct:* A mediator should not *aid* a party to lie or make misrepresentations in negotiations to the other side, while of course recognising that these are common practices in direct negotiations and indeed that the disclosures and comments made to the mediator (even in caucus) may not reveal the true or complete picture.

  (d) *Protection of third party safety/property:* There may be isolated cases where information emerges in mediation which indicates imminent danger to the health, lives or property of third parties (for example disclosure of a defect in new vehicle equipment). In such instances mediators arguably may be under a legal or moral duty, higher than their duty of confidentiality, to ensure that appropriate third party agencies are informed by the party or themselves. This is one of the most difficult ethical situations for a mediator to face, and fortunately likely to be a rare occurrence. Mediator codes of ethics may address this concern, or it may be incorporated as a term in the mediation agreement.

7.2 MEDIATOR ROLES

Mediators can play a wide range of roles within the context of a single mediation. To a large extent, the type of case and personality of the mediator will determine what mix of roles is played. The important point is that mediators should be alert to the varying styles and emphases they can bring to the situation, and be flexible enough to adapt their approach to meet the circumstances of the case.

- *Facilitator:* The mediator always has a role of easing communications by defusing a hostile or provocative atmosphere, channelling communications into a constructive mode, clarifying complex points, and allowing or encouraging discussion of sensitive areas.

- *Problem-solver:* The mediator can assist the parties, as someone with no stake in the outcome, to explore potential areas for solution, to review obstacles and options for overcoming them, to help identify where expert advice may be worth calling in, to review previous proposals for settlement and to discover if adjustments can be made to make these more acceptable.

- *Deal-maker:* The mediator often will bear between the parties, or himself make suggestions for, offers and counter-offers, concessions, or 'packages' that represent party negotiations channelled through the mediator. In sensitive or difficult negotiations, the mediator may be much better placed to do this than the parties could in direct face-to-face negotiations.

- *Reality-tester:* The mediator's neutrality is very important. It allows each party to have someone independent reflect on their case. While a mediator should generally avoid giving opinions, he can help shift party positions by questioning and reviewing their evidence and arguments (in a non-partisan manner) as a 'devil's advocate'. This can bring a greater sense of reality to the existing views of clients or advisors. (Mediators chosen for their expertise in a field may have been given an even clearer role of case assessment and evaluation and more scope to challenge each party's case, but should still avoid doing this until they have a good sense of the issues from both parties, and should preferably acknowledge that any views they express are based on the limited evidence presented to them.)

- *Scapegoat/lightning rod:* Mediation gives aggrieved clients/advisors their 'day in court' more frequently than settlement negotiations within traditional litigation, in that there is a neutral third party to 'hear' the case and the problems/damage caused by the other side, even possibly to 'blame' for a poor settlement when reported back to the company.

Furthermore, it certainly provides a more satisfying 'day in court' than a court hearing, since the informality of the process allows for a much freer and franker exchange in the parties' own words.

– *Non-advisor:* Mediators should beware of taking on an advisor role and should remind parties of this at appropriate times, as well as including reference to it in a mediation agreement. Parties will often seek from the mediator approval of their case, a stance mediators should resist (even when in simple terms of a question from a party – 'isn't that reasonable?'). Mediators should take particular care to avoid an advisor role when parties are unrepresented unless the issues are straightforward and the party has already received legal advice.

7.3 REPRESENTATIVE AND PARTY ROLES

7.3.1 Negotiators or advocates?

The object of mediation is to achieve a mediated settlement. Parties and their advisors need therefore to plan their negotiation strategy and objectives, retaining sufficient flexibility to reappraise these if new angles emerge as a result of the joint and caucus meetings. They should ideally know enough about the background of the party on the other side (financial, technical, etc) to be able to speak to them in terms they will understand. Demonstrating how effectively they have prepared will also convey a message about their competence to take the case through to arbitration or trial.

Advisors will generally achieve more in mediation if they take a principled rather than positional negotiation stance, guided by a real assessment of their best alternative to an agreement reached in mediation. Advisors should be able to assist their clients (and the mediator's task) by a clear preparation of the legal and non-legal options, and the likely sequence and cost of going to (or continuing with) arbitration or litigation if these are the alternatives available. Information which strengthens their case can be fed to the other party through the mediator or in the opening statement.

Whilst there is often a temptation for advisors to adopt a very hard-line, negative stance in mediation, the effectiveness of such positioning is questionable. Ultimately it may simply have the effect of confirming to the other party an absence of good faith and driving them away from the mediation. Mediation needs to be regarded as an opportunity (quite probably the best opportunity) to reach settlement without the need for trial. Undue negativity or aggression may simply waste that opportunity, whereas a more constructive, problem-solving approach will at least help to ensure that every option is explored in the mediation, even if agreement cannot ultimately be reached. In short, much of the ability to derive maximum benefit from the process lies with the parties and their advisors, and the approach they choose to adopt.

Parties should come with authority to settle and a clear commercial sense of the value of the relationship or settlement options. They can also help themselves and the mediator by identifying whether they can make progress by engaging in a meeting of principals only at some stage of the mediation, or by encouraging their legal advisors or other experts to meet the other side's experts to seek direct agreements on any areas of common ground.

In summary, parties and advisors should not come to mediation placing all their reliance on the mediator. Rather they should regard the mediation as providing a forum within which they can investigate the scope for settlement in a way that might not otherwise be possible before or afterwards. For the same reason it is completely inappropriate for legal advisors to approach mediation as if it was a trial, dogmatically insisting on the strict application of legal principles and refusing to acknowledge any limitations on their client's case, or to consider any other proposals for settlement.

7.3.2 Authority to settle

This is a normal prerequisite for mediation and mediation agreements. However it is not always achieved directly – managers may have implied or explicit limits on how much they can offer/accept; with some public bodies, charitable organisations or partnerships, a referral back may be required to an appropriate committee, just as high value or special commercial settlements may need Board approval.

If this problem arises during or before mediation ensure that the steps to achieve authorisation are clearly known by all parties and can be implemented soon after the mediation. For example:

- arrange for an appropriate telephone contact system to be in place if this will suffice to check approval;
- adjourn if necessary to ensure the presence of a more senior manager;

- keep all settlement terms conditional on the relevant approvals being obtained.

As a general rule parties should enter mediation with authority to settle up to the level of the other side's claim. The more senior the manager present the more likely a case will settle. Furthermore, senior management presence may be more likely to generate exploration of the wider commercial possibilities of a settlement, and may well be required to sanction any such arrangements.

7.3.3 Party involvement

Legal advisors should if necessary encourage client participation in joint and private meetings where the client is likely to strengthen the credibility of the case and drive the negotiations effectively. Careful rehearsal is appropriate both on what information should be revealed in joint meetings and on the negotiation strategy. In some cases legal advisors may be able to use mediation in an indirect way to assist their client to reappraise his case – because the mediator may be able to reinforce earlier advice to the client on weaknesses in the case (previously ignored by the client), or because a formal mediation may encourage the client to focus on the case or to send along a more senior or more effective manager. Indeed it is a regular complaint amongst lawyers that clients often do not address in detail the problems presented by litigation or arbitration until very late in the day. Mediation provides a forum to bring these discussions forward in time.

Good mediators will normally go out of their way to involve clients in joint and private sessions. Commercial settlements involve clients in decision-making. Also, enabling clients to talk often helps to develop or renew relationships with other principals which in turn will contribute to settlement momentum.

7.4 DURATION

The duration chosen for a mediation has to be a matter of experience, intuition and what the parties feel comfortable with in terms of time commitments and potential costs. Where the case can be quickly moved into settlement offers over a few central issues, a short timescale can be proposed. If the case will demand that the mediator and parties work through a range of information and case investigation before a sensible stage of settlement discussion can occur, then a longer timespan will have to be set. Parties used solely to working with litigation will normally expect the mediation to take longer than it need, although mediators should not brush aside party expectations. At the same time, setting aside only a day or two for mediation can be a useful discipline on both the parties and the mediator, focusing their objectives primarily on mediation as a settlement process rather than an investigation process and avoiding concerns that mediation may be used as a deliberate time-wasting exercise.

Standard commercial cases involving claims for damages up to say £1million can often be mediated within a day, albeit a day which can sometimes stretch into the evening before settlement is achieved. Very high value, complex or multi-party cases may need two to three days set aside, and even more complex cases or cases with many parties may require between a week or several months (usually in a series of separate meetings rather than continuous mediation). In such cases it may be unrealistic or inadvisable to keep all parties together for the length of the case, but care should be taken with this as a sense of meeting together at some stage helps settlement momentum.

The key objective for mediators, whatever the case duration set, must be to ensure that parties feel that the process continues to make or promise progress towards settlement. Open-ended timescales should be avoided. Setting a deadline for the mediation to be completed helps discipline the parties into looking to make realistic decisions on settlement. ADR contract clauses with mediation as a stage prior to arbitration or litigation proceedings, generally set time limits from initiation of the mediation. Parties can always agree to extend a deadline if they are satisfied progress can, or is likely to, be achieved.

7.5 LOCATION ARRANGEMENTS

Mediators should inspect location arrangements before parties arrive to confirm that room layout is appropriate and to confirm or amend any requirements set out in preparations for the mediation. The following points should be remembered:

- rooms of appropriate size for joint and caucus meetings (remember parties sometimes bring along additional unexpected participants);
- room layout appropriate to round-table negotiations rather than courtroom advocacy (and of sufficient size to avoid too much or too little distance between parties);

- separate private room for each party (or coalition of parties);
- soundproofing adequate for private discussions;
- flip charts available in rooms and any audiovisual aids parties have requested;
- catering arrangements covered (buffet style, in an open setting between rooms can if available assist parties to make informal contacts between sessions);
- telephone, fax facilities and other business services available;
- overnight arrangements for rooms to be locked or other document storage facilities where mediation to go over a day;
- availability of rooms for discussions to continue late into the night.

7.6 DOCUMENTATION

The parties should have exchanged before the mediation and copied to the mediator a brief case summary (and objectives they seek if appropriate), together with essential supporting documentation – contract or leases, expert witness reports to be used to substantiate the case, etc (see Chapter 6). An agreed bundle may be produced if advisors are in active contact or some way towards litigation or arbitration proceedings. A mediation contract should have been signed or should be signed at the beginning of the mediation. Many mediators use a simple notebook to take with them from meeting to meeting to emphasise the informality of discussions but a ring binder with separate tabs may be more helpful with blank sheets of paper behind each tab and a sequence such as:

- first tab with seating chart of name and occupational details, for easy reminder of who's who;
- mediation contract and notes of any other agreed details on procedure;
- a personal memory-jogger list of key mediation tactics;
- separate tabs for each party's statements and any essential documents;
- chronology of significant dates/list of issues;
- damages data/calculations;

111

- section for recording key points made in opening meeting;
- separate sections for caucus meetings (NB it is vital not to leave pages open in caucus revealing notes of private discussions with the other party);
- section for offers, counter-offers or statements that the mediator has permission to reveal to the other party;
- draft of a settlement agreement with blank schedule for details of terms;
- tab with address details of ADR organisation administering the case, of parties' contact details, details of any other parties involved but not present (eg insurance company, government department, etc).

7.7 ARRIVALS

The mediator should ensure that parties will be shown to their caucus rooms or to the joint meeting room as appropriate to the case and venue. In general it is helpful to allow parties a short time alone with their team for a final briefing. The mediator should call into each room to allow for informal introductions, to check if everyone will be ready to move into the opening meeting and to deal with any final queries on procedure which parties prefer to air in confidence before the opening session.

7.8 MEDIATOR'S OPENING TO MEETING

Most mediators have their own style and approach to their opening remarks. However, in every case mediators should be looking to establish their authority, win the parties' confidence, set an appropriate tone for discussions (in terms of formality/informality), and begin to create momentum. This is particularly important where the parties or their advisors have not previously met the mediator. First impressions can be vital in terms of the mediator's effectiveness during the mediation itself.

The length of the opening remarks should also be thought through beforehand; too long may frustrate parties who are keen to get to grips with the issues, and may tend to over-formalise; too short may lead to key points being omitted, and the parties lacking understanding or clarity about the process.

In general, the following points should be borne in mind:

- preferably seat parties between their advisors and the mediator to help them feel more comfortable about contributing;

- formal introductions – mediator fills in seating chart;

- mediator's opening statement, preferably concise rather than too long:

  - background and qualifications (keep to a minimum – they should have seen mediator's CV beforehand);
  - purpose of the mediation;
  - key legal points of mediation agreement; authority to settle, confidentiality, without prejudice, etc (this can be done where appropriate by directing attention to the mediation agreement provisions);
  - structure of the day; opening statements (duration?), questions, caucus meetings, possibility of further joint meetings or of occasions where the mediator may want to meet only principals or advisors to assist in achieving progress towards a settlement;
  - effect of settlement if reduced to writing and signed;
  - any other ground rules.

It is a matter of personal preference and judgment as to whether the mediator opens on more informal note by explaining that he will use first names or by removing his jacket (best adopted where relationships are already relatively amicable, otherwise perhaps leave informality to the caucus sessions);

- mediator may wish to ask parties to state formally that they have full authority to settle in order to emphasise again the purpose behind the meeting. This should normally have been confirmed, however, at a preparatory stage. Mediators should not labour this issue or it may spark off early destructive arguments. In some cases parties will only have authority up to certain limits and may have to refer back if the mediation moves them potentially beyond those limits;

- check parties expect and are available for the mediation to run into the evening if required, or any time constraints if not available;

- if not previously done, explain any previous contacts with parties or advisors and allow adjournment for parties to consider if they wish to withdraw if unexpected conflicts of interest emerge at this opening phase (this should really be done at the time the mediator accepts the appointment);

- timescale;
- any questions or problems?
- in that case invite party A to start because ... (they are making the claim/they called for the mediation/they are first alphabetically – mediators should have a reason for selecting the first party to prevent arguments or uncertainty).

7.9   OPENING STATEMENTS BY PARTIES

The opening statement should be concise yet forcefully demonstrate the strength of the case. Aim for impact on the other parties (particularly the client if you have not had an opportunity to meet before) as much as on the mediator – the mediator has no power to make an award or judge the merits but a good presentation may help confirm the strengths and weaknesses the mediator will choose to explore with each party;

- Stress your alternatives to settlement and their credibility;

- aim to highlight and emphasise rather than read the written statement which the mediator and the other side should have read prior to the mediation;

- identify any 'fair' or objective standards which support your claims;

- respond where appropriate to new points raised by other parties' submissions;

- bring in other team members to corroborate some key claims, reinforce sense of injustice/grievance, demonstrate credibility as potential witness;

- acknowledge the other party's just arguments/grievances;

- make clear if 'concessions' are being made that will not be available at trial/arbitration for the purpose of achieving a settlement in mediation that saves everyone's time and costs;

- end on what it is hoped to achieve by this mediation.

A few further points should be borne in mind:

1. Do not underestimate the importance of the opening statements in terms of making an impression on the other party(ies). It may well be the first time that a senior decision-maker on the other side has

heard your case put in a succinct and cogent manner. Even more importantly, it may well be the first time that the case has been put to him without being filtered through his own advisors, thereby perhaps losing much of its initial impact. The impression created by a short, cogent, articulate, polite and eminently reasonable presentation can have a significant effect on the settlement position which he will ultimately adopt.

2. Listen carefully to the other side's presentation. It may well contain hints about their true aspirations, and in any event attentiveness will demonstrate a good faith approach to the mediation.

3. Give considerable thought to how much of the presentation should be made by advisors, and how much by the parties themselves. It may be instinctive to assume that advisors will make them, and indeed that may be appropriate, particularly if, for example, complex legal arguments are to feature. However, the presentation phase of a mediation is the closest that the process comes to providing a 'day in court'. A party may well want the opportunity to address the other party directly, to convey the depth of feeling and the importance with which the dispute is regarded. Indeed, this may be a vital factor in enabling that party to express his emotions properly and thereby be able to move on to discuss specific settlement proposals. That kind of party contribution is made easier by the informal environment of a mediation. At the very least, if advisors are to make the opening statement then parties should be asked if they wish to add anything.

4. Consider in advance the length of time given over to opening statements. The intention is to generally to provide a short succinct summary, and therefore brevity is usually regarded as important (indeed, if a lengthy presentational phase is accepted as being important, a mini-trial format might well be more appropriate). However, in complex mediation cases it may also be important to spend time conveying to the other side the exact nature of a detailed argument, and if the opening statement is too short, this may not be achieved.

   The mediator should have formed a sense, from reading the case summaries and from initial pre-mediation discussions with each side, of what will be appropriate.

   It can be useful to agree a specific timetable for opening statements, so that each side knows how to prepare its statement, and so that the issue does not become too contentious within the mediation. However, as with any mediation procedure, an agreed timetable will need to be flexible enough not to impose a rigid structure on the mediation, and much of the skill of handling these situations will rest with the mediator.

7.10 QUESTIONS AND DISCUSSION

Following the opening statements, there will often be a period for general questions and discussion.

7.10.1 The advisors

- Encourage an early sense of a constructive approach to negotiations particularly if you feel that your previous contacts have not allowed for the development of an effective negotiating relationship (you may need to build on this later in the day or after the mediation if no agreement is achieved in mediation);
- avoid antagonistic or provocative questions;
- stress a willingness to search for a settlement if it meets your client's understanding of the merits of the case.

7.10.2 The mediator

- Ensure no interruptions from other parties (preferably by restating this ground rule just before the opening presentations, rather than by quelling later interruption) and stress that there will be plenty of opportunity for each party to put its case/respond to comments;
- ask silent team members at the end of each presentation if they wish to add anything at this stage (to encourage involvement in the settlement process);
- keep this period short if the parties are clearly antagonistic or going over well-trodden ground or repeating themselves;
- ask neutral questions for general clarification;
- avoid questions in open session that might imply an early view of the case or predisposition to one side;
- avoid questions that may require parties to touch on sensitive areas

in front of the other parties – these can be left to the caucus sessions if they have not been raised by other parties already (eg do not ask if they wish to continue in a business relationship in a joint session);

–   some venting of emotions may be appropriate if there are strong feelings in the case and the parties have not had any real opportunity to have such a 'day in court' before; the mediator needs to judge when and how to move beyond such emotional contributions to further questions, information or caucus sessions;

–   thank the parties for their contributions;

–   explain next stage and reinforce earlier explanation that:

  –   caucuses are confidential, nothing said to the mediator will be conveyed to other parties without express authority;
  –   nothing should be read into the time the mediator may be taking with each side as to whether support or criticism of their case is implied;
  –   when the mediator is absent, this is an opportunity for each party to reflect further on the case or on any requests for further work the mediator may leave with them, or to make contact with their office or to relax;
  –   try to provide, for the party(ies) not in caucus, an estimate of the time you will take with the other party (and keep to it).

7.11 PRIVATE MEETINGS (CAUCUSES)

7.11.1 Purpose

These meetings between the mediator and the individual parties are usually vital to progress in a commercial mediation. They are an opportunity for the mediator and each party/advisors to explore frankly and in confidence the issues in the case and options for settlement. A mediator should always seek authority to convey to another party anything specific said in caucus.

In addition to ensuring an easier setting for open discussion, private sessions:

–   give the mediator an effective forum for making progress and the opportunity to build good relationships with the parties;

–   prevent a party becoming locked in to positions and judgments stated in front of the opposing party;

117

  - allow for deeper, sustained discussion on issues without arguments or interruptions or the necessity of posturing;

  - give more time and space for offers or counter-offers to be thoroughly examined and analysed rather than requiring the direct reaction that tends to be demanded in joint negotiations;

  - make it easier for mediators to discuss a proposal's strengths and weaknesses without appearing to take sides;

  - allow the parties to build up more trust in the mediator.

Generally the mediator should caucus first with the claimant or the party who most recently declined to respond to an offer. Mediators should also beware of becoming locked in to the caucus formula of shuttling back and forth until agreement. In some mediation settings, such as family and neighbourhood disputes, caucus meetings are more rare. They work well in commercial mediations but mediators should remember that there are other options.

Caucus meetings may for example be mixed with further joint meetings on particular areas of disagreement. This helps to build up relationships across the parties and to encourage the parties to feel that the mediation is a 'joint venture' and a more fluid and dynamic process. The more time spent on private meetings with the mediator, the more the mediator will tend to be a shuttle negotiator. Finally the more the settlement is likely to involve parties working together afterwards, the more the mediator should structure joint meetings to help this new phase get started on an appropriate note. The mediator may also encourage meetings between principals only (on commercial issues or to see if a figure can be struck), or legal advisors or experts to establish points of agreement or differences and their implications in terms of further information requirements, etc. The mediator may or may not choose to attend these meetings depending on his judgment as to likely progress.

7.11.2 Issues to address in caucus

Since the aim behind the process is to achieve agreement between the parties, the mediator should endeavour to leave each caucus (with the possible exception of the first caucus meetings) with some change of offer or counter-offer to put to the other party, or some new issues/emphases that need to be explored. If there is no real change over two caucus sessions, the mediator should be beginning to consider ways of changing the dynamics of the meetings or identifying new information that needs to be researched.

In early caucus meetings, there should be an emphasis by the mediator on the use of open-ended questions and clarification of what parties would ideally like from a settlement. There will then often be a series of caucus meetings discussing the gap between the parties and searching for options to overcome their remaining differences. The pattern of caucus sessions is often similar to the core phases of the negotiating process, namely – Discussion–Bargaining or Problem-Solving–Closing the Deal.

7.11.3 Issues the mediator should raise

The choice of issues to raise will depend on the case and the mediator's judgment. It is a useful principle to follow that the mediator should allow the parties to lead with their agenda at the start of early caucuses. Subject to that a mediator should generally ensure he covers:

(a) *Ventilation of grievances/justifications:* Parties will often feel freer to 'sound off' in private session. This is an important phase of letting off steam where parties can 'have their day in court'. Mediators should acknowledge that they recognise parties have these strong feelings without necessarily sympathising or agreeing. Such ventilation should not be cut off or suppressed but should after an appropriate period be diverted into more positive issues.

(b) *Strengths and weaknesses on both sides:* Where a settlement will be primarily geared to potential trial outcome, the mediator will need to address with each party the strengths and weaknesses of their claims, again avoiding any appearance of personal judgment or evaluation (unless explicitly part of his requested role). Thus, for example: 'What do you feel are your strongest points?', 'Are there any areas where you think you might be vulnerable on the facts/principles/expert testimony/costs/rules/real chances of recovery?', 'What about the other side? How do you see their case?' ... 'How do you think they see it?'.

A good understanding of the issues helps the mediator challenge each side's claims using material from the other party to challenge rather than his own views, so acting as a neutral devil's advocate.

In this context, there may well be a temptation for legal advisors to want to focus exclusively on the legal arguments in a dispute, and to 'address' the mediator on those points. Certainly the legal issues in a case are generally important, and will inform the negotiating stance that a party is willing to take. However, legal arguments are usually most valuably dealt with, in caucus, by an open discussion of the strengths and weaknesses of a given argument, followed by discussions on the degree to which it should alter a party's current position. Legal advisors in particular need to remember the shift from advocate to negotiator which the majority of their role in mediation entails.

(c) *BATNA/WATNA:* 'What is your Best Alternative To a Negotiated Agreement (BATNA) if you fail to settle? Your Worst Alternative (WATNA)?', 'How confident are you? Where are you vulnerable?', 'What else would make a difference in terms of these alternatives?'. This area will generally involve a mediator testing the advice being given to the client on likely trial outcomes, and the costs and time elements associated with that, and in exploring the commercial context of the conflict.

(d) *What do you need? What do they need?* The mediator's goal, even in a case with no future relationships likely but merely a question of early settlement of damages, is to help parties to start thinking about the present and the future. What are their needs and wants? What lies behind these that might be met by other means than currently claimed (Interests)? What would they ideally like to see in an agreement at the end of today?

Similarly how do they see the other side? Is there a way to help them say 'yes' to a deal you would like?

(e) *What's been on the table?* The history of settlement negotiations should be explored to establish how close the parties have been in the past and the obstacles to settlement then. It may be that a previous offer is now acceptable under changed circumstances or can be made acceptable with sufficient adjustment/new elements.

(f) *What else could be relevant?* Explore all possible settlement options in terms of:

- figures (and how they could be amended, where they come from, how they can be justified to colleagues);
- timescale of payments;
- services;
- future business relationship possibilities;
- performance criteria/guarantees;
- apologies or other actions;
- anything else?

(g) *What other information/comfort would you need to settle this?* Keep searching for options.

(h) *What are you willing to offer?* This ensures a specific settlement momentum can be established. Sometimes parties will be unwilling to be specific unless the mediator reassures them on the confidentiality of the statement, but he can say he needs something to be able to encourage the other party also to show willingness to move – again in confidence. They may be nearer than they think.

(i) *Is there anything else?* Always a valuable question to ensure you have covered all they want to tell you.

7.11.4 Disclosure of information

The instinct to conceal information from the other side is pervasive in disputes. Within mediation, there are two issues to address – disclosures to the other side and disclosures to the mediator.

(a) *Disclosures to the other side.* If a mediation is to be effective in generating movement from entrenched positions, much of this will come from a fresh assessment of the respective merits, facts, risks and other circumstances of each party. Such an assessment will be prompted, though not delivered, by the mediator, acting in a 'devil's advocate' capacity. That in turn will often flow from fresh information brought to bear on the discussions. It follows, therefore, that the disclosure of information can be important in generating movement. Indeed, the failure to disclose may well only serve to make settlement impossible until a later date, and much of it will come out at trial in any event.

On the other hand, the possibility that the dispute may not settle in mediation, leading to the commencement or continuation of proceedings, will always act as a check on the willingness of parties to make disclosures to each other.

In mediation, a balance has to be achieved between these two competing priorities – sealed lips may prevent settlement, but an over-willing tongue may prejudice a position. This balance is something which parties and their advisors should discuss at length. Although there are no fixed rules, a useful guideline is to have to justify each non-disclosure, rather than each disclosure.

Much, though not all, of the problem is resolved by the 'without prejudice' nature of the proceedings. Thus offers and admissions made in the context of a mediation may not be produced or referred to in subsequent proceedings relating to the same dispute. However the 'without prejudice' rule does have limitations (see Chapter 4).

121

The rest is a matter of judgment for the parties and their advisors. In fact, that judgment, and the considerations on which it will be based, are exactly the same whether the parties are in direct negotiations or in mediation.

(b) *Disclosures to the mediator:* The structure of mediation is designed to generate an environment in which frank and open debate is possible, so as to increase the likelihood of settlement. Recognising that such debate is unlikely to take place directly between parties protective of their positions, the caucus becomes the primary tool for the mediator. As we observed in Chapter 4 all discussions between the party, their advisors and the mediator which take place in caucus are confidential between them and may not be discussed with other parties without the disclosing party's consent. If the mediator feels that disclosure to another party would assist settlement he may seek permission to make the disclosure, but if it is not forthcoming, he remains bound not to disclose it. It is the parties themselves who control the outflow of information from them to the other side, irrespective of what is discussed in caucus with the mediator. This structure should, and does, encourage parties to be frank with the mediator. There is in fact little to be gained from hiding information from the mediator.

Some parties are prone to 'negotiate with the mediator', as well as with the other side. For example, they might only partially disclose their position on a given issue to the mediator, hoping by so doing to affect the way he presents it to the other side. In practice, however, the net result is likely to be that the mediator's task is harder and settlement less likely or at least that the whole process will take considerably longer than necessary. Mediators need to be alive to this happening, but parties should be encouraged where possible to avoid it.

7.11.5 At the end of the caucus

It is a useful practice for mediators at the end of a caucus to summarise or clarify the points of information or offers they are able to reveal to the other side, anything else being confidential.

It is also important to leave behind some questions for the party and their advisor to consider or work on until they see the mediator next. This can help generate further evaluation or movement as well as just filling the time. Otherwise make clear they have time to call the office or explain where they can find refreshments, and that the amount of time you spend as mediator with the other side has no special significance as to where the case is going.

In a multi-party case, this may also be a good time to suggest that some of the parties seek to work together towards agreement on some of the issues while the mediator caucuses with another.

7.11.6 Between caucuses

The mediator does not have to shuttle directly from caucus to caucus. In a complex case or where a caucus session has been particularly tough, it may be wise to spend a little time reflecting on the case, reviewing the issues raised in the previous caucus or where to go on the next one.

Representatives can use the time to review negotiating strategy with their clients, to do some recalculation of figures involved, or to research further information relevant to discussions with the mediator.

7.12 EVALUATION

Evaluations should only be given if the parties have requested the mediator to give them and the mediator has the expertise (if a technical issue) or frames a judgment in terms of commercial common sense from the viewpoint of a detached observer. Even where evaluations are requested, mediators should avoid giving them until they have tested how much facilitative mediation will achieve. If evaluations are given, they should be given in private session to each party and should be consistent as between the parties in order to preserve the mediator's integrity. (Otherwise mediators might be tempted to tell both parties they have a terrible case in order to force a settlement on them!) Mediators should avoid being drawn into arguments with advisors in giving evaluations and listen carefully to any grounds of objection made.

Advisors might wish to encourage evaluations if they are uncertain of the real strength of their case or have differences with their client on assessment of the strength of the case.

7.13 AT THE END OF THE DAY – NO AGREEMENT?

If a scheduled time for ending a mediation is approaching (at the end of the first or subsequent agreed days), the mediator must determine whether to continue working with the parties in the hope of reaching a settlement that day, whether to suggest a return to mediation at a future date, or whether to terminate the mediation. As well as a question of whether the days set aside for the mediation are coming to an end, there may be an issue of time limits in a contractual ADR procedure.

If a mediator has a strong sense that there is sufficient momentum to achieve an agreement, it is usually worth pressing on even late into the night. If undecided, it is still worth consulting with the parties (in caucus) if they wish to press on. Otherwise the mediator should encourage an adjournment – a week or two will help the parties reflect, unless it is obvious the gap between the parties gives no grounds for belief that a settlement is achievable. This last position should rarely be adopted and only when at least one party tends to agree with it. Mediation experience suggests solutions are very often achievable with sufficient patience and persistence. A final suggestion from the mediator on a new proposal can be tested privately with each side.

Where the mediation is being terminated without settlement, the mediator's role remains one of doing what can be done to leave room and an atmosphere for future settlement or cost-effective outcomes. After caucusing, he should reconvene a joint meeting, and congratulate all parties on the efforts they put in to trying to achieve a settlement, reminding them of the advantages of settlement over litigation and expressing the hope that the process will have at least brought them closer, clarified the issues dividing them and enabled them to have a further meeting more easily or to reconvene in a further mediation. He can point out that most such cases end up settling within a few months after mediation. Indeed if the case merits it, the mediator should have explored in the final caucus sessions whether the parties might consider another cost-effective dispute resolution procedure, with a view to clinching settlement. For example if the parties are effectively arguing about a reduced gap between them on a few items, a 'pendulum' or final offer arbitration might be acceptable as the next stage, or an arbitration which can award only between agreed limits ('hi-lo' arbitration) after summary presentations (or the mediator may have suggested in caucus a final 'splitting the difference' proposal as a last resort).

Normally the mediator should not take on the role of arbitrator unless both parties are enthusiastic about this and clear on the potential procedural and legal pitfalls of 'med-arb' (see Chapter 3).

7.14 DRAFTING AN AGREEMENT

In the majority of cases the parties reach agreement. In the final caucus sessions the details of this agreement will have been hammered out so that the mediator should have a clear summary that he has confirmed with the parties. Alternatively the last sessions may have involved either joint meetings, meetings to resolve commercial details between principals, or between legal or other professional advisers. The mediator should help confirm all the elements agreed in a final joint session and deal with any final uncertainties or demands. It can be a mistake at times to bring parties together prematurely when key items have not been agreed in caucus. It can also create problems to allow parties to leave after an oral agreement without ensuring they sign up to a formal agreement in writing. A signed memorandum (even if not legally binding) ensures greater commitment with less chance of rescinding.

The legal aspects of settlement agreements are considered in Chapter 8. The commitment value of writing and signatures still holds even where an agreement is expressed to be not binding in law.

If parties are all legally represented it may be simplest to ask the advisers to recess in order to agree a draft, and to ensure clients stay around to sign this. The waiting period is a good opportunity to end on a personal and amicable note, again reinforcing commitment to the implementation of the agreement.

CONTENTS

CHAPTER 8

Settlement and Follow Up

It is late. Hours of hard negotiation and caucusing have eventually resulted in a mutually agreeable set of terms on which the dispute can be settled. The parties and the mediator are relieved and pleased. What remains to be done?

8.1 SETTLEMENT AGREEMENT

8.1.1 Written or oral?

It is vital that the agreed terms should be reduced to writing and that the parties should indicate their consent to these terms. First of all, this ensures that the terms of agreement are commonly understood by all concerned. Mediators will be well aware of the difficulties that arise in translating an apparently agreed oral position into an agreed written one!

Secondly, it gives the opportunity for further detail on the agreed points, and indeed further substantive points, to emerge. Although hearts may sink if they do, it is far better to have this happen during the mediation than a few days later.

Thirdly, some mediation agreements (including the CEDR one at Appendix 3) provide that no agreement reached between the parties during the mediation will be binding unless and until it is reduced to writing and signed. This helps to create a freer atmosphere for debate and consideration of offers during the mediation but obviously imposes a need for any binding settlement agreement to be in writing.

8.1.2 Binding or non-binding?

The settlement agreement, whether oral or written, can be made binding or non-binding in law. This is a matter for agreement between the parties (most agreements are likely to be legally binding subject to normal contractual principles, in the absence of this point being explicit in the agreement itself). In most cases, particularly where the dispute is in litigation, the parties will opt for a binding agreement. An agreed and executed binding document will commit the parties to the positions they have agreed in the mediation. Considerable momentum should have been generated during the mediation, and parties may have arrived at a different view of the dispute to that with which they began the mediation. It is important to harness that momentum in the form of a written commitment.

Inevitably that leaves mediations open to the charge that parties, worn out by the process, will commit to terms which in the 'cold light of day' they would reject. If this is an overriding concern, then of course they are free to conclude some form of non-binding 'memorandum of understanding' or 'gentleman's agreement', or implement a 'cooling-off' period during which the terms can be rejected. In practice, however, the agreement will reflect terms at which they have freely arrived, albeit in a tough negotiating environment. There is no reason why the agreement should not be binding. Furthermore, if those of their colleagues not present at the mediation find it hard to understand why such terms were accepted, that is more than likely a reflection of the fact that they were not present to hear the arguments, participate in the discussions with the mediator, and watch the positions emerge. It is not necessarily an indication that the terms agreed were 'unfavourable' or 'wrong' in any objective sense.

In some disputes, however, a non-binding agreement might more accurately reflect the agreed terms and the nature of the future relationship which the parties are trying to create. A 'cooling-off' period may also be appropriate in consumer cases or where one party is not legally represented.

8.1.3 Detailed agreement or heads of terms?

The question of how much detail to put into a settlement agreement at the end of a mediation will often arise. Where the nature of the dispute is relatively simple, the drafting of a document incorporating all the relevant detail should not pose a problem. If, however, the dispute has been highly complex, the settlement agreement may itself need to be a lengthy document. In addition, the terms of settlement reached may contemplate a new contractual arrangement between the parties, such as a new distribution agreement, which may itself require detailed drafting. Further formalities may also be required to implement any agreement reached, for example, to transfer land from one party to another.

A balance needs to be achieved in the drafting process. Clearly detail is more likely to provide clarity and less scope for future argument. On the other hand, it may simply be unrealistic for the parties to be able to produce a highly detailed document during the mediation itself. If that is the case, heads of agreement, setting out the main points, will often be prepared, which themselves contemplate a further, more detailed agreement being drafted over the coming weeks. The only note of caution which needs to be sounded is as to the degree to which such heads can be made binding, prior to the signing of the more detailed agreement. They will need to contain sufficient detail to avoid being unenforceable due to uncertainty as to the terms. Furthermore, they may end up constituting merely an 'agreement to agree' if too much detail is left for agreement in a later formal agreement, and thus also become unenforceable.

8.1.4 Standard form of terms of settlement

Much of the substance of a settlement agreement, whether a contract or a consent order, will be fairly standard 'boiler-plate' drafting including the identity and addresses of the parties, the recitals and even some of the substantive clauses. This, coupled with the fact that in many mediations the drafting of agreed terms will take place after many hours of arduous negotiations, leads some mediators to use standard form settlement agreements. An example of this is to be found in Appendix 7.

Clearly the content of any settlement agreement will need to be agreed between the parties and much of the detail cannot be prejudged. However, as an outline structure, a standard form can be a valuable 'skeleton' on which to hang the flesh of the agreement. This is particularly so where the substantive terms of the agreement can simply be inserted as an Appendix, or as one clause of the existing outline agreement.

It also serves as a checklist for the parties as to some of the clauses they may want to consider including. Thus, for example, the agreement at Appendix 7 includes:

1. A warranty by each signatory of his/her authority to sign the agreement.

2. A checklist, at clause 2, of issues which might need to be considered in relation to the substantive terms of agreement.

3. Consideration of the effect that breaches of the settlement agreement will have on the remainder of its terms.

4. Provision for dealing with disputes arising out of the settlement agreement (see also para 8.3 below).

5. Provision for dealing with matters still in dispute, if the mediation has only resolved part of the dispute.

6. Consideration of whether any elements of the mediation agreement remain in force following settlement, and how those should be addressed.

Parties and their advisors may conclude that many of these provisions are not in fact required in their particular case, but at least the points will have been raised and considered.

8.2 ENFORCEABILITY

Many parties, and their advisors, will want to be sure that an agreement reached in mediation is going to be enforceable, should the need arise. Sceptics who criticise the process for 'having no teeth' forget that many, possibly most, mediated agreements are, in fact, binding and enforceable. In addition the terms of agreement reached in mediation are likely to be simpler and clearer for the purposes of enforcement (or summary judgment) than the original matters in dispute.

Assuming that the agreement itself is intended to be binding, the following options exist.

8.2.1 Contract

The settlement agreement can take effect between the parties as a contract and bind them under normal contractual principles. Thus there will need to be the usual contractual elements of an offer and acceptance, consideration and intention to create legal relations. In practice, these are very likely to feature in any event. Where concern exists about consideration, the 'forbearance to sue' is very often an option.

Furthermore, any relevant contractual formalities, such as those governing the transfer of an interest in land, will need to be observed.

Assuming that the correct content and formalities exist, the agreement can be enforced in the same way as any other contract.

8.2.2 Consent or 'Tomlin' Order

If litigation proceedings have been commenced, terms of settlement reached between parties can be endorsed by the court in the form of a

Consent or 'Tomlin' Order. This applies whether the agreed terms have been arrived at through mediation or direct negotiation and is a relatively straightforward procedural formality to implement. A precedent form of Tomlin Order is set out in Appendix 7.

The advantage of such an order is that it can be enforced through the court as if it were a judgment. The enforcement of the kind of contract referred to in para 8.2.1 would require the issue of fresh proceedings.

8.2.3 Arbitration Consent Award

As with litigation, the arbitration process can be used to record terms of settlement reached between the parties before final hearing and the equivalent of a Tomlin Order, a Consent Award, is available. The agreed terms of settlement are drawn up and submitted to the arbitrator for approval. The Consent Award, in those terms, is then issued and published. Parties should remember that there are formalities for a Consent Award to be considered, details of which can be found in standard textbooks on the subject. A precedent form of Consent Award is set out in Appendix 7.

Where arbitration proceedings have not been commenced, it is still possible to use the Arbitration Award to record a mediated settlement. This may be a useful technique where concern over enforcement exists. The parties, having reached agreement in the mediation, appoint the mediator as arbitrator, purely for the purpose of recording the terms of settlement. Once appointed, the mediator (now arbitrator) can issue and publish a Consent Award encompassing the agreed terms of settlement.

8.3 CONTINUING ROLE FOR THE MEDIATOR FOLLOWING SETTLEMENT

Some settlement agreements can be performed almost immediately, for example, by the payment of cash, release of goods, signing of documents, etc. Others, however, by their very nature, will be performed or implemented over a period of time following agreement. Where this is the case, parties may well welcome the idea of the mediator (or ADR organisation) continuing to perform some 'overseeing' role. If the mediator has performed effectively, the parties will by then see him as impartial, committed to resolution of the dispute and informed as to its detail. He is therefore ideally placed to contribute in an on-going way.

8.3 Settlement and Follow Up

1. As a mediator

It is not uncommon for a settlement agreement arrived at in mediation to provide that any disputes arising out of the agreement will be referred, in the first instance, to mediation, perhaps with the same mediator. The fact that mediation is stipulated at all suggests that the parties have been relatively satisfied with the process thus far, and of course the use of the same mediator will be cheaper and more efficient, since he is already familiar with the issues.

This approach is particularly effective where the agreement envisages the performance of various future events, and there is concern about whether and how that will occur.

2. As an adjudicator/arbitrator

If the settlement agreement involves, for example, the subsequent sale of assets, the parties may choose to appoint the mediator to adjudicate on the valuation of those assets. This appointment can be included as a term of the settlement agreement.

3. As an 'overseer'

The future role of a mediator might be less formal than that of mediator or arbitrator. For example, if a partnership dispute is settled on terms which provide for the future management of the partnership to be conducted according to certain general principles, the parties might appoint the mediator as an 'overseer' of their conduct. His role, in essence, would be to assist the parties in the practical implementation of their agreed principles, and to be available to discuss and resolve with the parties any problems which might arise.

8.4 OPTIONS WHERE MEDIATION 'FAILS'

8.4.1 Partial settlement

It is an interesting feature of mediation that in the small percentage of disputes that do not settle in the mediation itself, the parties nonetheless usually express themselves satisfied with the process. Furthermore, a high proportion of such disputes do then proceed to settlement in the immediate aftermath of the mediation. It is therefore difficult to talk in

132

terms of the mediation having 'failed', since manifestly it may well have played a pivotal role in generating settlement. Very often, the parties to a 'failed' mediation will comment that they now understand both their own and the other side's case more fully, and that the gap between their respective positions, although not closed, is significantly narrower than before. If nothing else, this may make a subsequent trial quicker and cheaper because only some of the original issues may remain to be decided.

Furthermore, the mediation may result in a partial settlement – ie, where some but not all of the issues in dispute have been resolved. In this situation, it can be very valuable to draft a document which is not legally binding, but which sets out those matters that have been agreed, and the parties' positions in respect of those that have not. This has the effect both of encapsulating, and therefore in some way 'preserving', the progress that has been made, and at the same time reminding the parties that it is only the remaining issues which prevent final agreement being reached.

If the issues are separable, it may even be possible to reach a binding agreement on some without resolution of the others.

8.4.2 Further mediation

Further mediation should not be ruled out. Some mediations have lasted up to five days or more, sometimes spread across several months. The adjournments provide important time for reflection (parties should not be 'pushed' too fast into settlement), information gathering (without which the decisions about settlement may not be capable of being made), reassessment of positions and perhaps the generation of further options for settlement.

Mediation should not be seen as a fixed, one-session process. One of its great strengths is its flexibility. Mediators, parties and advisors should be alive to the possibility of adjournments and reconvening where necessary. Thus, for example, the parties might send in a fresh negotiator or negotiating team, or add some additional 'experts' to the old team. The presence of fresh minds (perhaps with wider settlement authority) may help break the log jam. The parties may even elect to appoint a new mediator, or an additional expert to advise the mediator.

It is often the case that a subsequent session, perhaps with time for reflection in the interim, can bring a change of approach.

If they cannot be persuaded to meet, the parties may nonetheless be

8.4.2 *Settlement and Follow Up*

prepared for the mediator to continue discussions with each of them in private. This he could do by visiting each of them in turn as a 'shuttle diplomat', or indeed by continuing the mediation more informally over the telephone, or via telephone/video conferencing.

8.4.3 Further direct negotiation

It may well be that the mediation has brought the parties to the point where they need further direct talks, without the assistance of the mediator. By coming to mediation in the first place they have indicated a willingness to talk. The mediation process may well have encouraged the perception that, although settlement has not (yet) been reached, further talks may make progress. It may even be that, at the end of the mediation, the parties will be prepared to sign a declaration of intent to have further talks and even to commit themselves to a date.

8.4.4 Different ADR process

The reason that many different ADR processes exist is that each can play a different role in generating settlement. What is applicable for one situation may not be for another. It may well be that, during a mediation, problems emerge which might best be dealt with through a different ADR process.

Typically, for example, one element of a dispute may prove hard to settle in a mediation because the parties had, and have maintained, a genuine good faith disagreement about a particular point of law, or technical issue. Depending on the view they take, they can come up with diametrically opposing views on the implications, and the whole settlement is put in jeopardy. However effective the mediator, he may be unable to break this impasse through mediation. One option would be for the parties to submit the particular issue to, for example, a judicial appraisal or neutral evaluation. This would provide a non-binding but authoritative view, to the parties jointly, on the issue in question. Armed with that, they may well be in a position to return to the mediation and progress beyond the earlier obstacle.

Similarly a mediation might have settled five out of six issues dividing the parties. They might therefore agree to commit to settlement of those on condition that the sixth issue be referred to some form of short-form binding adjudication process (eg, binding judicial appraisal, documents-only arbitration).

134

The use of combinations of processes such as these exemplifies the way in which ADR can, with a little imagination and flexibility, be used to provide a settlement forum designed to address the particular problems of a given situation.

CONTENTS

CHAPTER 9

The Mini-Trial (Executive Tribunal; Executive Appraisal)

9.1 PURPOSE AND FORMAT

The mini-trial has been described as a 'hybrid' or 'blended' ADR procedure because it combines a more formal legal advocacy procedure with elements of information management, negotiation, neutral facilitation and case evaluation. It is a channel for a streamlined information exchange between parties with a view to subsequent negotiation between clients. In essence lawyers or other advisors for each party present a 'mini' version of their case to a panel consisting of a senior executive of their client and of the other party(ies) to provide the appropriate base from which the clients can get to grips with the problem and negotiate resolution, having been given a foretaste of what would occur at a trial of the action. The term 'mini-trial' was apparently coined by a New York Times journalist reporting on an early 'information exchange' procedure.

The procedure may take place without a neutral's involvement but will usually be more effective with a capable neutral to chair the presentation stage and be available to facilitate negotiations or to offer a case evaluation towards the end of the negotiations if there is still a gap between the parties. Strict rules of evidence and strict cross-examination procedures are normally dropped from the procedure. Typically, the panel consists of senior executives from the companies involved who have not had previous direct involvement in the disputed matter. However the procedure may vary in these and other respects as the parties choose, so that panel 'members' may be the managers involved in the dispute or even a plaintiff in a complex personal injury case.

The scope for procedural variations in mini-trials helps to indicate the

137

essential objectives behind the mini-trial. It provides a forum for an exchange of views on case merits that is more formal than a mediation, but more streamlined than an arbitration or trial of the case. It allows advocates on each side to speak directly to the other side's client on the weaknesses of their case in law or fact (or ethics). And it puts clients in a position of greater 'detachment' from their professional or in-house advisors by physically placing them on a panel or 'tribunal' format where they can try to listen more objectively to an overview of the evidence before negotiating directly with the other side's client. The 'neutral advisor' (as he or she is often described in this process) provides a vital mechanism to referee the joint meeting and subsequent negotiations, and sometimes also to referee and advise on the preparatory stages of the mini-trial.

The process can be described more simply in diagrammatic format.

TYPICAL NEGOTIATING STRUCTURE

L1		L2
D1 ... M1		M2 ... D2
W1		W2

L1	=	lawyer for Party 1
M1	=	manager for Party 1 who has been 'running' the case
W1	=	witness (expert or factual) for Party 1
D1	=	director of Party 1 with some knowledge of the case but not previously directly involved.

MINI-TRIAL FORMAT : PRESENTATION STAGE

The senior representatives of each party, plus a neutral advisor, constitute the 'tribunal'

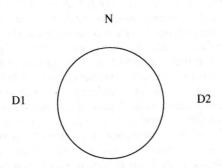

N = Neutral advisor

MINI-TRIAL FORMAT : NEGOTIATION STAGE

The neutral advisor and the senior representative of each party adjourn for private negotiations.

9.1 *The Mini-Trial (Executive Tribunal; Executive Appraisal)*

MINI-TRIAL FORMAT : MEDIATION OR EVALUATION STAGE

The neutral advisor and the senior representatives of each party adjourn for joint mediation session, or evaluation.

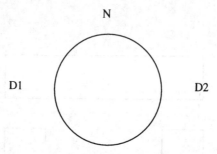

and (giving each side a chance for private caucuses with the neutral advisor)

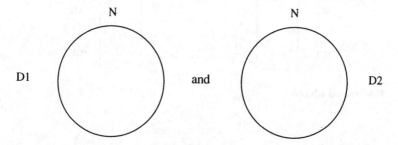

9.2 APPROPRIATE CASES FOR MINI-TRIAL PROCEDURES

There is substantial overlap between mediation and the mini-trial (and indeed many mediations have most of the elements of a mini-trial other than the name and the seating arrangements). Since the mini-trial is typically more formal and more costly, it is normally used in cases where (a) there is a great deal at stake for the parties; (b) the parties have significant differences in their interpretation or evaluation of the law and/or facts of the case; (c) all parties for reasons of cost, publicity or corporate relations would prefer to reach an amicable resolution if possible rather than go to trial or arbitration. Such cases might include situations where for example a serious difference arises between joint venture partners, between companies over intellectual property rights or between defendants over how to apportion liability contributions or indemnities. Ironically, however, there is no particular reason why disputes of that nature should not be dealt with in straightforward mediation, and indeed many have been. It seems then that the rationale for using a mini-trial format rather than mediation lies in:

(i) The psychological attraction of a more procedurally-formal process. This might, for example, create a stronger feeling of having had 'a day in court' than a mediation, due to the use of a more formal presentation phase, witnesses, etc. This may appeal in particular to the lawyers involved, as the forum is slightly closer to a court-room, with which they are likely to be more familiar.

(ii) The element of 'justification' of this process, and therefore of any terms of settlement reached, to a third party, or other constituencies within each party. It is often the case in very high-value or commercially-sensitive cases that the parties will feel that the case somehow merits a correspondingly formal resolution process (albeit that they have chosen to avoid the court-room if possible). There is a sense in which the formality of a mini-trial will enable the parties to feel that the case has been fully heard and explored. They might feel that a mediation was somehow too informal to be appropriate for such a significant dispute. This might be particularly significant for those senior representatives of each party who attend and who will ultimately sanction, or not, any settlement terms. They may well find the terms easier to 'sell' to their respective boards, third party insurers, or whoever, if the process has been seen to be a relatively formal and thorough one.

(iii) The presentational stage may well provide a better opportunity to assess the performance of key witnesses than would be available in mediation. Thus if the contributions of such witnesses are critical to the outcome of the case, a mini-trial may create a better environment for testing those contributions. (There may also be cases where lawyers or middle managers have reasons to resist putting the case before senior directors. These may in fact be appropriate for mini-trials, but contain political grounds for one side's resistance to the suggestion.)

9.3 MAJOR STAGES IN MINI-TRIAL PROCEDURE

9.3.1 Pre-hearing stage

1. Initiating agreement

As with other procedures the parties have to reach the point of agreement that they will use the process. If not based on contract or court-referred,

9.3.1 *The Mini-Trial (Executive Tribunal; Executive Appraisal)*

parties may choose to work from a simple contractual agreement, working out at a later date a more detailed protocol describing the mini-trial procedure.

2. Procedural details

The agreement or protocol on the mini-trial should normally cover the following issues:

(a) Agreement on identity of neutral advisor, and his or her fees and role, including if appropriate a role in helping parties agree details of mini-trial procedures and pre-hearing preparation or procedures. (It is generally helpful for an experienced neutral or ADR organisation to assist in at least some preliminary discussions and for the neutral advisor to meet the respective teams and panel representatives before the hearing.)

(b) Setting down timescale and schedule of actions.

(c) Extent to which the parties will be negotiating their own rules or relying on the neutral advisor or an ADR organisation's standard rules.

(d) Agreement on venue, dates for mini-trial, arrangements at venue (including hearing and caucus rooms, catering, office facilities etc).

(e) Agreement on abbreviated discovery process (if required).

(f) Agreement on procedures at the mini-trial – length of presentations, replies, panel question and answer session, whether witnesses used, questioning by other counsel or by panel only, post-hearing negotiations, neutral role, grounds for withdrawal or continuation.

(g) Agreement on bundle of documents.

(h) Notice of witnesses (if used), advocates and other panel members, and panel members' authority to settle the case.

(i) Date for exchange of notice of exhibits, witness statements, other material.

(j) Agreement on costs (usually each side bears its own costs and shares equally the other costs of the procedure).

(k) Notice of others who will attend mini-trial.

Given the range of activities involved, mini-trial pre-hearing procedures are likely to take at least two-three months.

3. Legal framework

The mini-trial agreement should also deal with the key legal questions discussed in relation to mediation agreements – effect on other proceedings, authority to settle, confidentiality between parties, neutral and ADR organisation, privilege, immunity, costs. Because of the similarity between the processes, a mediation agreement is a useful starting-point from which to draft a mini-trial agreement, certainly insofar as issues of confidentiality and 'without prejudice' are concerned.

9.3.2 The mini-trial stage

Typically the presentation stage is abbreviated compared with a trial, taking up only a few hours or a half-day or day per party. The aim is to give each party time to deliver its presentation effectively to the panel and the panel time to consider it – for instance:

Day 1	9.00	12.00	Plaintiff presentation
	12.00	1.00	Defendant reply
	2.00	3.00	Question and answer session with panel
Day 2	9.00	12.00	Defendant presentation
	12.00	1.00	Plaintiff reply
	2.00	3.00	Question and answer session
Days 3,4			Panel negotiations

Longer hearings may be encountered in multi-party or more complex cases, but care should be taken to avoid the procedure duplicating arbitration or trial because of lawyer expectations. The procedure is meant after all to be an abbreviated version, a *'mini-trial'*, in order to optimise executive time in dealing with the case and to resolve it on a reasonable and realistic basis.

For this reason, too, it may be best to allow each party to present its case as it sees fit, subject only to clear rules on timetable, on use of witnesses and exhibits, and on whether cross-examination is to be allowed (not a good idea in most cases).

Presentations can be done with more fluidity than an opening or closing address in court, involving an extended display of one's best case, perhaps calling on two presenters and interspersed with some exhibits, references to key passages in documents, and short statements from important witnesses of fact or opinion.

9.3.2 *The Mini-Trial (Executive Tribunal; Executive Appraisal)*

Rebuttals to such presentations should also be compact and able to highlight major weaknesses in the other's presentation.

Cross-examination may be best avoided since it may heighten adversarial attitudes but some scope should be given for opposing counsel to invite the panel to include some key questions in a panel question session following the presentation and reply phase.

There may also be value in building in short summary 'closing addresses' to remind the panel of the major features of the case.

9.3.3 The negotiation/mediation stage

Negotiations can commence after an adjournment, possibly mid-morning on the third day through to day five or as set out in the protocol. (The neutral's role is discussed more fully below.) If negotiations succeed, the parties' advisors can be called in to draft or execute the agreement. If they fail, parties are free to reconvene by agreement, can allow a 'cooling-off' period to consider proposals or neutral recommendations, or can return to continuing litigation or arbitration procedures. Negotiations may commence without the neutral being present, with the neutral being called on only if an opinion or mediation role would assist. However there are advantages in the neutral at least spending a short period with the parties to obtain an initial sense of their positions.

9.4 MAKING MINI-TRIAL PROCEDURES EFFECTIVE: PARTICIPANT ROLES

It has been said that mini-trials are effective because everyone involved gets a chance to do what they are best at, to 'do their thing'. Lawyers get an opportunity to present legal argument and analysis in a semi-formal setting and what is more to address themselves directly to the other party(ies). (This is a feature of mediation as well, and its value to the settlement process can be immense. In the normal course of litigation/arbitration, parties are generally only confronted with the other side's case via their own lawyers and experts, until, that is, the case gets to trial. The element of 'raw' exposure of each party to the other side's case, which most ADR processes provide, is often critical in generating settlement.) Experts and other witnesses get a chance to summarise their evidence in their own words without the stress and distortion of trial cross-examination; managers get the chance to take commercial decisions in the light of expert advice, probability assessment, the commercial context and their 'feel' for the situation and the people involved; 'neutrals' can nudge the process along with a detached yet considered contribution to discussions. It is worth bearing this overall perspective in mind in deciding on procedure and on the way to allot and perform the various roles involved in the mini-trial.

9.4.1 Role of the lawyer

The lawyer's role in the mini-trial can be more easily described formally than in mediation, although lawyers should not make the mistake of assuming that mediation requires less preparation than a mini-trial. However there is a more overt advocacy and research element in the mini-trial. The stages a lawyer must review are:

(i) organising procedure, particularly with regard to information collection, presentation and exchange;

(ii) selecting the neutral and agreeing on the neutral's role (if any) in organising pre-hearing procedures;

(iii) counselling client and witnesses pre-hearing and at the hearing;

(iv) presenting case at the hearing;

(v) counselling client where appropriate during negotiation or mediation phase;

(vi) drafting and/or executing settlement agreement.

Key practice pointers for lawyers involved in a mini-trial are:

(a) remember at all times the objective – to persuade the other party and the neutral advisor of the credibility of your case, and to strengthen the confidence and skills, where appropriate, of your own client for the negotiation and evaluation stage;

(b) be careful to avoid the trap of becoming over-rigid in negotiations on pre-hearing procedures – your goal is not to prove you can 'win' over your legal opponent but to lay an effective foundation to achieve your objectives in (a). Neither clients nor a neutral adviser are likely to be impressed with a lawyer scoring technical points, and such an approach is likely only to delay proceedings and add to costs;

(c) similarly consider whether your case might be assisted by consenting to the other side's choice of neutral – if you can 'win over'

9.4.1 *The Mini-Trial (Executive Tribunal; Executive Appraisal)*

their choice during the mini-trial, how will they fare when they have less control before a judge?

(d) coach your own client to respond effectively to strong arguments likely to be put across by the other side or by the neutral; to have a structured negotiating plan; to be aware of the possibility of calling an adjournment in negotiations if further advice may be needed;

(e) select and prepare witnesses so that their presentation is compact yet telling, and so that they are able to respond in a similar vein to questions from the panel;

(f) remember the goal at the advocacy stage is not merely to 'win over' the neutral. First and foremost, you need to help the other party adjust their expectations on the outcomes of the negotiation stage and alternatives to a reasonable settlement;

(g) in the same vein remember that an over-adversarial presentation can lead to resistance to your case from the other party or neutral – you need to be part of their solution to this dispute, not the biggest problem in it.

9.4.2 Role of the neutral advisor

The neutral advisor's role in the mini-trial may also be more wide-ranging in a complex case than that of a mediator. Like the lawyer the neutral needs to review his or her role in:

(i) pre-hearing procedures or disputes arising at this stage;

(ii) the hearing itself;

(iii) negotiations and mediation subsequent to the hearing.

(i) Pre-hearing procedures

Where involved at this stage, the neutral should adopt as much as feasible the role of facilitative mediator rather than adjudicator of procedure. This will help avoid either party deciding that the neutral is biased at an early stage. Such a development may undermine the neutral's credibility if a later evaluative stage becomes necessary. On the other hand where the parties have a high regard for the neutral, they may be prepared to defer to that neutral's greater experience. Even in such circumstances an effective neutral should ensure the parties feel they have had a full airing of their concerns.

146

(ii) The hearing

The neutral's role is very much to demonstrate capability as a fair chair of proceedings and an insightful questioner, again to reassure the panel members and their advisors of his or her fairness, credibility and experience. The neutral should in particular ensure that he or she uses the various breaks in proceedings to develop a good relationship with the executives on the panel, and to avoid indications of favouritism to either party.

(iii) Post-hearing negotiations

This is perhaps the most delicate stage of the procedure for a ..eutral. Classical 'theory' on the mini-trial suggests that the executives should spend a period of time on their own in order to attempt to negotiate a settlement before resorting again to the neutral. However the neutral advisor should be alert throughout the hearing phase to whether a more active role may be called for, and in particular:

(a) whether to spend a short period after the hearings reviewing with the panellists their initial reactions and helping summarise the key issues and evidence in a non-evaluative way;

(b) whether to step immediately into the role of facilitative mediator.

These approaches may be justified if the neutral senses that relations between the executives are initially so sensitive or rigid that a direct negotiation session may be fruitless or unproductive without the assistance above.

Whichever route is adopted, the neutral should remind the panellists of the timetable and of how and when to recall him if negotiations seem to be floundering.

Determining the appropriate tactics is a matter of professional judgment based on the neutral's experience and sense of the type of case and type of parties or personalities involved. In particular, however, neutrals should be aware that if they intervene too early the parties may not have developed fully their negotiating sense of the situation; intervene too late and the parties may have frozen into resistance to movement even on the basis of the neutral's evaluation.

Again it is a matter of judgment as to how the neutral plays the role if negotiations have not produced a settlement. In general the neutral should first obtain a sense from each side of the extent and cause of progress or lack of it. If required, evaluation of the case should initially be given in private caucuses, but should be a review of strengths and weaknesses on each side that is consistent and detached between them.

In some cases this may lead to discussion of a flexible settlement proposal; in more narrow cases a suggested monetary figure or bargaining range.

The neutral should bear in mind at this stage that there may be some need for 'face-saving' to justify further movement by one or both parties. It may even be necessary to help the parties 'revisit' some of the witnesses or legal advisors to help matters forward, or to suggest a 'cooling-off' period followed by a further meeting to have a 'last shot' at settlement. An offer to take the executives to dinner for a final attempt may not go amiss!

The power of the mini-trial lies in the range of techniques and roles it draws into the more informal mediation process. It is an extremely valuable option in major corporate disputes and used perhaps less frequently than its potential impact merits.

CONTENTS

CHAPTER 10

Adjudication and Expert Determination

It is not within the scope of the book to consider the processes of adjudication and expert determination in detail, but a brief description and analysis may be of assistance.

10.1 ADJUDICATION

10.1.1 Definition

We referred in Chapter 1 to 'adjudicative processes', and in Chapter 3 to 'adjudication', to describe, conceptually, a range of processes in which some form of adjudication (ie, decision on the outcome of a case by a third party) takes place. This should not be confused with 'adjudication' as dealt with in this chapter, which is a very specific type of adjudicative process.

Adjudication, in this context, is a process that some consider bestrides ADR and litigation/arbitration. The feature emphasised by ADR commentators, when differentiating adjudication from other ADR processes, is that the latter are essentially consensual, whereas the function of the adjudicator is to reach a decision having considered submissions from both sides.

Unlike litigation and arbitration, adjudication is not subject to the rules of the Supreme Court, the appropriate statutes or the Arbitration Acts. Nor is the adjudicator afforded any immunity in carrying out his function.

10.1.2 Features

10.1.2.1 Speed

Most adjudication procedures contemplate a very short timetable with the appointment taking place within 7–14 days, submissions being delivered within the same timescale with a requirement that the adjudicator produces his decision shortly thereafter.

10.1.2.2 Documents only

Because of the constricted timetable it is normally contemplated that submissions will be by documents only with little or no allowance for oral submissions to be made. Obviously the documents that are produced are those upon which the party relies – there being no time or allowance for any sort of discovery.

10.1.2.3 Inquisitorial procedure

The adjudicator is commonly allowed to investigate areas he deems appropriate and this may involve, in technical disputes, a visit to, or an inspection of, the matter in dispute.

10.1.2.4 Qualification of the adjudicator

Normally it is contemplated that he will be an expert in his field (hence the allowance for an investigation). Expertise also avoids the necessity of briefing the adjudicator fully on the technical subject matter. It may also be helpful if the adjudicator has some knowledge of court or arbitration procedures in order for him to conduct himself in a judicial manner. It is therefore likely that he will come from a background of either litigation or arbitration practice.

10.1.2.5 Enforceability of decision

The Court of Appeal in *Cameron v Mowlem* [1990] 52 BLR 24 held that (in respect of a particular form of building contract) a decision of an adjudicator was binding only until the determination by an arbitrator on the disputed claim to a set-off, and so was not 'an award on an arbitration agreement' within the meaning of section 26 of the Arbitration Act 1950, and could not be enforced summarily under that section. However, in *Drake & Scull v McLaughlin & Harvey* (1992) 60 BLR 102 an Official Referee enforced an adjudicator's decision by granting a mandatory injunction requiring the defendant to pay monies to a trustee-stakeholder. It is uncertain whether the injunction would have been granted if the adjudicator had ordered that the money be paid direct to the plaintiff. These two decisions illustrate that there are many unanswered questions relating to the status of an adjudicator's decision that still need to be determined by the courts.

10.1.2.6 Appeal

Adjudicators are not encouraged to give reasons as this lays their decisions open to attack. The underlying principle behind the concept of adjudication is to produce what has sometimes been described as 'rough and ready' justice, upon an interim basis, with a view to diffusing the argument, easing the claimant's cash flow and allowing the parties to proceed with their contract. Adjudication rules normally provide that the decision is binding upon the parties subject to the right to take the matter to litigation and/or arbitration upon the giving of notice within a specified period after the adjudicator's decision. It is this feature that primarily distinguishes adjudication from some types of arbitration. Furthermore, the procedure is not conducted on a 'without prejudice' basis and therefore submissions made to the adjudicator and his decision can be referred to in later proceedings.

10.1.2.7 Immunity

As stated above, the adjudicator has no immunity. Indeed, he is subject to normal professional standards and can be liable to a claim in negligence – another reason to avoid giving reasons. Any plaintiff contemplating an action for negligence against an adjudicator will, of course, have to take into consideration the information that was supplied to the adjudicator and upon which he based his decision coupled with the time frame within which such a decision was reached.

10.1.2.8 Identity of the adjudicator

As with arbitration clauses, it may not be appropriate to identify a particular adjudicator in the contract clause. This is not only because the parties will not know the expertise required of the adjudicator until a particular dispute arises, but also because of the element of speed. The adjudicator needs to be readily available, possibly not already committed on any other adjudication at the time.

10.1.2.9 Usage

The provision for adjudication is sometimes found in standard forms of building contract. There has been a recent trend to encourage its wider use. It is true to say that widespread use in the construction industry is still in its infancy. Elsewhere it can be found mostly in areas of valuation be it in property or in the financial field.

10.2 EXPERT DETERMINATION

Often the dispute between the parties is one of valuation or of a purely technical nature. Following legislative restrictions on the parties' rights of appeal, coupled with a growing dissatisfaction with formal arbitration, parties often opt for such a dispute to be determined by an independent third party acting as an expert rather than in a judicial or arbitral capacity. Whilst there are many parallels with the function of adjudicator, nevertheless, there are significant differences.

10.2.1 Acting as expert

It is important that the clause providing for the dispute to be determined by an expert specifically records that he is to be acting 'as expert'. Firstly, this helps to ensure that the procedure is not governed by the Arbitration Acts and secondly (if that is the case) there is no right of appeal, thereby giving the parties finality. However, merely using the term 'expert' will not suffice if in reality the person concerned is, de facto, acting as an arbitrator.

10.2.2 Procedure

Again there are parallels with adjudication. The parties are likely to make their submissions by way of documents only. As the expert is acting as expert, he is normally clothed with the power to investigate, ie, act inquisitorially. He must, however, be mindful of his overriding duty to act fairly as between the parties.

10.2.3 Appeal

There is no statutory right of appeal. The only circumstances in which a decision can be challenged is where the expert has asked himself the wrong question or decided the wrong issue. Because there is no immunity either, the expert can, like the adjudicator, be vulnerable to a claim for negligence if he fails in his professional duty.

10.2.4 Identity

As in adjudication it may be preferable not to name the expert in the contract. However, unlike adjudication, it is helpful to identify the particular expertise needed; for example, a surveyor in respect of rent reviews, an accountant for share valuations and an actuary in respect of pension disputes. There is nothing to stop a lawyer being appointed as an expert in respect of a legal dispute. In practice, however, such an appointment is more likely to be made where a dispute arises after the contract has been agreed as most lawyers (and indeed their clients) would like to think the document that they have agreed is clear.

10.2.5 Finality

By way of contrast to adjudication, it is intended that the expert's determination is final and binding on the parties. In other words, provision is not usually made for the parties to have a time limit, following the determination, within which to take the matter to arbitration or litigation.

CONTENTS

CHAPTER 11

ADR and Practice Development

11.1 INTRODUCTION

The development of ADR has been thought to present many professionals, not least lawyers, with an apparent dilemma. Indeed, one might even say that for all professionals involved in the litigation process, ADR exposes a fundamental and uncomfortable tension within their work, between obtaining a good (which often includes fast and cost-effective) solution for the client, and maximising the income required to run a business.

. The dilemma, therefore, is whether or not to endorse processes which often bring the litigation process to an end more quickly. On the face of it, the question is easily answered. A lawyer has a duty to act in his client's best interests, and if early resolution serves those interests, then all appropriate ways of achieving it should be (and often are) pursued. In practice, however, the question may be much harder to resolve. It is probably this factor, more than any other, which explains the initially slow growth of ADR both in the UK, and in other jurisdictions where it now prospers.

Furthermore, there has been a considerable degree of 'hype' surrounding the development of ADR, much of which has blurred the very important issues facing professionals, in their response to ADR. Stripping away the hype, a picture emerges of a mixture of 'negative' and 'positive' reasons for dispute professionals to endorse ADR. In other words, ADR presents both a 'carrot' and a 'stick'. The arguments merit considered analysis by anyone operating in the field of disputes.

11.1.1 ADR and Practice Development

11.1.1 'The carrot'

(a) Good results

The client comes to the litigation professional with 'a problem' and wants 'a solution'. He measures the effectiveness of the lawyer's service by a number of factors – clearly by whether he 'wins' or 'loses', but also by such factors as the time and cost required to obtain the result; the relevance of the result to his own commercial or personal situation; and whether any pre-existing commercial or personal relationships survive the process. Indeed, it is probable that the client judges the value of the lawyer's service to him by a broad range of criteria – perhaps even broader than the lawyer's judgment of his own service.

ADR will frequently obtain for a client a 'better' result than might otherwise have been achieved, particularly where 'better' includes reference to the wider commercial or personal priorities of the client. Since the practise of law is essentially demand-led, it must make sense to be offering services that the clients want (or would want, if they were informed about them).

(b) Reputation

Reputation is critical to any professional, and certainly to those engaged in disputes. Different professionals covet and pursue different reputations, but few would shy away from a reputation for getting 'good results'. There is little doubt that in the longer term (if not already) lawyers and other professionals will emerge with reputations for using ADR to resolve problems quickly and effectively – indeed some are already pursuing that. This is even more significant for those seeking 'repeat business' clients – those, such as insurance companies or banks, for example, who tend to have a regular throughput of litigation. Clearly, the benefits accruing to the client are multiplied for each piece of litigation which is successfully and quickly resolved. For repeat litigants, the benefits of ADR, and hence the reputation and kudos falling on those of their advisors who offer it, can be very considerable.

Furthermore, there will always be a significant tranche of cases which are considered 'uneconomical' to litigate, but which would be considered appropriate for ADR, thus bringing new work to those who can offer ADR.

(c) ADR reflects well on non-ADR work

There can be little doubt that an informed commitment to ADR can send a powerful message to clients. This applies not only where ADR is used, but also where it is not. A client whose lawyer uses ADR properly will at least know that where the lawyer is not doing so, it is because ADR is not appropriate or possible, rather than because he is not informed or willing. It is much easier to convince a client of the necessity of continuing with the litigation process if he knows that the ADR option has been canvassed and validly rejected.

(d) Competitive edge

The current professional climate is extremely competitive, with strong downward pressure on fees from an increasingly sophisticated client base well accustomed to 'shopping around' for advisers, and negotiating strongly on fees. Thus the arguments about individual reputation transfer easily to firm reputation. For a firm seeking a competitive edge over their competitors, ADR offers a wide range of possibilities – from general prominence in a 'beauty parade' to specific litigation tenders based on significant numbers of cases going to ADR, and costed accordingly. It is fair to say that, so far, few if any law firms in the UK have begun fully to exploit the true potential of ADR.

11.1.2. 'The stick'

(a) Reputation

Essentially, many of the 'stick' arguments are the reverse of the 'carrot' ones, and none more so than those of reputation and the competitive edge. A reputation for not using processes which other lawyers or other professionals can use to good effect is never likely to attract business.

(b) Litigation practice developments

ADR in the UK has travelled a great distance in a relatively short time. The involvement of the courts has been demonstrated through two Practice Directions (see Chapter 5) and the use of a specific direction at the summons for directions stage. To that extent, ADR has 'arrived' on the legal scene, and it is therefore neither credible nor possible for lawyers in particular to remain uninformed about it. At the very least, the question now has to be discussed with clients and the other parties to the action (see for example Commercial Court Practice Direction, Appendix 6). This can only realistically be done by those who are properly informed, and preferably who have some experience of ADR in practice.

In short, ADR has shifted from being essentially fringe to increasingly within the mainstream of legal practice. Although it is not easy to judge future developments, it seems clear that this trend will continue to intensify. If it is not the case already, it will soon be impossible to practice litigation or arbitration without a solid grounding in ADR.

(c) Potential liability

Given the value which ADR can deliver to a client, it is not hard to argue that the failure to alert a client to the existence of ADR is, at best, falling short of best practice. The more widespread its use becomes, the more likely such a failure is to become an act of professional negligence although the question has not yet been tested in the English courts. Naturally, it might be difficult to prove causation and loss in such circumstances, but the mere fact that the conduct itself may come close to, or even be, negligent gives an indication of the significance which ADR has achieved within the legal process. In any case, and more cynically, it is always useful if a lawyer can say to a client who, following lengthy litigation, complains about the cost or result – 'I did tell you about ADR but you rejected it'.

11.2 ADR CHOICES

As with all areas of practice development, professionals have essentially three options:

(1) Oppose ADR – ADR can be expressly opposed, presumably on the grounds that it is not a process which serves clients' interests. That is all very well, but it is not easy to maintain that a process with a proven track record, and which can offer clients faster, more cost effective and more constructive settlements than litigation or arbitration, is not in their interest.

(2) Ignore it – ADR can be ignored (subject to public lip service being paid in appropriate circumstances). This may be an attractive short-term view but it takes no account of the fact that clients

increasingly shop around for advisors, and are attracted to those who are capable of offering imaginative, effective and, above all, commercial solutions.

(3) Use it – ADR can be incorporated into the mainstream of litigation and commercial practice, and offered to clients on the same basis as any other legal services. This does not mean that it will replace all litigation and arbitration. It means that those engaged in disputes will be sufficiently informed and experienced to guide their clients through ADR when it will be of benefit.

11.3 DEVELOPING AN ADR CAPABILITY

Once a decision is taken to endorse ADR, and develop a capability for it, practical questions arise as to how to put that into effect. The following points, at least, may merit some consideration.

(a) Decision and policy

Any serious use of ADR needs to stem from a conscious decision to use it, rather than from a drift into it. Not only is this a more intellectually and professionally credible position, it is also likely to result in a more coherent approach to ADR and greater success in using it. It is also generally critical that those in more junior positions within an organisation are aware of the firm or company's decision and policy on ADR. If they are to be expected to grapple with new practices, they will need the comfort of knowing that their efforts are sanctioned by their superiors. If not, there will always be a tendency to adopt the 'safe' option and continue with traditional methods.

(b) Training

As with any new area of practice, good training is important. ADR presents legal and tactical questions for the professional, about which his client will require advice. It also presents lawyers in particular with a new challenge – representation of the client within ADR. As we suggested in Chapter 7, this can differ markedly from representation in the traditional adversarial forums. Furthermore, the negotiating structure of, for example, a mediation is probably different from anything most lawyers have previously experienced. In order to understand fully how the process will operate and develop and so derive the maximum benefit for the client, lawyers should acquaint themselves with the subtleties of the process through an appropriate training programme.

(c) Budget

It is not possible to launch any new product without a budget, covering for example planning, development and marketing costs. The same applies to ADR. However, the 'start-up' costs of ADR are in reality fairly limited, covering perhaps some training and marketing. In fact, given the benefit that ADR is capable of delivering over the medium to long term, the minimal start-up costs can make it an attractive proposition. This is mainly because it operates within the context of an existing litigation and arbitration practice, on to which it can be grafted with relative ease.

(d) Publicity and marketing

Professionals today are more conscious than ever of the importance of publicity and marketing. In many ways, ADR fits very easily into that arena because the essential message is a very positive one. It is, in short, a relatively 'easy product to sell', particularly to those accustomed to buying litigation services. It therefore makes sense to give such a product good exposure, whether in firm brochures, seminars with clients, newsletters, or however else the firm's marketing is conducted.

(e) ADR units

Some firms have gone to the length of establishing ADR specialist units within the firm. These consist of practitioners who have some knowledge and training, and hopefully experience, of ADR, and who are therefore able to offer specialist advice to colleagues within the firm and their respective clients. This could range from advice on ADR clauses through to the preparation and conduct of a mediation. These units were probably at their most effective a few years ago, when ADR was novel and such knowledge limited to a few. There is probably still an argument for concentrating particular expertise in a few people, but that should not cloud the fact that a working knowledge of ADR is something all litigators should now have.

(f) ADR schemes, tenders, and beauty parades

Following the 'competitive edge' argument (para 11.1.1 above), ADR can clearly play a role in tenders for new work, or 'beauty parades'. The financial implications of the consistent and strategic use of ADR can be very significant, and that is not likely to be lost on any client who regularly buys litigation services. It may well be that the client requires some considerable guidance in working out, with their legal advisors, how best ADR can be integrated into their existing dispute-handling process. That in itself can be advice that the lawyer can give, and can also create a context in which to develop a good working relationship with the client as well as a sense that the lawyer is interested in reducing the client's exposure to litigation, rather than simply dealing with the results of it.

11.4 THE LAWYER AS MEDIATOR

So far we have assessed the relevance and value of ADR to professionals (particularly to lawyers) in the context of their own clients – ie, where they represent one party to a dispute. There is, however, a significant role for lawyers as mediators.

At present, it is probably fair to say that there is more benefit to be derived (financially and otherwise) from the former role than from the latter, since the amount of work available for mediators in the UK is still not large. Over the medium to long term, however, that is very likely to change. Many of those already acting as mediators are lawyers. The mental shift from adversarial representative to mediator is not always an easy one, and indeed not one which all lawyers can, or would want to, make. But for those who do, it has proved an extremely satisfying and challenging role. The likelihood is that, as the field develops, an increasing number of lawyers will see a role for themselves as mediators. In the nature of the work, it can easily be an 'extension' to an existing legal practice, rather than there being any need to become a full-time mediator.

Furthermore, it is certainly the case that the best understanding of the subtleties and potential of ADR stems from immersion in it, both as representative of a party and as mediator. Many lawyers have already sought to train as mediators not because they expect to generate much income from it, but because it enhances and informs their ability to represent their own clients in the process.

In passing, it is worth noting, however, that the delivery of ADR services from within the context of a law firm can raise its own particular problems. In particular, the sensitive nature of the mediator's position requires scrupulous attention to be paid to any possible conflicts of interest. In any one mediation, the mediator may well receive confidential information from at least two parties which in itself may impact upon his firm's ability to act for or against either of those parties in the future. In addition, indications from the United States suggest that there is something of a conflict between a law firm offering its services as a representative of a party, and doing so as mediator. It may be, in the long term, that the reality of a mediator's position is that the services have to be delivered from an essentially independent base, and not one which is also engaged in partisan representation.

11.5 NON-CONTENTIOUS LAWYERS

Disputes do not always suddenly spring into being. They often emerge, sometimes quite slowly. In reality, there is often a 'grey area' near the outset of a dispute, between a 'commercial negotiation' and a fully-fledged 'dispute'. Of course, vast numbers of potential disputes are settled at that stage, with or without the intervention of lawyers. But for those that do not, considerable thought needs to be given to the transition process, and particularly to the way in which it is handled within the law firm. Even a change of solicitor, as a case is handed from for example the commercial department to the litigation department, can send a powerful message (intentionally or otherwise) to the other side.

ADR can be a powerful tool in this transitional phase. Indeed, the mere offer of ADR (perhaps as a final attempt at resolution before the issue of proceedings) can help to preserve a negotiating environment that may be lost as soon as a writ is issued. It follows that the non-contentious lawyer, perhaps well accustomed to handling negotiations up to a certain point prior to handing the case to a litigator, has as much need of fluency in and knowledge of ADR as the litigator. Indeed, the ADR processes themselves, supremely mediation, are in many respects more instinctive and habitual for, for example, a commercial lawyer than for a litigator. The environment of the mediation is much more akin to a typical commercial negotiation than it is to a court.

Even more importantly, perhaps, it is non-contentious lawyers who control the drafting of commercial agreements, and hence the opportunity to include a contractual commitment to ADR use. Without doubt, this is an area where the draftsman can significantly affect the future relationship between the parties. That, on one analysis, could be said to be legal drafting at its best. A fuller discussion of ADR clauses appears in Chapter 12, but their importance cannot be overstated.

11.6 IN-HOUSE LEGAL ADVISORS

In-house advisors may especially be able to find a role for promoting ADR and have been in the forefront of its development in the USA. Not only do they not have the fear of lost fees, by contrast they have an incentive to control costs for their employers.

In-house lawyer litigation management can include ensuring that outside lawyers are required on a regular basis to quote predicted costs and outcomes if they recommend litigation, and assessment of ADR potential at regular stages of litigation. In particular outside lawyers should be required to specify the risks of using ADR if they advise against it.

In addition to litigation management in-house lawyers may be able to consider the strategic potential for adding value to their employer's business – by contract procedures, joint venture agreements, corporate policy statements on relations with suppliers and customers, ADR schemes for customer disputes or disputes between internal operating units of the company. As with their external colleagues, in-house lawyers should seek to ensure that they fully understand the practicalities of ADR by involvement in training and by testing its use in cases which are not too sensitive for company politics, if there is limited knowledge of ADR amongst managers. Education programmes for managers will also assist corporate readiness to use ADR.

11.7 OTHER PROFESSIONS

There is a wide variety of professionals engaged in the delivery of 'dispute services'. ADR has implications for all of them.

11.7.1 Accountants

So far the use of ADR processes by accountants has been limited. Mostly it has been confined to their role as expert witnesses in litigation proceedings, when they attend the mediation of that dispute to advise their clients. In itself this is an extremely valuable role, and such expert input at a mediation can sometimes help generate movement (see Chapter 6 for use of experts). It is, however, curious that their involvement has not yet been greater. Accountants often inhabit the 'grey area' between negotiation and dispute referred to above, and as the lead professionals involved at that stage, they are in an ideal position to steer a dispute into ADR, perhaps

165

even without the lawyers becoming involved. Accountants regularly have such early involvement in disputes concerning share valuations, partnerships, financial services and many other business areas, as well as in more personal areas such as family businesses and trusts, and even divorce. It is the early nature of their involvement, often prior to any legal input, which creates opportunities of its own in relation to ADR.

Accountants also have a considerable role to play as mediators. Whilst being an accountant is no guarantee of possessing the appropriate personal qualities to be a good mediator, there is no reason why accountants should not join other professionals in working as mediators. In particular, some complex financial disputes, for example concerning loss of profit in business interruption, might benefit from an accountant mediator.

Finally, the accountancy profession includes management consultancy, an area where ADR could have extensive implications. At its best, ADR represents an opportunity for a business to rethink its entire approach to the handling of disputes, rather than merely use ADR processes on an ad hoc basis from time to time. Such a rethink can incorporate issues as diverse as corporate policy and governance, relations with suppliers, customers and employees, and public image. Furthermore, it can have a significant impact on the time and cost attributable to the handling of disputes.

All these factors indicate that, taken seriously, ADR could with comparative ease become an integral part of a management consultancy review of a business.

11.7.2 Construction industry professionals

The construction industry is a source of many disputes, and there is no reason why the professionals who work in it (quantity surveyors, engineers, architects, etc) should not, with appropriate training and experience, offer their services as mediators. Furthermore, the greater use of mediation (or other ADR techniques) has the potential significantly to improve the efficiency and profitability of the industry, and all professionals should be considering the use of ADR in situations where they represent one party.

11.7.3 Other disciplines

The same principles apply to more or less any disciplines or professional sectors, whether in the field of medicine, charities, local government, information technology, or elsewhere.

CONTENTS

CHAPTER 12

ADR Contract Clauses

12.1 WHAT IS AN ADR CONTRACT CLAUSE?

An ADR contract clause is a clause in an agreement by which the contracting parties agree to attempt to resolve any disputes between them by the use of one or more ADR processes. It may be a very simple, short clause, or alternatively set out a lengthy and complex process. It may specify a particular ADR procedure (eg, mediation) or leave the parties to agree on one as and when a particular dispute arises. Where it contemplates the use of a non-binding ADR procedure (eg mediation, mini-trial, judicial or expert appraisal, etc) it can clearly only require the parties to *attempt* resolution, whereas a clause containing a binding ADR procedure (eg, binding expert appraisal, adjudication etc) can oblige the parties to abide by any award which results from it.

ADR clauses are now in relatively widespread use in the UK. A number of examples of standard form clauses are set out in Appendix 2 (and a useful commentary on those clauses appears as Annex 3 to Appendix 5).

12.2 WHAT DO ADR CLAUSES AIM TO ACHIEVE?

The whole philosophy of ADR tends towards a non-binding, 'without prejudice' approach, designed to provide an opportunity for the dispute to be discussed, and resolution explored, in a relatively risk-free and confidential environment. The use of a contract clause to compel parties to take part in, for example, a mediation might therefore be regarded by some as contrary to the whole notion of ADR. After all, any mediation which the parties are only attending because they are contractually

169

obliged to do so may be difficult to settle. Mediation pre-supposes some degree of willingness on the part of both/all parties at least to explore the various settlement options and to listen to the other side's arguments, whatever view is eventually taken. This may be absent among parties compelled to attempt ADR.

However, the primary value of an ADR clause lies not in its element of compulsion, but in the fact that it puts ADR 'on the agenda'. It is a reminder to the parties that, when they signed the agreement, ADR was viewed as a sensible step to take in the event of a dispute arising. It may even remind them that there was a time when relations between them were better! Most importantly, it overcomes any reluctance to suggest ADR when a dispute arises, for fear that that may be viewed as an indication of weakness. ADR can be discussed and attempted merely because it is in the contract. It is difficult to overstate the importance of such clauses in enabling parties to set up an ADR procedure. There is a widespread assumption that the suggestion by one party of a willingness to use ADR will be perceived by the other(s) as a sign of weakness (see also Chapter 5 above). Whatever the truth of this, it acts as a significant barrier to many disputes reaching mediation (or other ADR processes). ADR contract clauses constitute by far the most effective way of circumventing this fear. The existence of the clause provides ample justification for a mediation to be suggested and discussed. If it is not felt suitable, the parties can always agree to waive the requirement. Indeed, since many ADR clauses are not enforceable as a matter of law (see para 12.4 below), either party can often unilaterally avoid the obligation in any event.

In fact, the inclusion of ADR clauses in contracts is a vital element of good dispute avoidance or management. It is an attempt to pre-empt future disputes by putting in place the appropriate resolution structure while the parties are still on good terms.

For this reason it is important to note that ADR begins at the contractual, non-contentious stage. Those involved in drafting and preparing contract documentation (eg, non-contentious commercial lawyers) need to be as informed and aware of the various ADR possibilities as those who will eventually handle the resulting disputes. Creative organisation of contractual dispute systems ought to be considered their responsibility.

12.3 TYPES OF ADR CLAUSE

There is a wide variety of types of ADR clause, some examples of which are set out in Appendix 2. Although the precise wording of the clause may matter less if it is unenforceable, the clause should nevertheless be the subject of considerable thought, since if the parties do choose to implement it when the dispute arises, it will need to meet the demands of their situation effectively. The nature of the agreement in which the clause appears may well have a bearing on the choice and drafting of the clause. For example, a partnership agreement would suggest the use of a very flexible, facilitative process (eg mediation) whereas a highly technical engineering contract might call for an expert appraisal/neutral evaluation.

12.3.1 Considerations

There are a number of considerations to bear in mind.

(a) Length and detail

Essentially, the clause merely needs to stipulate that in the event of a dispute arising, the parties will attempt to resolve it by ADR. A very short form of clause can accomplish that with ease (see Appendix 2, short form clauses). However, a clause such as that may beg as many questions as it answers, such as which ADR process will be used, who will the neutral be, is the ADR process a condition precedent to litigation/arbitration, what (if any) should the timetable be for carrying out the ADR process, and so on.

Surprisingly, this may in fact be of benefit. It leaves the details of the process open for the parties to decide at the time the dispute arises. The most appropriate type of ADR process might only become clear at that time, and the parties would not want to be restricted by reference to an earlier stipulation. Furthermore, some contracting parties might find it distasteful to draft too detailed a disputes clause at a time when no dispute exists between them.

On the other hand, leaving the parties with a choice when the dispute arises can also present problems. If they are unable, when a dispute does arise, to agree the requisite details, the whole value of the clause may be lost. Furthermore, parties wanting some objective justification for not complying with a clause will find it easy to disagree on the details and hence prevent any progress.

The drafting of each clause should therefore be approached freshly each time, with thought given to the context in which disputes will arise, each party's likely attitude, the results which the clause is intended to achieve, and so on. In fact, the principle that contracting parties should discuss the resolution of any disputes *at the time of contracting* is a

171

sound one, and is more likely to increase rather than diminish the trust between the parties, since the otherwise taboo subject will be brought out into the open. That discussion will serve as a much more solid base for the parties to refer to when the dispute does arise.

Ideally, the drafting of ADR clauses should be much more than the reproduction of a standard form ADR clause, and in particular the parties themselves, and not just their advisors, should be drawn into discussion about the optimum dispute resolution structures. Drafting should also be approached with imagination. There is no reason why each contractual context should not have its own dispute resolution process (see para 3.9 on dispute system design in Chapter 3 above). Parties will become increasingly aware of the approaches that prove most effective for them through a process of trial and experience.

(b) Content

In terms of the detailed contents to be included in an ADR clause, the following points at least should be considered:

- Will the clause refer to an ADR process to be agreed, or stipulate a particular one (eg, mediation)?

- Is there to be a timetable for compliance with the clause or with procedural stages within the clause (eg, appointment of a mediator, exchange of case summaries etc)?

- Is the ADR process intended to be a condition precedent to the commencement of litigation or arbitration proceedings, or not? (See para 12.4 below for the implications of this.)

- Is the identity of the neutral/mediator to be spelled out in advance? If not, what provision should there be for appointment?

- Is an ADR organisation to be used to provide a mediator and administer and supervise the process?

- How will any costs of the process be apportioned?

- Is a tiered process to be used? (eg, direct negotiations, followed (if necessary) by mediation, followed (if necessary) by arbitration).

(c) Tiered clauses

ADR clauses present an opportunity for the use of a 'tiered structure' within the clause – that is, a series of steps in the overall dispute resolution process, each designed to handle the dispute if it has not been resolved by the previous step. These can be particularly effective. Indeed, this approach has already been widely used in the past, for example the introduction of a negotiating phase as a prerequisite to the commencement of litigation or arbitration, and the 'engineer's decision' in some construction contracts. ADR techniques allow for this principle to be developed and used in greater detail.

The principal strengths of a tiered structure are that:

(i) The dispute resolution mechanism in use at any particular stage of a dispute will be the one most likely to resolve it. For example, it may be that the issue of proceedings too early in a dispute will drive out certain settlement possibilities which have not been achievable through initial direct negotiations. The introduction of a mediation phase between the negotiation and litigation phases may well provide a process more capable of teasing out a settlement in that particular environment.

(ii) The resolution processes can increase in formality and structure as it becomes clear that the dispute itself requires that. All the benefits of the litigation/arbitration processes remain available to the parties, but the formality and rigidity they bring is delayed until it is considered indispensable.

Some detailed examples of tiered ADR clauses are set out in Appendix 2. Particular attention is also drawn to paras 6.3–6.6 and 9.7, and Annexes 1 and 3 of the CUP Guidance Note (Appendix 5). Paragraphs 6.3 and 6.6 discuss the value of tiered clauses, and Annex 1 gives a diagrammatic illustration. Annex 3 sets out the ADR clauses which also appear in Appendix 2 of this book, together with commentaries.

In terms of drafting, the guiding principle should again be an attempt imaginatively to anticipate likely dispute scenarios, and to match them with relevant methods of resolution.

It is also worth noting that the choice of dispute clause can constitute a powerful form of 'policy statement' to those with whom one deals. For example, the CUP Guidance Note (Appendix 5) sets out best practice for the handling of disputes arising in government procurement contracts. The tiered ADR clauses all anticipate mediation being attempted before litigation or arbitration has been commenced, but not thereafter. This reflects the policy approach not to commence litigation until other avenues have been exhausted, but equally not to use any ADR processes once proceedings have been commenced. Those advising government departments or their contractors clearly need to be aware of this approach.

12.4 ENFORCEABILITY

We suggested earlier that the primary value of an ADR clause does not lie in its enforceability as a matter of law, but rather in its role as a pretext for discussion of possible ADR solutions. Indeed, even before addressing the legal position on the enforceability of such clauses, there is considerable debate on whether it is appropriate or even desirable for ADR clauses to be enforceable and enforced. The arguments were neatly summarized by Giles J in the Australian case of *Hooper Bailie Associated Ltd v Natcon Group Pty Limited* (unreported, 12th April 1992 at pp 24–25):

> 'Conciliation or mediation is essentially consensual, and the opponents of enforceability contend that it is futile to seek to enforce something which requires the consent of a party when co-operation and consent cannot be enforced; equally they say that there can be no loss to the other party if for want of co-operation and consent the consensual process would have led to no result. The proponents of enforceability contend that this misconceives the objectives of alternative dispute resolution, saying that the most fundamental resistance to compromise can wane and turn to co-operation and consent if the dispute is removed from the adversarial procedures of the Courts and exposed to procedures designed to promote compromise, in particular where a skilled conciliator or mediator is interposed between the parties. What is enforced is not co-operation or consent, but participation in a process from which co-operation and consent might come.'

12.4.1 The position under English law

To our knowledge the enforceability of an ADR clause has not yet been tested in the English courts. We must therefore work from first principles to see what conclusions can be reached.

12.4.1.1 An agreement to negotiate is unenforceable

Until the decision of the House of Lords of *Walford v Miles* [1992] 1 All ER 453, there was still some doubt about this proposition, stemming from the dictum of Lord Wright in *Hillas & Co v Arcos Ltd* (1932) 38 Com Cases 23. However the position following *Walford v Miles* is clear, namely that an agreement to negotiate is not enforceable in law. This case followed and endorsed the decision of the Court of Appeal in *Courtney & Fairbairn Ltd v Tolaini Brothers (Hotels) Ltd* [1975] 1 All ER 716. It is worth looking at *Walford v Miles* in some detail.

The case concerned the sale of a photographic processing business, and the central issues were the enforceability of a contract to negotiate and the terms of a 'lock-out' agreement (ie, an agreement not to negotiate with any other parties whilst negotiations were continuing with one party). In 1986 the Vendors decided to sell the business and received an offer of £1.9 million from a third party. In the meantime some other purchasers (the Purchasers) had entered into negotiations with the Vendors and in March 1987 the Vendors agreed in principle to sell the business and premises for £2 million. It was also further agreed in a telephone conversation that if the Purchasers provided a comfort letter confirming that their bank had offered them loan facilities, the Vendors would 'terminate negotiations with any third party or consideration of any alternative with a view to concluding agreements' with the Purchasers, and that even if the Vendors received a satisfactory proposal from any third party before that time they would 'not deal with that third party and would not give further consideration to any alternative'.

Subsequently the Vendors withdrew from negotiations and decided to sell to a third party. The proposed Purchasers brought an action against the Vendors for breach of a lock-out agreement under which the proposed Purchasers had been given an exclusive opportunity to try to come to terms with the Vendors and which was collateral to the 'subject to contract' negotiations which were proceeding for the purchase of the business and the premises. The proposed Purchasers alleged that it was a term of the collateral agreement, necessarily to be implied to give business efficacy to it, that so long as the Vendors continued to desire to sell the business and the premises, the Vendors would continue to negotiate in good faith with the proposed Purchasers. It was contended that the consideration for the collateral contract was the proposed Purchasers' agreement to continue negotiations.

On appeal, the Court of Appeal held that the alleged collateral agreement was no more than an agreement to negotiate and was therefore unenforceable. On further appeal, the House of Lords held that a lock-out agreement, whereby one party for good consideration agreed for a specific time not to negotiate with anyone except the other party in relation to the sale of his property, could constitute an enforceable agreement. However, an agreement to negotiate in good faith for an unspecified period was not enforceable, nor could a term to that effect be implied in a lock-out agreement for an unspecified period, since a vendor was not obliged under such an agreement to conclude a contract with a purchaser and he would not know when he was entitled to withdraw from the negotiations, and furthermore the court could not be expected to decide whether, subjectively, a proper reason existed for the termination of the negotiations. It followed that the alleged collateral agreement was unenforceable.

12.4.1 ADR Contract Clauses

Lord Ackner gave the lead judgment. In it he said (at p 459):

'Mr Naughton accepted that as the law now stands and has stood for approaching 20 years an agreement to negotiate is not recognised as an enforceable contract. This was first decided in terms in *Courtney & Fairbairn Limited v Tolaini Brothers* where Lord Denning MR said:

'If the law does not recognise a contract to enter into a contract (when there is a fundamental term yet to be agreed) it seems to me it cannot recognise a contract to negotiate. The reason is because it is too uncertain to have any binding force . . . It seems to me that a contract to negotiate, like a contract to enter into a contract, is not a contract known to the law . . . I think we must apply the general principle that when there is a fundamental matter left undecided and to the subject of negotiation, there is no contract.'

In the *Courtney* case Lord Denning rejected as not well founded the dictum of Lord Wright in *Hillas & Co v Arcos Ltd*:

'There is no bargain except to negotiate, and negotiation may be fruitless and end without any contract ensuing: yet even then, in strict theory, there is a contract (if there is good consideration) to negotiate, though in the event of repudiation by one party the damages may be nominal, unless a jury thinks that the opportunity to negotiate was one of some appreciable value to the injured party.'

Having considered (in *Walford v Miles*) a proposition put forward by Lord Bingham in the Court of Appeal that there was an obligation upon the Vendors not to deal with other parties which should continue to bind them 'for such time as is reasonable' Lord Ackner concluded:

'However, as Bingham LJ recognised, such a duty, if it existed, would indirectly impose upon the Respondents a duty to negotiate in good faith. Such a duty, for the reasons which I have given above, cannot be imposed. That it should have been thought necessary to assert such a duty helps to explain the reason behind the amendments to paragraph 5 and the insistence of Mr Naughton that without the implied term the agreement, as originally pleaded, was unworkable – unworkable because there was no way of determining for how long the Respondents were locked out from negotiating with any third party.

Thus, even if, despite the way in which the *Walford* case was pleaded and argued, the severance favoured by Bingham LJ was permissible, the resultant agreement suffered from the same defect (although for different reasons) as the agreement contended for in the amended Statement of Claim, namely that it too lacked the necessary certainty and was thus unenforceable.'

In essence then, *Walford v Miles* confirmed that a contract to negotiate is unenforceable since a court cannot say with sufficient certainty what the obligations are that it is being asked to enforce, and in any meaningful way monitor or assess compliance.

176

12.4.1.2 A court can require compliance with certain procedures as a condition precedent to the issue of litigation or arbitration proceedings

This general principle was established in the case of *Scott v Avery* [1865] 5 HL Cas 811, 10 ER 1121. Whilst the eventual jurisdiction of the court cannot be ousted, it can nevertheless be validly delayed, in that the parties can properly impose on themselves, by way of agreement, a series of intervening steps which have to be completed as a condition precedent to either party commencing litigation or arbitration.

This principle translates easily into the ADR arena. Many ADR clauses simply require parties to attempt resolution by an ADR process (eg, see Appendix 2, short-form clauses). However, it is equally possible (indeed, increasingly common) for the clause to express compliance with, and exhaustion of, the ADR phase as a condition precedent to the issue of any proceedings. Such a clause at least has the effect of introducing a slightly clearer, and therefore more certain, set of steps into the process, which arguably a court might find easier to enforce. Even so, however, the uncertainty problems raised in *Walford* persist, since the court would still have to determine whether compliance with that condition precedent had been achieved, so that proceedings could be validly issued. For example, would a party who attended a mediation but terminated it by leaving after an hour be said to have 'attempted to mediate'?

It is likely, in our view, that this 'problem' exists far more in theory than in practice. Whilst it may be difficult to produce a set of criteria or rules by which compliance can be judged in every situation, it is in practice often very clear to the parties whether they have attempted to settle a case through ADR or not. It is, of course, even clearer to the mediator, but he or she is not in a position to confirm or deny compliance after the event, partly because of the contractual commitment to confidentiality and partly because his role during the mediation would be fatally compromised if the parties felt he could eventually pass judgment on their conduct.

The problem is, of course, exacerbated by a lack of comprehension of what ADR actually involves. Thus, the uncertainty argument is strengthened because it is assumed that ADR procedures are inherently either too unclear or too flexible to be able to require compliance. As ADR use grows, however, this argument will lose some of its impact, since there will be greater familiarity with ADR practice and the processes themselves will become more regularised. Indeed, although mediation is a very flexible and adaptable process, it is already possible to say with some consistency what constitutes, in procedural terms, a 'typical' mediation. It must also follow that the more detailed the ADR process spelt out in an ADR clause, the greater the likelihood of it being enforceable.

12.4.1 *ADR Contract Clauses*

Thus a simple commitment to attempt an ADR process leaves unresolved too many procedural issues (not least which ADR process will be used). Conversely an agreement to use mediation, under the auspices of a particular ADR organisation, or using a certain individual mediator, where the procedural requirements for the process (eg, timetable for submitting case summaries and holding the mediation, who will attend the mediation, etc) are spelt out in detail, must inherently be more capable of enforcement.

It is worth noting, however, that such detail may in fact be counterproductive. Mediation (of all the ADR processes) has a unique flexibility to respond to the very particular exigencies of a given situation. The greater the emphasis on a pre-arranged structure, the less the opportunity to adopt a particular approach and format of mediation which the situation demands.

There is therefore some measure of balance to be achieved in the drafting of such a clause.

It is also important to distinguish between various kinds of ADR processes. Some, such as early neutral evaluation, contain no element of negotiation about them. In that case, the parties simply make oral and/or written submissions to an agreed independent expert, who makes a non-binding 'evaluation', which the parties can then use to inform their negotiations. There is no reason in principle why the uncertainty objections raised in the *Walford* case should apply to such a process. Indeed, since the process is not inherently one of negotiation at all, the *Walford* case is not relevant to any assessment of it.

Finally, the uncertainty objections in *Walford* can be very largely minimised by the use of specific time periods, or 'lock-out' agreements. For example, rather than requiring the parties to mediate prior to issuing proceedings, an ADR clause may simply impose a time period between the dispute arising and proceedings being commenced. Provided it follows the *Scott v Avery* form, there is no objection to such a clause. During the intervening time period, the clause can either impose an obligation to use ADR, or simply offer it as an option, subject to the parties' consent at the time (see Appendix 2, Clause 2, long-form clauses). As a matter of law, this changes little. An obligation to use ADR would still be vulnerable to the uncertainty arguments and an option to use ADR is in fact no more than the parties already have in any event, even without such wording.

In practice, however, the position is very different. A specific breathing space is created, during which the parties are unable to issue proceedings. ADR is 'on the agenda' during that period, whether by obligation or option, and there can therefore be little concern about raising it with the other side. Many parties, faced with an intervening period during which they may either negotiate and/or use ADR, or do nothing, will sense the value in trying to use all available means to resolve the dispute. If the breathing space were not imposed on them, it is likely that some of them would be tempted to miss out the ADR, and even the negotiation, phase, and a valuable settlement opportunity might be lost.

Finally, where there is a concern that the imposition of a 'breathing space' may prejudice a party's position in the event that, for example, immediate injunctive relief is required, express provision for that can easily be made in a clause giving rights to by-pass the ADR or negotiation phases in such circumstances (see for example Appendix 2, short-form clauses, 'additional clause').

12.4.1.3 Is ADR equivalent to negotiation, such that the law regarding agreements to negotiate applies equally to ADR?

So far in this section, we have assumed largely that ADR is a form of negotiation, and thus that the law regarding the enforceability of agreements to negotiate applies equally to agreements to use ADR. However, we have already drawn a clear distinction between ADR processes which involve a large element of negotiation (eg, mediation, mini-trial, etc) and those which do not (eg, judicial appraisal, early neutral evaluation, etc). Clearly, the latter category is exempt from any of the problems relating to agreements to negotiate. The remainder of this section therefore applies to the former category of ADR processes.

On the face of it, those processes are extremely similar to negotiation. Indeed, their aims and objectives are almost indistinguishable from those of direct negotiations. Both seek a consensual result, with no ability to mandate any concession or change of position from the other side. Both can be disbanded by either party at any time. Neither requires or permits the imposition on the parties of any form of binding judgment. The outcome of both types of process is either a mutually acceptable agreement (which the parties can agree should have binding or non-binding status) or no agreement at all. Following this rationale, the law applicable to negotiation should also apply to ADR.

However, whilst ADR and negotiation may share the same aims and objectives, there are fundamental differences of process. Anyone familiar with both will immediately appreciate this. The introduction of a third party (a mediator/neutral) into the process fundamentally changes the terms and conditions of the negotiating process. The parties submit themselves to a third party process, with an independent dynamic and momentum of its own, to a far greater degree than they do in direct negotiations. Indeed, the mere fact that the process has such a momentum and a structure beyond that generated by the parties themselves, distinguishes it very significantly from direct negotiations. The process elements of a mediation are to a large extent governed by the mediator's own input and perceptions of what will prove effective, even allowing for the fact that the parties must at least consent to any such process decisions.

It is therefore possible to say, at least to some extent, that ADR processes exist as structures independent of the parties themselves. The implication of this is highly significant. If it is possible to identify such processes or structures with sufficient clarity, the uncertainty objections raised in the *Walford* case begin to fall away. By agreeing to use ADR, the argument runs, the parties are not agreeing to negotiate, but rather to submit themselves to a series of objectively definable processes, the effect of which is likely to be greater on them than if they merely entered the direct negotiation process. To quote again from Giles J in the *Hooper Bailie* case:

'What is enforced is not co-operation and consent, but participation in a process from which co-operation and consent might come.'

If that rationale is adopted, it becomes much easier to countenance enforcement of an ADR clause.

To use an analogy, assume that a husband and wife have a particular problem in their marriage. They may agree between themselves to attempt to resolve it by discussion. Clearly they cannot be compelled to resolve the problem. Realistically, neither can they be compelled to 'discuss it' since that is too vague an obligation to define effectively. How productive do discussions have to be in order to constitute compliance? If they set aside an hour to do so, and simply sit in silence, or scream at each other, have they complied? And for how long do the discussions need to continue?

On the other hand, they might agree to attempt to resolve the matter by seeking the assistance of a counsellor. Even more expressly, they might commit to have 10 weekly sessions with the counsellor. This is an easy obligation to monitor. It contains no assumptions that they will succeed in reaching resolution but merely a commitment to submit themselves to a particular and definable process. Implicit in it is an assumption that the counselling process constitutes something independent of the parties, a pre-existing structure into which the parties will submit their differences.

Necessarily, the counselling process itself is not easy to define in advance, in terms of the detail of how a particular session will progress. But that does not mean that it does not have enough of a structure of its own to enable the parties to know in advance what obligations they will take on when they agree to use it. Exactly the same is true of, for example, the mediation process. Indeed, the only difference between the two (in terms of ensuring compliance) is that counselling is currently better known and more widely used than ADR and thus more easily permits an immediate and objective recognition of what is involved.

In summary then, we tend to the view that ADR is 'more than' direct negotiation, in a way which tends to distinguish the two processes and therefore the law applicable to each and we can envisage circumstances in which an ADR clause requiring mediation might be enforceable.

12.4.2 The position under Australian law

Whilst obviously not binding in any way on the English courts, the legal status of ADR clauses in Australia nevertheless sheds considerable light on the central issues concerning the enforceability of ADR clauses in England.

There are two schools of thought. For some time the established position was that an ADR clause (requiring conciliation/mediation) was not binding. There were two principal reasons for this:

(a) An ADR clause may be unenforceable because it seeks to achieve too much, by ousting the jurisdiction of the court (per the Supreme Court of Queensland in *Allco Steel (Queensland) Pty Ltd v Torres Strait Gold Pty Ltd* (unreported, Supreme Court of QLD, 12th March 1990, Master Horton QC). In that case, the court refused to stay proceedings in that court while a contractual conciliation clause was implemented.

(b) An ADR clause is no more than an agreement to negotiate and is therefore unenforceable because it lacks the necessary certainty required to create legally binding decisions (per NSW Court of Appeal in *Coal Cliff Collieries Pty Ltd v Sijehama Pty Ltd* (1992) 24 NSWLR 1). The reasoning here is, of course, essentially the same as that followed by the House of Lords in *Walford*.

However, doubt has since been cast over the application of both principles to ADR clauses. A decision by the New South Wales Supreme Court held that an agreement to conciliate, in the form permitted by *Scott v Avery*, would be enforced by the court staying arbitration proceedings under the contract until the conciliation phase had been properly concluded. Furthermore, the judge (Giles J) expressly stated that such a stay would also have been granted had there been court proceedings on foot equivalent to the arbitration proceedings. The case in question was *Hooper Bailie Associated Ltd v Natcon Group Pty Ltd* (supra). The facts of the case were summarised as follows (from Robert S Angyal in the

181

12.4.2 ADR Contract Clauses

'Mediation Agreements and Enforceability of ADR Clauses' paper to the First International Conference in Australia on Dispute Resolution):

'Hooper Bailie was the Contractor for the construction of dry wall partitions and ceilings of the New Parliament House Building in Canberra and Natcon was sub-contracted to perform that work. Disputes arose under the Contract; the disputes were submitted to arbitration; and in that arbitration Natcon claimed more than $3,000,000 from Hooper Bailie. Before the arbitration could start, it was found by Giles J that the parties reached agreement that they would conciliate a number of issues and that the arbitration would not take place until the conciliation had concluded. A conciliator was retained and a series of successful meetings took place in which the conciliator took the role of facilitating the voluntary agreement of the parties without making any determinations in relation to disputed items. Before the conciliation could conclude, Natcon was wound up. About a year later, the liquidator of Natcon sought to proceed with the arbitration rather than continuing with the conciliation meetings. At that point Hooper Bailie commenced proceedings to establish that Natcon was unable to continue with the arbitration basing its claim in part on the argument that the parties had agreed that the arbitration would not continue until the conciliation had concluded, and that it had not concluded.'

The judgment of Giles J contains a lengthy and detailed analysis of the issues, out of which the following principal points arise:

(i) The *Allco Steel* case had found that a conciliation clause could not operate as a pre-condition to litigation. Part of the rationale for this seems to have been a belief that conciliation was futile in view of the apparently entrenched and divergent positions of the two parties. In *Hooper Bailie* the judge found no evidence to suggest that further conciliation meeting would not prove fruitful (earlier ones had been fruitful) and even the fact that Natcon would not participate in the conciliation without an order to do so did not necessarily imply that the process was pointless.

(ii) This point was substantiated by remarks of Rogers CJ in *AWA Limited v Daniels* (unreported, Supreme Court, NSW of 24th February 1992). In that case, Rogers CJ concluded that there was 'utility in requiring parties, who are clearly bent on being difficult, to submit to conciliation processes ... In my view initial reluctance is not necessarily fatal to a successful mediation. If the parties enter into [it] as they all said they would, the skill of the mediator would be given full play to bring about consensus'.

(iii) Rogers CJ also criticised the *Allco Steel* decision on the basis that 'The Master ought to have required the parties to adhere to their freely agreed contractual obligations'. This argument has, in our view, quite some force. Where parties, particularly sophisticated commercial ones, have freely constructed for themselves a dispute resolution procedure which they clearly anticipate should be used in the event of a dispute arising, the courts should be straining wherever possible to give effect to their intentions.

(iv) Giles J assessed the English authorities on the question of an agreement to agree, acknowledging that the established position (following *Walford v Miles*, *Courtney v Tolaini* and *Paul Smith Ltd v H&S International Holding Inc* [1991] 2 L1R 127 was that an agreement to negotiate was not enforceable. However, he drew a clear and important distinction between a contract to negotiate and a contract to mediate or conciliate, and accorded to the latter process sufficient procedural certainty to permit enforcement.

> 'An agreement to conciliate or mediate is not to be likened (as Lord Ackner likens an agreement to negotiate, or negotiate in good faith) to an agreement to agree. Nor is an agreement to negotiate, or negotiate in good faith, perhaps necessarily lacking certainty and obliging a party to act contrary to its interests. Depending upon its express terms and any terms to be implied, it may require of the parties participation in the process by conduct of sufficient certainty for legal recognition of the agreement.'

He then applied that consideration to the present case and held that:

> 'There was a clear structure for the conciliation for which Natcon was to attend before Mr Schick [the conciliator], put before him such 'evidence' and submissions as it desired and receive his determinations. As has been seen, ancillary to this arose an exchange of information between the parties for the purposes of the conciliation and there were no determinations in any sense other than in the sense of suggested solutions. In my opinion, Natcon promised to participate in a conciliation by doing those things and the conduct required of it is sufficiently certain for its promise to be given legal recognition.'

It is also worth stressing that the judge did not impose any obligation to compromise any of the matters which would be the subject of the ensuing conciliation, nor did he express any view on whether there was an implied term that the parties would conduct themselves in good faith during that conciliation.

(v) The judgment in *Hooper Bailie* also expressly reflects a recognition of the increasing profile and usage of ADR in Australia and, in particular, the enactment of legislation enabling courts to refer cases to mediation in certain circumstances. Whilst it remains unclear what view an English court might take of a similar case, the position in Australia does reflect the way in which the increased use and profile of ADR has begun to have an impact upon the law relating to it.

12.5 AREAS OF RELEVANCE

ADR clauses of different types can be used in a wide variety of contexts. Examples of these might include general commercial contracts, partnership agreements, terms and conditions of business, construction contracts, development contracts, and so on. In each case, thought should be given to the type of ADR process most likely to generate resolution.

It is also important to remember the value of ADR 'clauses' in corporate policy statements. Thus many large American companies have adopted a public 'corporate pledge', to use ADR processes in appropriate situations. Although not legally committing the company to the use of ADR in any particular dispute, this pledge has been used to send a powerful message to those with whom this company deals, and promote the company's public image.

APPENDICES

Note Where standard form documents appear in the Appendices, the majority of those used are CEDR documents, for reasons of convenience. Standard form documents from other ADR organisations can be obtained by writing to them.

Glossary of Terms[1]

ADR

ADR stands for 'Alternative Dispute Resolution' defined as 'any method of resolving an issue susceptible to normal legal process other than by an imposed binding decision.'NB: In general usage 'decision' means an authoritative decision imposed on the parties other than by their consent by a judge or arbitrator.

ADJUDICATION

'Exercise of a power delegated by contract to a third party to resolve disputes on an interim or final basis as they arise without recourse to formal arbitration or litigation.'

CAUCUS (ALSO KNOWN AS PRIVATE MEETING)

'A private session with any one party in which the mediator explores ways of resolving the dispute.'

COMPREHENSIVE MEDIATION

'Mediation on all, rather than selected, issues, particularly in family disputes.'

---

1 All terms defined in this glossary are reproduced by kind permission of the Academy of Experts from their Glossary 'The Language of ADR'.

CONCILIATION

'A without prejudice non-binding dispute resolution process in which an independent third party ("neutral") assists the parties to settle their differences but may, if necessary, deliver his opinion as to the merits of the dispute.'

Note: A Conciliator (neutral) may be required to make a 'Recommendation' as to how the dispute should be settled if agreement cannot be reached by the parties during the process.

In some contracts the parties agree that a Conciliator's Recommendation is binding unless challenged within a stated period. 'Conciliation' and 'Mediation' are often used interchangeably and indiscriminately.

COURT-ANNEXED ADR

'Any ADR process which parties may be required or advised to undertake by the court or an ADR facility which is offered by the court (eg, in a "multi-door" courthouse).'

COURT-ANNEXED ARBITRATION

'A form of court-annexed ADR in which an "arbitrator" gives a preliminary decision which, in some circumstances, may thereafter become binding upon the parties (esp USA).'

DISPUTE REVIEW PANEL/BOARD

'A panel set up under the terms of a contract to adjudicate, mediate, or settle claims, disputes or controversies referred to them, either on an interim or a final and binding basis.'

EARLY EXPERT EVALUATION

The use of an independent Expert to investigate and give his Expert opinion on any matter referred to him by the parties. Normally this will be used by the parties to assist them in reaching a settlement or narrowing the issues.

EARLY NEUTRAL EVALUATION

The use of a neutral to give his opinion on a matter often of the potential outcome of the dispute.

EXECUTIVE HEARING (ALSO KNOWN AS MINI-TRIAL OR EXECUTIVE TRIBUNAL)

A without prejudice formalised settlement procedure in which advocates present their client's best case and reasons for settlement within strict time limits to a panel composed of one executive decision-maker representing each party. It is followed immediately by direct negotiation. The parties are often assisted by a neutral retained to assist the panel to assess the presentations. The procedure will vary according to ground rules agreed by the parties. If a neutral is retained, he may be requested to preside and maintain the rules and any agreed timetable, to assist with negotiations and, if so agreed, to give an opinion on the likely outcome of litigation.

EXPERT DETERMINATION

The use of an independent Expert to investigate the referred matters and to give his opinion which becomes binding on the parties. Not strictly an ADR process.

EXPERTS MEETING

These can be either party arranged or Court (or Tribunal) ordered. The object is to enable the Experts to determine those matters upon which they agree and those upon which they disagree. Not strictly an ADR process.

FACT-FINDING EXPERT

'Independent expert appointed by agreement of the parties to investigate and report to them on all or any specified issues of fact and/or opinion in dispute between them, either to assist them in reaching a settlement by any ADR process or, as may be agreed, to determine those issues for the purpose of any on-going litigation or arbitration.'

GRIEVANCE PROCEDURE

A prescribed procedure agreed by a public or private body which it and/or its members are normally obliged to follow for the consideration and redress of complaints or grievances brought against it or them, by employees, clients or members of the public.

MED-ARB (MEDIATION-ARBITRATION)

'A dispute resolution process whereby a neutral first attempts to mediate the dispute but, if mediation is unsuccessful in whole or in part, the remainder of the dispute is arbitrated upon by the same or a different person.'

MEDIATION

'A without prejudice non-binding dispute resolution process in which an independent third party ("neutral") assists the parties to settle their differences but does not advise them of his own opinion as to the issues and merits of the dispute.'

Note: 'Conciliation' and 'Mediation' are often used interchangeably and indiscriminately.

MINI-TRIAL

See Executive Hearing.

MODERATED SETTLEMENT CONFERENCE

'A settlement conference promoted and supervised by the court.' (Many variations.)

MULTI-DOOR COURTHOUSE

'A court of law in which facilities for arbitration and/or ADR are also provided.'

NEGOTIATION

'The process of working out an agreement by direct communication.'

NEUTRAL

'Independent third party who acts as mediator, conciliator or chairman in various ADR procedures.'

OMBUDSMAN

'Usually an independent person whose role is to deal with complaints by the public against administrative (and, in some countries, corporate) injustice and maladministration, with the power to investigate, criticise and publish reports on his findings. He will normally have some power to recommend the payment of compensation.'

PRE-HEARING REVIEW

In arbitration – as for pre-trial review.

PRE-TRIAL REVIEW

In litigation, the preliminary consideration of a case with a view to giving directions as to its speedy future handling.

Note: This should not be confused with Mediation although it should be noted that some judges specifically draw attention to the benefits of mediation but leave it to the parties to make their own arrangements if they wish to proceed with that route.

Appendix 1

PRELIMINARY MEETING

In arbitration – as for pre-trial review.

SETTLEMENT CONFERENCE (IN SOME TERRITORIES)

A pre-trial review by a Judge who acts as a Mediator. In the event the Mediation is not successful the matter is tried by a different judge.

Note: Although 'suggestions' may be made by a trial judge that the parties should settle this should not be confused with Mediation.

STRUCTURED SETTLEMENT CONFERENCE

In some territories it is an Executive Hearing but in others it is a specialist process in personal injury litigation.

TERMS DESCRIBING PARTICIPANTS IN ADR

'Parties should be referred to by their proper names or by their generic description (eg "Employer", "Insurer", etc).'

Contract Clauses[1]

CEDR MODEL CLAUSES

Many disputants find it easier to enlist the assistance of CEDR if they wish to incorporate an appropriate ADR clause into their initial contract. This can act as a form of dispute prevention as much as a dispute resolution procedure.

The attached model clauses are intended to give professional advisors and their clients an indication of how ADR can be introduced simply into a contract. There are various versions from examples of a very succinct approach to a longer variant.

Please note that these are only models and should be used/adapted to suit parties' own requirements and in the light of their own legal advice. Please let us know of any issues which arise concerning these ADR Clauses and also keep us in touch with your own versions. We try to keep a library of variations to assist in advising members and in monitoring ADR developments.

William Marsh, Director of Mediations

CEDR SAMPLE DISPUTE RESOLUTION SHORT FORM OF CLAUSES

Short form alternatives

(a) If a dispute arises out of or in connection with this Agreement, the Parties will, with the help of the Centre for Dispute

---

1 All material in this Appendix is reproduced by kind permission of the CEDR, Centre for Dispute Resolution, 100 Fetter Lane, London, EC4A 1DD, tel: 0171 430 1852, fax: 0171 430 1846.

Resolution (CEDR), seek in good faith to resolve it by alternative dispute resolution.

(b) If a dispute arises out of or in connection with this Agreement, the Parties will, with the help of the Centre for Dispute Resolution (CEDR), seek in good faith to resolve it by alternative dispute resolution. If the parties fail to agree terms of settlement within [ ] days of the [initiation][commencement] of the procedure the dispute shall be referred to arbitration in accordance with the [as appropriate]/or litigation. [The [initiation][commencement] of the procedure is defined as [the request to CEDR by both/all parties for an ADR procedure][the commencement of the first ADR meeting]].

(c) The parties will attempt in good faith to negotiate a settlement to any claim or dispute between them arising out of or in connection with this Agreement. If the matter is not resolved by negotiation the parties will refer the dispute to mediation in accordance with CEDR (Centre for Dispute Resolution) procedures. If the parties fail to agree terms of settlement within [ ] days of the [initiation][commencement] of the procedure the dispute shall be referred to arbitration in accordance with [as appropriate]/or litigation. [The [initiation][commencement] of the procedure is defined as [the request to CEDR by both/all parties for a mediation][the commencement of the first ADR meeting]].

(d) Unless settled by prior negotiation a claim or dispute arising out of or in connection with this Agreement shall be submitted to mediation by CEDR (Centre for Dispute Resolution) within [ ] days of one side giving written notice to the other of such dispute and of their intention to refer it to mediation by CEDR.

Additional

The following paragraph may be added to any of the Short Form Clauses above.

'Both Parties reserve all their respective rights in the event that no agreed resolution shall be reached in the [mediation][ADR procedure][and neither party shall be deemed to be precluded from taking such interim formal steps as may be considered necessary to protect such party's position while the mediation or other procedure is pending [or continuing]].'

CEDR SAMPLE DISPUTE RESOLUTION
CLAUSE 2

Disputes

1. The parties will attempt in good faith to resolve any dispute or claim arising out of or relating to this Agreement promptly through negotiations between the respective senior executives of the parties who have authority to settle the same.

2. If the matter is not resolved through negotiation, the parties will attempt in good faith to resolve the dispute or claim through an Alternative Dispute Resolution (ADR) procedure as recommended to the parties by the Centre for Dispute Resolution.

3. If the matter has not been resolved by an ADR procedure within [ ] days of the initiation of such procedure, or if either party will not participate in an ADR procedure, the dispute shall be referred to arbitration in accordance with [as appropriate/or litigation].

4. The construction performance and validity of this Agreement shall in all respects be governed by the [Laws of England].

CEDR SAMPLE DISPUTE RESOLUTION
CLAUSE 2 (LONG FORM)

Disputes

1. In the event of any dispute or difference arising between the parties in connection with this Agreement, [senior representatives/members of the board of directors] of the parties shall, within [10] days of a written request from either party to the other addressed to [the managing director], meet in a good faith effort to resolve the dispute without recourse to legal proceedings.

2. If the dispute or difference is not resolved as a result of such meeting, either party may (at such meeting or within 14 days from its conclusion) propose to the other in writing that structured negotiations be entered into with the assistance of a mediator or neutral advisor ('Mediator').

3. If the parties are unable to agree on a Mediator or if the Mediator agreed upon is unable or unwilling to act, either party shall within fourteen days from the date of the proposal to appoint a Mediator

or within fourteen days of notice to either party that he or she is unable or unwilling to act, apply to the Centre for Dispute Resolution ('CEDR') to appoint a Mediator.

4. The parties shall within 14 days of the appointment of the Mediator meet with him/her in order to agree a programme for the exchange of any relevant information and the structure to be adopted for the negotiations [to be held in [ ]]. If considered appropriate, the parties may at any stage seek assistance from CEDR to provide guidance on a suitable procedure.

5. Unless concluded with a written legally binding agreement all negotiations connected with the dispute shall be conducted in confidence and without prejudice to the rights of the parties in any future proceedings.

6. If the parties accept the Mediator's recommendations or otherwise reach agreement on the resolution of the dispute, such agreement shall be reduced to writing and, once it is signed by their duly authorised representatives, shall be binding on the parties. [Such agreement shall be implemented in full within [ ] days of signature failing which it shall be rendered null and void (and may not be referred to any subsequent legal proceedings) unless legal proceedings have been initiated to enforce it by either party within a further [ ] days.]

7. Failing agreement, either of the parties may invite the Mediator to provide a non-binding but informative opinion in writing, who need only comply with their request if he considers it would be helpful. Any such opinion shall not be an attempt to anticipate what a court might order but rather the Mediator's suggestions as to the settlement terms which are considered appropriate in all the circumstances. [Such opinion shall be provided on a without prejudice basis and shall not be used in evidence in any proceedings arising in connection with this Agreement without the prior written consent of both parties.]

8. If the parties fail to reach agreement in the structured negotiations within [60] days of the Mediator being appointed then any dispute or difference between them may be referred to the Courts unless within [such a period/a further period of 30 days] the parties agree to refer the matter to arbitration before an arbitrator whose method of appointment is agreed between them.

9. The construction performance and validity of this Agreement shall in all respects be governed by the [Laws of England.]

Mediation Agreement[1]

CEDR MEDIATION AGREEMENT

THIS AGREEMENT is between:

(1) EUROPEAN DISPUTE RESOLUTION LIMITED trading as CENTRE FOR DISPUTE RESOLUTION (CEDR) of 100 Fetter Lane, London EC4A 1DD.

(2) [of] ('Party A').

(3) [of] ('Party B').

(4) [of] ('the Mediator').

(5) [of] ('the Pupil Mediator').

MATTER: (Please complete)

AGREEMENT

1. Party A and Party B (herinafter referred to as 'the Parties') agree to use their best endeavours to resolve the dispute by mediation and to the appointment of [   ] as Mediator and [   ] as Pupil Mediator.

2. The Representatives of the Parties for the Mediation will be:

1 This agreement is reproduced by kind permission of the CEDR, Centre for Dispute Resolution, 100 Fetter Lane, London EC4A 1DD, tel: 0171 430 1852, fax: 0171 430 1846.

[   ] for Party A
(Advised by   )

and

[   ] for Party B
(Advised by   )

3. The Representatives (or such other representatives as the Parties may from time to time appoint) will represent the respective Parties at the Mediation and will have full authority to settle the dispute.

4. The Mediation will take place at [   ] am on the [   ] day of [   ], 199[ ] at [   ]. If the issues are unresolved at the end of the meeting, then with the unanimous agreement of the Parties and the Mediator, the Mediation may be adjourned to such time and place as may be agreed.

5. Prior to the Mediation both Parties will have submitted to the Mediator and will have exchanged copies of a written summary of their case and relevant background documentation.

6. Procedure at the Mediation will be determined by the Mediator, in consultation with the Parties.

CONCLUSION OF THE MEDIATION

7. The Mediation will continue during the day(s) agreed until agreement is reached; or one of the Parties withdraws from the Mediation; or the Mediator is of the view that further efforts at mediation would not be worthwhile.

8. If the Parties require and the Mediator agrees that this would be helpful, the Mediator may produce for the Parties a written report of the case with recommendations on terms of settlement. This will not constitute an attempt to anticipate what a court might order but rather the Mediator's suggestions as to the settlement terms which are considered appropriate in all the circumstances.

SETTLEMENT

9.1 If an agreement is reached between the Parties, Heads of Agreement will if appropriate and required by the Parties be prepared and signed by the Parties. No agreement as to the terms of any settlement reached during the Mediation shall be legally binding unless and until it is reduced to writing and signed by the Representatives for and on behalf of the Parties. The Parties shall however be legally bound by any settlement so reduced to writing and signed and undertake to give effect to such settlement in accordance with its terms.

9.2 All Parties reserve their respective rights should the Mediation not result in a settlement agreement being reached between them.

CONFIDENTIALITY

10.1 By taking part in the Mediation the parties undertake to each other and agree that:

(i) the entire Mediation is and will be kept confidential;

(ii) the Parties, the Representatives and their advisers and the Mediator shall keep all statements and all other matters whether oral or written including any settlement agreement relating to the Mediation confidential except insofar as disclosure is necessary to implement and enforce such settlement agreement;

(iii) the entire process of the Mediation shall be treated as privileged and will be conducted on the same basis as without prejudice negotiation in an action in the courts (or similar proceedings). All documents, submissions and statements made or produced for the purposes of the Mediation whether oral or written shall be inadmissible and not subject to discovery in any arbitration, legal or other similar proceedings except that evidence which is otherwise admissible or discoverable shall not become inadmissible or non-discoverable by reason of its use in connection with this Mediation.

10.2 The Mediator may not act for either Party individually in any capacity with regard to the subject matter of the Mediation, and the Parties acknowledge that in acting under this agreement, neither CEDR nor the Mediator is representing or giving legal advise to, nor assessing, upholding or protecting (or attempting to assess, uphold or protect), any rights of any of the Parties. The Parties are encouraged to take legal advice in respect of all matters pertaining to the Mediation and any agreement reached.

Appendix 3

10.3 Neither Party may have access to the Mediator's notes or call the Mediator as a witness in any proceedings relating to any of the issues between them, and the Mediator's opinion will be inadmissible in any subsequent proceedings which may take place between the Parties concerning the subject matter of the Mediation.

COSTS

11. Unless the Parties otherwise agree, the fees and expenses of the Mediator as well as any other administrative expenses of the Procedure will be borne by the Parties in equal shares. Each Party will also pay its own expenses of individual representation in the Mediation. In the first instance all Mediation fees and expenses will be paid to CEDR. CEDR will be responsible for reimbursing the Mediator. The fees and expenses of the Mediation, as estimated by CEDR, are payable in advance. Such estimate may be revised in the event of any further meeting(s) or other services being required of CEDR and/or the Mediator, and in any event, Parties will be invoiced in arrears for any additional costs or expenses not included in the initial invoice. If the Parties fail to pay the Mediator's expenses they, and not CEDR, will be liable for non-payment. In the even that the Parties settle the matter prior to the Mediation, but after fees payable in advance have become due, CEDR's standard cancellation terms shall apply.

EXCLUSION OF LIABILITY

12. Neither CEDR nor any Mediator appointed by CEDR shall be liable to the Parties or either of them for any act or omission whatsoever in connection with the services to be provided by them.

13. In clauses 4, 10, 11, 12, and 14 of this agreement the term 'Mediator' shall be deemed to include the Pupil Mediator, and those clauses will be construed and apply accordingly.

14. CEDR, the Mediator, and the Parties acknowledge that the Mediator is acting as an independent contractor under this

200

agreement, and not as agent, servant, employee or representative of CEDR.

15. This agreement shall be governed by and construed in accordance with English law, under the jurisdiction of the English Courts.

Dated the [   ] day of [   ] 199[ ]

SIGNED: ....
for and on behalf of Party A

SIGNED: ....
for and on behalf of Party B

SIGNED: ....
by the Mediator

SIGNED: ....
by the Pupil Mediator

SIGNED: ....
for and on behalf of CEDR

APPENDIX 4

Codes of Practice

MEDIATION – SPECIMEN CODE OF PRACTICE – PRACTICE INFORMATION[1]

I Principles of mediation

1. Mediation is a process in which a neutral mediator (or in some cases, two mediators) help parties in dispute to try to work out their own principles and terms for the resolution of the issues between them. Mediators do not arbitrate and have no authority to make or impose decisions regarding the parties' issues.

2. Mediation is voluntary, and any party or the mediator may terminate at any time.

3. Notwithstanding that a mediator may be a solicitor, barrister, accountant or other professional, when acting as a mediator he or she acts as a neutral facilitator of negotiations and does not give professional advice to the parties, individually or collectively, nor does he or she represent any party, and mediation is not a substitute for each party obtaining independent legal, accounting, tax or other professional or technical advice.

4. The mediator tries to assist the parties to reach a conclusion of the dispute which is appropriate to their particular circumstances, and not necessarily the same conclusion that might be arrived at in the event of adjudication by the court. That allows the parties to explore and agree upon a wider range of options for settlement than might otherwise be the case.

1 Reproduced by kind permission of Henry Brown and Arthur Marriott, authors of *ADR Principles and Practice*, and the Law Society.

5. The mediator may meet the parties individually and/or together and may assist the parties, for example, by identifying areas of agreement, narrowing and clarifying areas of disagreement, and defining the issues; helping the parties to examine the issues and their available courses of action; establishing and examining alternative options for resolving any disagreement; considering the applicability of specialised management, legal, accounting, technical or other expertise and generally facilitating discussion and negotiation; managing the process and helping them to try to resolve their differences.

6. A mediator will not act as such in a dispute in which he or she has at any time acted as a professional adviser for any party, nor in respect of which he or she is in possession of any information which was obtained by the mediator (or any member of his or her firm) as a result of having so acted or advised; nor having once acted as a mediator will he or she act for any party individually in relation to the subject matter of the mediation.

II Confidentiality and privilege

1. The mediator will conduct the mediation on a confidential basis, and will not voluntarily disclose information obtained through the mediation process except to the extent that such matters are already public or with the consent of the parties. If however the mediator considers from information received in the mediation that the life or safety of any person is or may be at serious risk, the duty of confidentiality shall not apply; and in such event the mediator shall try to agree with the person furnishing such information as to how disclosure shall be made.

2. Where the mediator meets the parties separately and obtains information from any party which is confidential to that party and which is not already public, the mediator shall maintain the confidentiality of that information from all other parties except to the extent that the mediator has been authorised to disclose any such information.

3. All discussions and negotiations during the mediation will be regarded as evidentially privileged and conducted on a 'without prejudice' basis, unless such privilege is waived by the parties by agreement, either generally or in relation to any specific aspect. No party is to refer in any proceedings that may subsequently take

place to any such privileged discussions and negotiations, or require the mediator to do so, nor may any party have access to any of the mediator's notes or call any mediator as a witness in any proceedings.

III Duty of impartiality

1. The duty of impartiality of the mediator is inherent in the mediation process.

2. If a mediator believes that any party is abusing the mediation process, or that power imbalances are too substantial for the mediation to continue effectively, or that the parties are proposing a result which appears to be so unfair that it would be a manifest miscarriage of justice, then the mediator will inform the parties accordingly, and may terminate the mediation.

IV Information and documents

1. The mediator will assist the parties, so far as appropriate and practicable, to identify what information and documents would help the resolution of any issue, and how best such information and documents may be obtained.

2. Mediation does not provide for the disclosure and discovery of documents in the same way or to the same extent as required by court rules. The parties may voluntarily agree to provide such documentation, or any lesser form of disclosure considered by them to be sufficient. This may be considered and discussed in the mediation.

3. The mediator has no power and does not purport to make or require independent enquiries or verification to be made in relation to any information or documentation sought or provided in the mediation. If this may be material to the resolution of any issues, consideration may be given in the mediation to the ways in which the parties may obtain any such information, documents or verification.

V Relationship with professional advisors

1. Solicitors, barristers or other professional advisors acting for the individual parties may, but need not necessarily, participate in the mediation process. Such solicitors and/or advisors may take part in discussions and meetings, with or without the parties, and in any

other communications and representations, in such manner as the mediator may consider useful and appropriate.

2. Professional advisors representing all the parties collectively, such as the accountants of a partnership whose partners are mediating their differences, may be asked to assist in the mediation in such manner as may be agreed.

3. Parties are free to consult with their individual professional advisors as the mediation progresses. The mediator may make recommendations to the parties as to the desirability of seeking further assistance from professional advisors such as lawyers, accountants, expert valuers or others.

VI Recording of proposed agreement

1. Agreements reached in mediation are ordinarily intended to be legally binding on the parties when (but not before) they have been recorded in writing and signed by the parties. Where appropriate, orders of the court or arbitration awards may be made by consent on the basis of such agreements.

2. At the end of the mediation, or at any interim stage, the mediator and/or the parties or their representatives may prepare a written memorandum or summary of any full or partial agreement reached by the parties, which may, where considered by the mediator to be appropriate, comprise draft heads of such agreement for formalisation by the legal advisors acting for the parties.

3. If the participants wish to consult their respective individual legal advisors before entering into any binding agreement, then any terms which they may provisionally propose as the basis for resolution will not be binding on them until they have each had an opportunity of taking advice from such legal advisors and have thereafter agreed to be bound.

CODE OF CONDUCT FOR MEDIATORS[2]

A Mediator on the British Academy of Experts' Register of Mediators shall:

2 This code of conduct is reproduced by kind permission of the Academy of Experts.

1. Not accept an appointment in any matter where there is an actual potential or apparent conflict of interest between the Mediator and any of the parties. If, however, full disclosure is made in writing to all parties the Mediator may in appropriate cases accept the appointment when all parties have specifically acknowledged the disclosure and confirmed their agreement to the appointment in writing.

2. Not enter into an agreement to receive a contingency fee in respect of the Mediation, or an arrangement whereby the loser pays the fee.

3. Ensure that he has time available to conduct the Mediation in accordance with the Academy's Guidelines.

4. Treat all information obtained during a Mediation with unquestioning confidentiality both during and after the Mediation.

5. Maintain a neutral stance at all times.

6. Refuse to act as a witness, advocate, or advisor for any party in any subsequent action concerning the matters in dispute in the Mediation.

7. Maintain Professional Indemnity Insurance to an adequate amount with a reputable insurer.

8. Not publicise his services in any manner which may be reasonably regarded as being in bad taste. Publicity must not be inaccurate or misleading in any way.

9. Adhere at all times in all matters to the *Code of Practice* of the *Academy of Experts*.

APPENDIX 5

CUP Guidelines[1]

NO. 50 DISPUTES RESOLUTION

This is one of a series of guidances prepared and issued by CUP on purchasing and supply procedures and practices. Its use is not mandatory, but a statement of good professional practice. Departments should consider incorporating it into their purchasing and supply manuals.

1. INTRODUCTION

1.1. Any dispute arising either during the life of a contract or at its termination can be expensive and time consuming. It can add substantially to the cost of the contract, as well as nullifying some or all of its perceived benefits or advantages. The importance of a fast, efficient and cost-effective dispute resolution procedure cannot be overstated.

1.2. *This guidance is drafted on the basis that the law of England and Wales applies, if Scots law or the law of Northern Ireland apply, consult your legal advisers.*

1.3 The following Practice Direction (which was handed down by the Lord Chief Justice in the High Court on January 24 1995 – The Times 25 January 1995) shows that the Courts will question whether an attempt has been made to resolve a dispute by alternative dispute resolution.

---

1 Central Unit on Procurement, HM Treasury. Reproduced by kind permission of the Controller of Her Majesty's Stationery Office.

Appendix 5

Practice Direction
(Civil Litigation: Case Management)

1. The paramount importance of reducing the cost and delay of civil litigation made it necessary for judges sitting at first instance to assert greater control over the preparation for and conduct of hearings than had hitherto been customary.
   Failure by practitioners to conduct cases economically would be visited by appropriate orders for costs, including wasted costs orders.

2. The court would accordingly exercise its discretion to limit:
   (a) discovery;
   (b) the length of oral submissions;
   (c) the time allowed for examination and cross-examination of witnesses;
   (d) the issues on which it wished to be addressed;
   (e) reading aloud from documents and authorities.

3. Unless otherwise ordered, every witness statement was to stand as the evidence-in-chief of the witness concerned.

4. Order 18, rule 7 of the Rules of the Supreme Court (facts, not evidence, to be pleaded) would be strictly enforced. In advance of trial parties should use their best endeavours to agree which were the issues or the main issues, and it was their duty so far as possible to reduce or eliminate the expert issues.

5. Order 34, rule 10(2)(a)(b)(c) of the Rules of the Supreme Court (the court bundle) would also be strictly enforced. Documents for use in court should be the A4 format where possible, contained in suitably secured bundles, and lodged with the court at least two clear days before the hearing of the application or a trial. Each bundle should be paginated, indexed, wholly legible, and arranged chronologically and contained in a ring binder or a lever-arch file. Where documents were copied unnecessarily or bundled incompetently, the cost would be disallowed.

6. In cases estimated to last more than 10 days, a pre-trial review should be applied for or, in default, might be appointed by the court. It should when practicable be conducted by the trial judge between eight and four weeks before the date of trial and should be attended by the advocates who were to represent the parties at trial.

7. Unless the court otherwise ordered, there must be lodged with the listing officer (or equivalent) on behalf of each party no later than two months before the date of trial a completed pre-trial check-list in the form annexed to the Practice Direction.

8. Not less than three clear days before the hearing of any action or application each party should lodge with the court (with copies to other parties) a skeleton argument concisely summarising that party's submissions in relation to each of the issues, and citing the main authorities relied on, which could be attached. Skeleton arguments should be as brief as the nature of the issues allowed, and should not without leave of the court exceed 20 pages of double-spaced A4 paper.

9. The opening speech should be succinct. At its conclusion, other parties might be invited briefly to amplify their skeleton arguments. In a heavy case the court might in conjunction with final speeches require written submissions, including the findings of fact for which each party contended.

10. This Practice Direction applied to all lists in the Queen's Bench and Chancery Divisions, except where other directions specifically applied.

Pre-trial check-list

[Short title of action]
[Folio number]
[Trial date]
[Party lodging check-list]
[Name of solicitor]
[Name(s) of counsel for trial (if known)]

Setting down

1. Has the action been set down?

Pleadings

2. (a) Do you intend to make any amendment to your pleading?
   (b) If so, when?

Interrogatories

3. (a) Are any interrogatories outstanding?
   (b) If so, when served and upon whom?

Appendix 5

Evidence

4. (a) Have all orders in relation to expert, factual and hearsay evidence been complied with? If not, specify what remains outstanding.
   (b) Do you intend to serve/seek leave to serve any further report or statement? If so, when and what report or statement?
   (c) Have all other orders in relation to oral evidence been complied with?
   (d) Do you require any further leave or orders in relation to evidence? If so, please specify and say when you will apply.

5. (a) What witnesses of fact do you intend to call? [names]
   (b) What expert witnesses do you intend to call? [names]
   (c) Will any witness require an interpreter? If so which?

Documents

6. (a) Have all orders in relation to discovery been complied with?
   (b) If not, what orders are outstanding?
   (c) Do you intend to apply for any further orders relating to discovery?
   (d) If so, what and when?

7. Will you not later than seven days before trial have prepared agreed paginated bundles of fully legible documents for the use of counsel and the court?

Pre-trial review

8. (a) Has a pre-trial review been ordered?
   (b) If so, when is it to take place?
   (c) If not, would it be useful to have one?

Length of trial

9. What are counsel's estimates of the minimum and maximum lengths of the trial? [The answer to question 9 should ordinarily be supported by an estimate of length signed by the counsel to be instructed.]

Alternative dispute resolution (see Practice Statement (Commercial Court: Alternative dispute resolution) (The Times December 17, 1993; [1994] 1 WLR 14).

10. Have you or counsel discussed with your client(s) the possibility of

attempting to resolve this dispute (or particular issues) by alternative dispute resolution?

11. Might some form of alternative dispute resolution procedure resolve or narrow the issues in this case?

12. Have you or your client(s) explored with the other parties the possibility of resolving this dispute (or particular issues) by alternative dispute resolution?

[Signature of solicitor, date]

Note: This check-list must be lodged not later than two months before the date of hearing with copies to the other parties.

2. SCOPE

2.1. This guidance provides advice on the process of dispute management and resolution where a dispute arises on a procurement contract which cannot be resolved between the contracting parties by 'simple negotiation' and third party or agency input is required. It identifies as one of the options the use of Alternative Dispute Resolution (ADR). This guidance is not a comprehensive manual nor is it a substitute for appropriate legal advice. It is a companion to guidance no 41 *'Managing Risk and Contingency for Works Projects'*; no 42 *'Contracting for the Provision of Services'* and no 47 *'Contract Management'*.

3. DISPUTE AVOIDANCE

3.1. Given the expense and disruption caused to any contract when a dispute arises, the importance of following dispute avoidance techniques cannot be over-emphasised. The principles and procedures for good contract management (see guidance no 47) should therefore be followed.

3.2. *Remember that the best way to deal with a dispute is not to have it in the first place.* Early warning of a possible dispute can be invaluable. All contract management techniques should include monitoring for the early detection of such problems. In any contract, the supplier should be obliged to give early warning of the possibility of any dispute, and regular discussions between the client and supplier should include reviews of possible areas of conflict (see guidance nos 42 and 47).

3.3. As early as possible (preferably at ITT) a clause should be identified, requiring both parties to adopt a suitable dispute resolution procedure (or procedures) which should include a reference to an appropriate appointing body if arbitration or an ADR procedure is to be used or both. There may be particular trade bodies or organisations which are appropriate in the case of a specialised contract. Legal advice should always be obtained on the suitability of such a clause for a particular contract.

4. DISPUTE MANAGEMENT

4.1. If a dispute arises, it is important to manage it actively and positively to encourage early and effective settlement. Unnecessary delays and inefficiency can lead to rapid escalation of costs and may impede (or even prevent) the successful resolution of the dispute. Moreover, there are statutory (and perhaps contractual) limitation periods for the issue of proceedings.

4.2. Risks should be continually assessed to prevent confrontation. The primary objective should be to achieve a satisfactory resolution of the dispute which will provide the best value for money solution.

5. DISPUTE RESOLUTION PROCEDURES

5.1. The four main categories of dispute resolution are:

—negotiation;
—ADR;
—arbitration; and
—litigation.

Negotiation

5.2. This is the most common, direct and effective method to resolve a dispute. It should take place on a 'without prejudice' basis. Direct negotiation should always be used and all possible avenues explored before progressing to other dispute resolution procedures. The main benefits of negotiation are that:

—it is free from any procedural formalities;
—the costs of any third party intervention are avoided; and
—a solution acceptable to all parties may be achieved.

The disadvantages are that:

—it may not result in a settlement;
—it can lead to acrimony between the parties which prevents effective communication; and
—the process of resolving a problem may drag on.

Alternative dispute resolution (ADR) procedures

5.3. ADR procedures have become more important since the 1980s as an approach to contract management. To be effective, it is recommended that they should be specified in the contract terms and conditions. ADR clauses normally ensure the use of ADR before arbitration of litigation. However, ADR procedures can be used at any time by agreement of the parties. The various ADR procedures are:

—mediation;
—conciliation;
—mini-trial;
—judicial appraisal;
—early neutral evaluation;
—adjudication; and
—dispute review board/dispute advisor.

5.3.1. *Mediation*: the most widely used of all the ADR techniques. It is a private voluntary dispute resolution procedure in which a neutral mediator assists the parties in reaching a mutually acceptable solution to the dispute. Mediators have no authority to impose a judgement. They work with the parties, both jointly and in private sessions, assessing with them the strengths and weaknesses of their positions, areas of common ground, and the possibility of creative forward-looking solutions. Mediations are conducted on a 'without prejudice' basis. Furthermore private meetings between the mediator and each party are confidential to that party, unless express authority is given to the mediator for disclosure. If a settlement is reached as a result of the mediation, it is usual practice for the parties to record the terms in writing, either by contract or (if available) by consent order. Parties may elect to have legal representation during a mediation. Several years experience, both here and in the USA, indicates a settlement rate in mediation of about 90 per cent.

5.3.2. *Conciliation*: differs very little in practice from mediation; often used synonymously. It has been argued that there is a technical difference in that the mediator gives a written evaluation (or recommendation) to the parties whereas a conciliator does not: but in other cases the terminology has been applied in reverse. In practice, the name of the process is irrelevant provided all parties agree and understand the procedure they wish to use.

5.3.3. Mini-Trial (Executive Tribunal/Executive Appraisal): despite its name, this is not a trial but a more formalised mediation. A panel is appointed, comprising a mediator together with a senior executive from each party to the dispute. Presentations are then made to the panel (by a representative of each party and/or their advisers) in the presence of all parties after which the panel retire to negotiate/mediate the dispute. Where there is extensive evidence, expert or lay witnesses can be called. However, as with mediation, there are no formal rules of evidence. Again, the procedure is voluntary and intended to generate a mutually acceptable agreement between the parties. Neither the panel nor the mediator may impose any judgment on the parties.

5.3.4. Judicial Appraisal: involves presentations (oral and/or written) being made to a senior legal figure (eg a retired judge or QC) who will then deliver an appraisal to the parties of the relative merits of each side's case. The parties contract in advance that the non-binding appraisal delivered will be open/ 'without prejudice', delivered in writing/orally, etc. In other words, the procedure may be adapted to take whatever form the parties agree in advance. The advantage of Judicial Appraisal is that parties have the opportunity at an early stage in a dispute to receive an authoritative, albeit non-binding, view of the merits of their respective cases, which can form the basis of settlement negotiations. It is most effective as a procedure where the parties cannot agree over a very specific point of law (eg interpretation of a statute or contractual provision). The appraisal given may resolve the dispute in its entirety, or simply pave the way for further negotiations or a mediation. It can also be adapted to produce a binding decision.

5.3.5. Early Neutral Evaluation: is broadly similar to the Judicial Appraisal and has similar advantages. It involves the appointment of an expert in the particular field (whether legal or technical), who, after hearing/reading the arguments/evidence, will present the parties with a non-binding evaluation of their respective cases. It can also be adapted to produce a binding decision.

5.3.6. Adjudication: as its name implies, this involves the appointment of an adjudicator, who will deliver a view on the case, having heard oral and/or written submissions. Most commonly, the adjudicator is appointed as a 'valuer' or 'expert'. This procedure falls outside the scope of an 'arbitration' and therefore is free from the formalities attaching to the latter. However adjudicators can be liable for damages if negligent (unless their contract of appointment provides otherwise). Unless the contract provides otherwise, awards are binding on the parties to the adjudication without rights of appeal. Often the contract will provide for the award to bind the parties during the performance of the contract, with rights of appeal thereafter.

5.3.7. Dispute Review Board and/or Dispute Adviser: It is a more formalised version of mediation. A Dispute Review Board is a group of experts appointed at the outset of a contract before disputes arise to foster co-operation between client and contractor and to advise informally or adjudicate on controversial matters as they arise during the contract. It is aimed at large complex contracts and is not suitable for small ones. Dispute Advisors are independent experts appointed soon after contracts are awarded. Their task is to assist the parties to resolve disputes, claims and other differences promptly and equitably by early, non-binding procedures. This avoids reference to more formalised dispute resolution procedures.

Arbitration

5.4. Historically the process of arbitration goes back to mediaeval times (or earlier), but the modern process is now governed by statute, principally the Arbitration Act 1950 (as amended) and the Arbitration Act 1979.

5.5. The process is contractual, arises from an agreement between the parties and is binding and enforceable. This can be achieved by including an arbitration clause in the original contract or by making an ad hoc arbitration agreement when a dispute arises. The arbitration clause will provide for the dispute to be referred to an independent authority (known as the arbitrator or arbitrators) for resolution. An arbitration agreement can provide for referral to a single arbitrator, or to panels of two, three or more arbitrators. The arbitration agreement and the authority and jurisdiction of the arbitrator (which derive from it) are irrevocable by either party individually; arbitration can only be terminated (other than by agreement between the parties) by order of the High Court. Similarly the arbitrator or arbitrators can only withdraw by consent of both parties or with leave of the court. (Model clauses can be found in GC Stores 1 Standard Conditions of Government Contract for Stores Purchases, Form GC/Works 1 etc General Conditions of Government Contacts for Building and Civil Engineering and guidance no 42 'Contracting for the Provision of Services.')

5.6. When a dispute is referred to arbitration, the arbitrator (or arbitrators)(who need not have any particular qualifications other than any specified in the arbitration agreement itself) is appointed by agreement between the parties or, in default of agreement, by the appointing authority (if any) specified in the arbitration agreement. If there is no appointing authority able and willing to act and no agreement, the appointment can be made by application to the court. Arbitrators are entitled to charge an agreed fee (or, if no fee is agreed, a reasonable fee) for their decision (called an award). They have power to order their fees and expenses (called the costs of the award) and the costs incurred by the parties (called the costs of the reference) to be paid by either or both of the parties in any proportion. The final award must deal with the question of costs.

5.7. After the appointment, arbitrators are subject to any rules contained in or incorporated by the arbitration agreement in addition to the provisions of the Arbitration Acts. Within these restrictions, they can determine their own procedures and give any reasonable or appropriate directions for the further conduct of the dispute resolution. Most major arbitrations eventually come to an oral hearing which is usually similar to a court hearing before a judge but which takes place in private with no wigs or robes etc. The arbitrator is bound by the same rules of evidence as a judge in court unless the parties agree to relax them. An interim award may be made in respect of any part of the dispute, with the final award being made at a later stage. Arbitrators are entitled to retain their awards until these fees are paid. Normally awards will not be published to the parties until payment is received.

5.8. In simple cases where the facts are not in dispute the parties may decide to ask arbitrators to conduct a 'documents only' arbitration. In such cases the parties each send arbitrators relevant documents (either serially or simultaneously as arbitrators request) setting out their case. Arbitrators make awards on the basis of those documents. This procedure implies that the parties have waived the strict rules of evidence. A further option is a 'short-form' procedure under which arbitrators hold hearings on some specific issues and deal with the balance on documents submitted. In other cases the parties agreed to adopt a set of rules under which arbitrators are given discretion over whether to have a hearing or not.

5.9. Arbitrators are the sole judge of all questions of fact or law which need to be decided in arbitration. However, arbitrators can appoint independent experts (known as 'assessors') either to advise them separately or to sit in on the arbitration. But any decision reached must be the arbitrators' own. No part of it can be delegated to the assessor. The costs of assessors are, initially, the responsibility of arbitrators, who can recover them from the parties as part of the overall costs of arbitration.

5.10. Rights of appeal against arbitrators' decisions are very limited.

Under section 1 of the Arbitration Act 1979 an appeal can only be made on a question of law and must be lodged within 21 days from the date of publication of the award. It must be made with the consent of all parties or with the leave of the court. The circumstances in which the court will give leave are strictly curtailed. The parties can, and often do, exclude the right of appeal by agreement.

5.11. Section 2 of the 1979 Act provides for points of law arising during the arbitration to be referred to the court as they arise, either by agreement of the parties or with the consent of the arbitrators. This may be useful if the arbitrator is not a lawyer. Sections 22 to 25 of the Arbitration Act 1950 give the court powers and discretion to control the conduct of arbitrators including the power to require them to reconsider an award or to remove them and appoint replacements.

Litigation

5.12. All the processes set out above require some degree of consent before being invoked, although in some cases the consent, once given, cannot be withdrawn. If the use of a consensual process cannot be agreed, the only alternative is litigation before the High Court or County Court. Although rights of access to a court should not be restricted by an ADR clause it can be by an arbitration clause. Litigation will involve trial before a judge, and may well be a lengthy, drawn out and costly process. Normally disputes involving sums of up to £50,000 go to the County Court, others above this figure go to the High Court. However, there may be other factors governing the choice of court, (eg disputes over technical matters go to a special type of Judge called an 'Official Referee').

6. CHOOSING THE BEST PROCEDURE

6.1. The variety of techniques available highlights the opportunity to select a procedure most suitable to a particular case. Even where the contract provides a specific dispute resolution procedure, it is not uncommon to agree to use some other procedure more relevant to the particular dispute. *Good dispute management involves selecting and using, wherever possible, the most appropriate resolution procedure available.*

6.2. In considering which process to adopt you will need to consider the need for expert and informed advice and:

—the overall cost effectiveness when balanced against risk. Dispute management involves consideration of constantly changing risk. Changing perception of risks may need to be reflected in the dispute management process. Remember, processes can be used either serially or in parallel;
—the effectiveness of the process. Whichever process is used, it may become necessary during the process to put pressure on the other side to reach a decision, or to enforce the decision reached;
—the comparative speed of the differing process. Some processes (particularly ADR and, to a lesser extent, arbitration) have considerable advantages of speed. However, some disputes may need the detailed consideration of a more formal process, and speed should not necessarily be regarded as the most important factor;
—the necessity to preserve the working relationship of the conflicting parties during the course of the contract (or other contracts involving the same parties). If this is important, careful consideration should be given before becoming involved in litigation or even the more formal type of arbitration. The conflict of emotions arising from a formal process can wreck the working relations of the parties so that any prospect of them working together in the future becomes impossible;
—fairness. This is important: the process adopted must be demonstrably fair to both sides in the dispute. Any possibility that an allegation of unfair conduct could be made by the supplier against a government department must be avoided; and
—audit. In all disputes it is important to maintain at all times a clear and visible audit trail.

6.3. Most approaches to the resolution of disputes involve a combination of procedures. Typically, parties may first attempt direct negotiation. If this fails, arbitration or litigation may start. The availability of a wider range of dispute resolution techniques allows departments to combine several techniques in a 'multi-step process'. This will ensure that the process being used is the one most likely to be effective in resolution, at any given stage of the dispute.

6.4. The processes, whether single or multi-step, can be put in place either at contract negotiation, or when the dispute itself arises. The former is clearly preferable, since the likelihood of obtaining consent from the parties to such a process is greater at this stage. Advice may be required from appropriate professionals. Factors influencing the choice of process (either single or multi-step) are described in section 7 below.

6.5. Government will normally exhaust all avenues of dispute resolution before embarking on arbitration or litigation proceedings (see flow chart at Annex 1).

6.6. Each process itself can be varied, the aim being to provide one which fits the requirement of the parties. Examples are:

—*Mediation:* either where the mediator facilitates a settlement without expressing any view on the merits or engages in a confidential evaluation (albeit non-binding) of each party's case, or a combination of the two;

—*Judicial Appraisal:* designed to deliver an appraisal which can be binding or non-binding, open or without prejudice: delivered either in writing or orally; and

—*Fast-track arbitration:* a useful alternative where a binding decision is required with the minimum of delay. The decision can be taken either on documents only or at short oral hearing. However, both require goodwill to succeed. Arbitrators' Awards must still be in writing, but they may be prepared to indicate their decisions orally. This process is particularly useful where an immediate and urgent decision is required before proceeding to the next phase of a contract.

7. ADVANTAGES OF ADR

7.1. The advantages of using an ADR procedure include:

—keeping costs down;
—a speedy resolution;
—confidentiality (avoiding publicity of a court hearing);
—the parties retaining control over the procedure and the outcome;
—the possibility of continuing satisfactory business relationships;
—maintaining and improving communication between the parties; and
—providing the possibility of a creative forward-looking solution, rather than simply an historic one.

7.2. Two specific criteria should be met if a dispute is to be referred to ADR:

—that sufficient legal, factual and other information is available to enable each party to make a realistic analysis and assessment of its case for a sensibly negotiated result (eg experts' reports, counsel's opinion, medical reports, damages calculations etc); and
—direct negotiations between the parties are not proving effective or efficient in resolving the dispute.

7.3. A dispute may not be suitable for ADR at an early stage, (eg if insufficient information is available), but it may become so later on. Disputes should therefore be reviewed on a regular basis.

221

8. ADVANTAGES OF OTHER DISPUTE RESOLUTION PROCEDURES

8.1. The advantages of using binding procedures such as arbitration and litigation, include the ability to:

—bring an unwilling party to the dispute resolution procedure;
—ensure from the outset that the solution will be enforceable without further agreement; and
—enforce the participation to third parties (litigation only).

9. USING ADR PROCEDURES

9.1. *Setting them up.* In the majority of cases, ADR procedures are set up and conducted under the auspices of an ADR organisation (see Annex 2 ADR Organisations). However, parties can set up the procedures themselves. If involved, an ADR organisation's role will generally include providing:

—a suitably qualified neutral individual, who will:
— contact and meet all parties to secure their consent to the procedure;
—design and administer the procedure;
—advise all parties of the procedures; and
—ensure the quality of the procedures.

9.2. *Obtaining consent of the other party(ies).* All ADR procedures are voluntary, and the consent of all parties is therefore required. Where an ADR contract clause exists this part of the process should simply be a formality. In other cases, most ADR organisations will, at the request of one party, approach the other(s) with a view to obtaining their consent to the procedure. Alternatively, the approach can be made directly between the parties/their advisors.

9.3. *The Agreement.* Most ADR procedures are governed by a short and straightforward agreement between the parties and the appointed individual, setting out the terms on which the procedure will be conducted. In the case of mediation, for example, this will include confirmation that it will be without prejudice and confidential, that the mediator may not be called as a witness subsequently and that the representatives have full authority to settle the matter at the mediation (subject, where relevant, to obtaining ministerial or other consents).

9.4. *Venue and Date.* A mutually acceptable venue and date will need to be agreed. As regards venue, most ADR procedures will require a room where all parties can meet together, (including the neutral) with additional private rooms for them to meet separately, again often with the neutral. The venue itself may also be a neutral one.

9.5. Identity of Neutral. This will need to be agreed between the parties, in conjunction with the ADR organisation if used. For example, a number of ADR organisations maintain a large panel of qualified mediators, drawn from a range of professional and commercial backgrounds. In some cases, the parties will wish the neutral not only to be experienced as a neutral, but also to have some expertise in the specific field in question, particularly if complex legal or technical questions are involved. However, mediation skills tend to be more important than any specific technical/legal expertise.

9.6. Representatives of each party. It is vital to the success of an ADR procedure that the individuals attending as representatives of each party have authority to settle the matter on behalf of their respective parties or at least to recommend the terms of settlement. This may be stipulated in the agreement, subject only to any requirements to refer to a minister or other source for final consent. Sometimes in ADR, particularly in mediation, the final settlement reached between the parties is more creative and wide ranging than anticipated. The ability of those present to sanction such arrangements is, therefore, vital and the scope of the representative's authority needs to be considered fully, prior to the ADR procedure taking place. *Where required, provision can be made in the settlement terms for those terms to be approved by someone not present at the mediation. This would apply in cases where ministerial content is required to the terms of settlement. In these circumstances, it should be made clear before mediation commences that any settlement terms will be subject to such consent.*

9.7. Some sample ADR clauses are set out at Annex 3. In using clauses, the following points should be noted:

—ADR procedures should be considered at the ITT stage;
—some of the clauses refer to 'an ADR procedure' and some specifically to 'Mediation'. It should be considered at the contract stage whether it would be appropriate to specify a process in the contract, or leave it to be decided in the light of any particular dispute that emerges;
—some of the clauses contain an element of 'multi-step' procedure. For example, clause 2 (long-form and short-form) specifies a direct negotiation phase before the adoption of any ADR procedure. Clearly the clauses can be amended to include a more complex multi-step approach;
—many ADR clauses are not enforceable in law — in other words, a

party cannot be mandated to participate in an ADR procedure, even where such a clause exists. However, the value of ADR clauses is that they focus the parties' minds, at the onset of a dispute, on the dispute resolution procedures adopted by them at the time of signing the contract. Indeed the non-binding nature of the commitment usually makes it easier for parties to accept its inclusion in the contract; and

—it should be clearly understood that the use of a non-binding ADR procedure does *NOT* require the parties to contract out of using arbitration or litigation proceedings.

10. USING ARBITRATION PROCEDURES

10.1. Arbitration procedures should be considered at ITT stage, when a decision must be made on whether to put an arbitration agreement clause into the contract, and, if so, what form it will take. A well drawn clause must contain a clear intention, binding the parties to refer any dispute to arbitration (see guidance no 42).

10.2. Some forms of contract contain arbitration rules, and some other bodies publish such rules for the use of parties to arbitrations (eg the Chartered Institute of Arbitrators, the Institution of Civil Engineers and the London Maritime Arbitrators Association). Examples of international rules are published by the International Chamber of Commerce and by the London Court of International Arbitration. Copies of these can be obtained from the relevant bodies. (Annex 4 sets out the 'Short Form Arbitration Rules 1991' published by the Chartered Institute of Arbitrators.)

10.3. When a dispute arises and there is an arbitration clause in the contract one party may attempt to ignore it and issue court proceedings. It is important that the other party should take no step in those proceedings, other than to apply as soon as possible for a stay of those proceedings and an order that the dispute be referred to arbitration.

10.4. When the arbitration procedure has started the first task is the appointment of the arbitrator or arbitrators (see Annex 2 for list of Arbitrators Organisations). If the agreement specifies someone having a particular skill or professional background, enquiries can be made of the relevant professional body which will usually keep lists of suitably qualified and experienced members. If the parties cannot agree, the appointing body specified in the agreement should be approached. If there is no appointing body specified, or none is able and willing to act, then application can be made to the court for an appointment to be made.

10.5. Arbitrators, when appointed, are in charge of procedures, subject only to any applicable rules and to the provisions of the Arbitration Acts. The way in which the arbitration process will proceed, therefore depends on the directions given by arbitrators. Usually the process follows fairly closely the process of court litigation (directions being given for pleadings, discovery of documents, oral hearings etc). Arbitrators have power to take evidence on oath, although frequently this is dispensed with. All hearings are in private, and no-one apart from the arbitrators, the parties and their witnesses is entitled to be present except with the consent of the parties. Occasionally the parties agree to deal with the dispute in whole or in part on documents only, but, unless the particular rules adopted provide for this procedure, arbitrators must have an oral hearing if either side requests it.

10.6. When arbitrators have considered all the submissions and evidence, whether orally or in documents, the award is prepared and published. Arbitrators are entitled to (and usually do) retain the award, and refuse to pass it to the parties until the appropriate fees have been paid. It should be remembered that the date of publication is the date on which the arbitrators tell the parties that the award is ready, and not the date on which the fees are paid and the award is taken up. Therefore, the 21 day period for making an appeal runs from the date of publication, and if the award is not taken up promptly the right of appeal may be jeopardised or even lost. The courts have emphasised in a number of recent cases that appeals from arbitrators must be pursued with promptness and diligence, and extensions of time are only given in exceptional circumstances.

10.7. When the award is published arbitrators' functions are terminated (known as 'functus officio'). There is, however, one exception. The final award must deal with costs (even if only to say 'no order as to costs') and arbitrators have the power to assess their level. If arbitrators do not exercise this power, then costs are assessed by the High Court Taxing Master.

11. ENFORCEMENT

11.1. *Non-binding ADR Procedures* — where settlement of a dispute has been achieved through a non-binding ADR procedure (including obtaining any final authorisation required), it is usual for the terms of settlement to be recorded and signed by the parties. As well as serving to clarify and confirm the agreed terms, this assists enforcement of the agreement. Broadly, the options are:

—parties agree and sign the main points of settlement (known as Heads of Terms) which will be followed by a more detailed contract documenting the full settlement. The Heads of Terms can be made binding as a matter of law or non-binding (either because it is too generalised or because it is merely as 'agreement to agree'). If it is unenforceable, either party can withdraw from the agreement prior to signing the main document;

—parties draft and sign an agreement as above, but use it as the basis for a consent award in Arbitration or 'Tomlin' order in the courts. This option is available only where court proceedings have been commenced, and has the advantage of making the agreement enforceable as a judgment of the court, without the need for fresh proceedings; or

—parties sign a contract setting out the full term of their agreement.

11.2. *Binding Procedures:* as court litigation eventually results in a court judgment this is enforceable through the usual processes of the court. An arbitration award can be enforced through the court by bringing an action on the award as if it were a new contract. A judgment will be made on the terms of the award. Alternatively, an application can be sought under section 26 of the 1950 Act seeking a summary order directing enforcement of the award as if it were a judgment. Neither an expert adjudication nor a judicial appraisal can be treated as an arbitration award, and therefore can only be enforced by bringing an action for a judgment in the same terms, and then enforcing that judgment.

ANNEX 1

ADR FLOW CHART MODEL

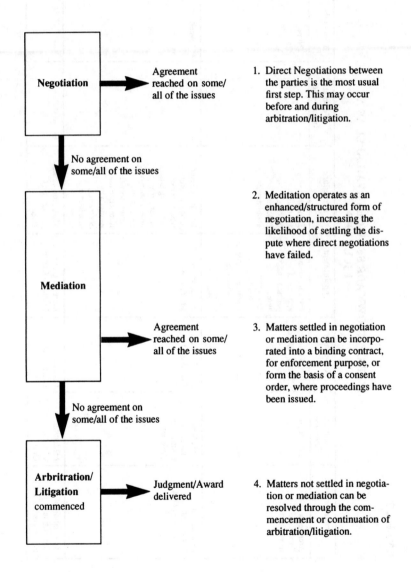

Negotiation → Agreement reached on some/all of the issues

1. Direct Negotiations between the parties is the most usual first step. This may occur before and during arbitration/litigation.

No agreement on some/all of the issues

2. Meditation operates as an enhanced/structured form of negotiation, increasing the likelihood of settling the dispute where direct negotiations have failed.

Mediation

Agreement reached on some/all of the issues

3. Matters settled in negotiation or mediation can be incorporated into a binding contract, for enforcement purpose, or form the basis of a consent order, where proceedings have been issued.

No agreement on some/all of the issues

Arbitration/Litigation commenced → Judgment/Award delivered

4. Matters not settled in negotiation or mediation can be resolved through the commencement or continuation of arbitration/litigation.

227

ANNEX 2

TABLE OF KNOWN ADR SERVICES AVAILABLE AS AT 1 JULY 1993

Organisation	Limit of Service	Reference	Appointment	Procedure	General Information	Timetable	Costs
Architects & Surveyors Institute (ASI)	Arbitration	All ASI Contracts Clauses 10.1 to 10.03	Institute President appoints if partners cannot agree. Appointment within 14 days Institute President if both parties agree to submit to arbitration	Standard arbitration process following appointment	—	None	Not stated
	Arbitration	Voluntary					
Association of Consultant Architects (ACA)	Adjudication Employer/ Contractor Optional	ACA Contract Clause 25.1 to 25.8	Parties appoint adjudicator	Dispute referred to adjudicator whose decision is binding unless either party gives notice of arbitration within 4 weeks. Reference may be made by contractor, architect or client	—	1 week	Not stated
Association of Consulting Engineers (ACE)	Mediation Client/Consultant Only	Conditions of Engagement Clause 4	Mutual agreement President CIArb	Mediation as an optional first stage	—	—	Not stated

			BAE appoints mediator from register of qualified persons or provides list of three	Discretion of mediator who assists in resolving dispute but does not impose decision	Guidelines published. Courses for qualifying mediators		
British Academy of Experts (BAE)	Mediation	—	BAE appoints mediator from register of qualified persons or provides list of three	Discretion of mediator who assists in resolving dispute but does not impose decision	Guidelines published. Courses for qualifying mediators	—	—
British Institute of Architectural Technicians (BIAT)	Mediation Client/ Consultant Only	—		Mediation scheme in preparation	—	—	Not stated
Building Employers Confederation (BEC)	See CEDR	None	CEDR Scheme (Fixed Fee)	See CEDR	—	—	Fixed fee on sliding scale
Centre for Dispute Resolution (CEDR)	Conciliation	—	CEDR	Informal	Guidance notes published / Qualifying courses for mediator/ conciliator	Not stated	Own costs plus costs of mediator/ conciliator
	Mediation	—	CEDR	More formal with attempts at settlement			
	Executive Tribunal	—	CEDR	One executive with powers to settle on each side plus mediator appointed by CEDR. Similar to CIArb mini trial procedure			

Organisation	Limit of Service	Reference	Appointment	Procedure	General Information	Timetable	Costs
Construction Disputes Resolution Group (CDRG)	Mediation	—	CDRG	Mediation		Limited to 5 days	Not stated
(Service available internationally)	Dispute Review Board	—	CDRG	Experts appointed at start of contract to advise on controversial matters	Guidance notes published	Duration of contract	Not stated
	Dispute Advisor	—	CDRG	Single experts as above		Duration of contract	Not stated
Chartered Institute of Arbitrators (CIArb)	Conciliation/ Mediation	—	Conciliator or mediator appointed by CIArb. Parties may also appoint one conciliator or mediator each with 3rd acting as referee.	Discretion of mediator/ conciliator	Guidance notes published	—	Joint
	Mini-Trial	—	CIArb appoint neutral advisor	Each side appoints a member of their senior management with powers to settle. Exchange of concise statements, documents and expert opinion. Formal meeting, followed by attempts at settlement with or without neutral advisor	Guidance notes published	—	Joint

Organisation							
Chartered Institute of Building (CIOB)	Conciliation service for members of Chartered Building Company Scheme	Rules of conduct	CIOB	As rules	Register being compiled	—	—
Electrical Contractors Association (ECA)	Referee	Contract Clause 19	By agreement or by CEDR	Referee acts as expert not as arbitrator. Decision binding for duration of contract	—	28 Days	Scale of fees
IDR Europe	Mediation	—	Mediators drawn from 24 members the National Network of Solicitors in Alternative Disputes Resolution	Details from IDR Europe Ltd Equity & Law Building 36–38 Baldon Street BS1 1NR	—	—	£175 plus VAT
Institution of Civil Engineers (ICE)	Conciliation	ICE contracts	ICE	Decision of conciliator binding unless referred to arbitration within specified period	Register of conciliators with appropriate training	2 months	Not stated
Joint Contracts Tribunal (JCT)	Adjudicator	Design and Building Management contracts (works section)	—	—	Preliminary to arbitration	—	—
	Conciliation/ Mediation	—	—	Under consideration for JCT 80 and other contracts	—	—	—

Appendix 5

Organisation	Limit of Service	Reference	Appointment	Procedure	General Information	Timetable	Costs
Landscape Institute (LI)	Mediation Client/ Consultant only	Conditions of Engagement Clauses 3.28–3.30	President	Not Known	—	—	—
London Maritime Arbitrators Association (LMAA)	Conciliation		President LMAA	Procedure by agreement. May formulate terms of settlement. Confidential and without prejudice unless otherwise agreed	Guidance notes available	Not stated	Own costs plus costs of conciliator
	Sole Arbitrator	Small claims	President LMAA	Informal procedure on documents only but hearing may be necessary. Award legally binding	Guidance notes available	Not stated	Arbitrators award
National House-Building Council (NHBC)	Conciliation for Members/clients	—	—	—	—	—	—
National Joint Consultative Committee for Building (NJCC)	—	—	—	—	—	—	—
Royal Institute of British Architects (RIBA)	Conciliation Client/ Consultant	In preparation	President RIBA	Informal conciliator does not impose decision	RIBA Practice Note 97	Not stated	Sliding scale starting with £200 for 1.5 days
Royal Institute of Chartered Surveyors (RICS)	Mediation	In preparation.	Applicant requests mediator from Information or Arbitration Service	Presidential nomination if contract or lease provides	Mediator assists in resolving dispute but does not impose decision	Guidance notes to be issued	Set by mediator and and agreed by parties

ANNEX 3

ADR clauses — examples

The examples set out below are ADR Clauses drafted and used by the *Centre for Dispute Resolution (CEDR)*, and those who use its services. They should be used only with legal advice and may need to be adapted.

Clauses	Remarks

Short Form Alternatives

(a) If a dispute arises out of or in connection with this Agreement, the Parties will, with the help of the Centre for Dispute Resolution (CEDR) seek in good faith to resolve it by alternative dispute resolution.

This single-step procedure provides only for an ADR procedure, leaving the exact choice of procedure to be agreed at the time of the dispute.

(b) If a dispute arises out of or in connection with this Agreement, the Parties will, with the help of the Centre for Dispute Resolution (CEDR) seek in good faith to resolve it by alternative dispute resolution. If the Parties fail to agree terms of settlement within [ ] Days of the [initiation] [commencement] of the procedure the dispute shall be referred to arbitration in accordance with the [as appropriate] /or litigation. [The [initiation] [commencement] of the procedure is defined as [the request to CEDR by both/all the parties for an ADR procedure] [the commencement of the first ADR meeting].]

This multi-step clause provides first for an ADR procedure, (again, the exact choice of which will be made at the time of the dispute), followed by either arbitration or litigation (this choice will be made at the time of contract execution and specified in this clause). The move from first to second phase is governed by a time limit. In practice, this limit may be extended by agreement between the parties at the time of the dispute, if an ADR procedure is being seriously considered.

(c) The parties will attempt in good faith to negotiate a settlement to any claim or dispute between them arising out of or in connection with this Agreement. If the matter is not resolved by negotiation the parties will refer the dispute to mediation in accordance with CEDR (Centre for Dispute Resolution) procedures. If the parties fail to agree terms of settlement within [ ] days of the [initiation] [commencment] of the procedure the dispute shall be referred to arbitration in accordance with [as appropriate] /or litigation. [The [initiation] [commencement] of the procedure is defined as [the request to CEDR by both/all parties for a mediation] [the commencement of the first ADR meeting].]

This three-step clause is similar to (b) above, except with the addition of a negotiation phase prior to the use of an ADR procedure. (See ADR Flow Chart at Annex 1 above.)

(d) Unless settled by prior negotiation a claim or dispute arising out of or in connection with this Agreement shall be submitted to mediation by CEDR (Centre of Dispute Resolution) within [ ] days of one side giving written notice to the other of such dispute and of their intention to refer it to mediation by CEDR.

This single-step clause specifies mediation, rather than any other ADR procedure.

The following paragraph may be added to any of the *Short Form Clauses* above.

Both Parties reserve all their respective rights in the event that no agreed resolution shall be reached in the [mediation] [ADR procedure] [and neither party shall be deemed to be precluded from taking such interim formal steps as may be considered necessary to protect such party's position while the mediation or other procedure is pending [or continuing]].

Where concerns exist about excluding the possibility of protective relief from the courts, by agreeing to an ADR procedure, this additional wording may be added.

Clauses

Remarks

Clause 2

Disputes: three-step clause

1. The parties will attempt in good faith to resolve any dispute or claim arising out of or relating to this Agreement promptly through negotiations between the respective senior executives of the parties who have authority to settle the same

Step 1: the negotiation phase.

2. If the matter is not resolved through negotiation, the parties will attempt in good faith to resolve the dispute or claim through an Alternative Dispute Resolution (ADR) procedure as recommended to the parties by the Centre for Dispute Resolution (CEDR).

No time limit for this transition to ADR, merely a failure of negotiations.

3. If the matter has not been resolved by an ADR procedure within [ ] days of the initiation of such procedure, or if either party will not participate in an

The litigation/arbitration phase can be triggered (as here) by a time limit on the ADR phase.

235

Appendix 5

ADR procedure, the dispute
shall be referred to arbitration
in accordance with [as appro-
priate/or litigation].

4. The construction performance
and validity of this Agreement
shall in all respects be governed by [Laws of England].

This Guidance Note is drafted in
the context of English Law.
Further guidance/advice should be
taken if other laws apply.

Clause 2 (Long Form)

Disputes: three-step clause

1. In the event of any dispute or
difference arising between the
parties in connection with this
Agreement, [senior represen-
tatives/members of the board
of directors] of the parties
shall, within [10] days of a
written request from either
party to the other addressed to
[the managing director], meet
in a good faith effort to resolve
the dispute without recourse to
legal proceedings.

Step 1: Good faith negotiations.

2. If the dispute or difference is not
resolved as a result of such meeting, either party may (at such
meeting or within 14 days from
its conclusion) propose to the
other in writing that structured
negotiations be entered into with
the assistance of mediator or
neutral adviser ('Mediator').

Step 2 - ADR procedure, triggered by
a time limit on failed negotiations.

'Structured negotiations' is a
deliberately vague expression
leaving the exact format fluid.
This can be replaced by 'mediation' (or some other process) if
more certainty is required.

3. If the parties are unable to
agree on a Mediator or if the
Mediator agreed upon is
unable or unwilling to act,
other party shall within fourteen days from the date of the

Selection of a mediator is often
assisted through a provider of
ADR services, who will ensure
appropriate quality/training, and
such matters as professional
indemnity insurance.

proposal to appoint a Mediator or within fourteen days of notice to either party that he or she is unable or unwilling to act, apply to the *Centre for Dispute Resolution (CEDR)* to appoint a Mediator.

4. The parties shall within 14 days of the appointment of the Mediator meet him/her to agree a programme for the exchange of any relevant information and the structure to be adopted for the negotiations [to be held in ....]. If considered appropriate, the parties may at any stage seek assistance from *CEDR* to provide guidance on a suitable procedure.

It may well be helpful if the parties met to discuss the format of the proposed procedure, information to be exchanged etc.

5. Unless concluded with a written legally binding agreement, all negotiations connected with dispute shall be conducted in confidence and without prejudice to the rights of the parties in any future proceedings.

This should also feature as a binding agreement term of the Mediation Agreement which the parties sign, governing terms of the mediation/other ADR procedure.

6. Failing agreement, either of the parties may invite the Mediator to provide a non-binding but informative opinion in writing, who need only comply with their request if he considers it would be helpful. Any such opinion shall not be an attempt to anticipate what a court might order but rather the Mediator's suggestions as to the settlement terms which are considered appropriate in

This envisages that, if agreement cannot be reached in mediation, the parties may request that the Mediator deliver a non-binding recommendation. Again this would need to feature as a term of the Mediation Agreement.

all the circumstances. [Such opinion shall be provided on a without prejudice basis and shall not be used in evidence in any proceedings arising in connection with this Agreement without the prior written consent of both parties.]

7. If the Parties accept the Mediator's recommendations or otherwise reach agreement on the resolution of the dispute; such agreement shall be reduced to writing and, once it is signed by their duly authorised representatives and all relevant consents have been obtained, shall be binding on the parties. [Such agreement shall be implemented in full within [ ] days of signature failing which it shall be rendered null and void (and may not be referred to in any subsequent legal proceedings unless legal proceedings have been initiated to enforce it by either party within a further [ ] days].

8. If the parties fail to reach agreement in the structured negotiations within [60] days of the Mediator being appointed then any dispute or difference between them may be referred to the Courts unless within [such period/a further period of 30 days] the parties agree to refer the matter to arbitration before an arbitrator whose method of appointment is agreed between them.

Step 3 - triggered by a time limit and the failure of the ADR procedure, the parties may resort to arbitration/litigation.

9. The construction, performance and validity of this Agreement shall in all respects be governed by the [Laws of England].

This Guidance Note is drafted in the context of English Law. Further guidance/advice should be taken if other laws apply.

ANNEX 4

The Chartered Institute of Arbitrators

SHORT FORM ARBITRATION RULES 1991

Preliminary

1. These Rules shall apply to arbitrations which the parties intend to be conducted according to short-ended forms of procedure, whether on the basis of:

   1.1 written submissions and documentary evidence only, without a hearing; or
   1.2 a hearing for the purpose of receiving oral submissions and evidence.

   The parties may vary any of the provisions of these Rules by agreement.

Commencement of arbitration

2. An application for arbitration shall be made to the Appointing Authority by the parties on the Appointing Authority's form, accompanied by the prescribed registration fee. At such time as the Appointing Authority thinks fit, it shall appoint an Arbitrator.

Jurisdiction and powers of the Arbitrator

3. Without prejudice to the jurisdictions and powers set out in the Schedule to these Rules, the Arbitrator shall have the widest discretion permitted by law to ensure the just, expeditious, economical and final determination of the dispute.

4. Without prejudice to any powers conferred on the Arbitrator by law or by the contract between the parties, the Arbitrator may exercise the powers set out in the Schedule to these Rules.

Procedure

5. The parties shall, if possible, agree whether the arbitration is to proceed on the basis of written submissions and documentary evidence only, without a hearing, or whether a hearing is required for the purpose of receiving oral submissions and evidence. If the parties fail to agree, the Arbitrator shall decide which procedure is to be followed and may, if he considers it desirable, call a meeting with the parties to consider the matter. The Arbitrator shall in any case confirm which procedure is to be followed by directions issued to the parties in writing.

6. Within 21 days of the Arbitrator's directions under article 5, the party making the claim ('the Claimant') shall submit to the Arbitrator and to the other party ('the Respondent') a brief statement of claim.

7. Within 21 days of receipt of the Claimant's statement of its claim, the Respondent shall submit to the Arbitrator and to the Claimant:

   7.1 a brief statement of its defence to the claim;
   7.2 a brief statement of any counterclaim.

8. Within 14 days of receipt of the Respondent's statement(s) under Article 7, the Claimant shall submit to the Arbitrator and to the Respondent:

   8.1 a brief statement of any reply to the defence which it wishes to make;
   8.2 a brief statement of its defence to any counterclaim.

9. Where the Claimant submits a defence to the Respondent's counterclaim, the Respondent may, within 14 days of receipt of the defence to the counterclaim, submit to the Arbitrator and to the Claimant a brief statement of its reply to that defence.

10. All statements submitted under Articles 6 to 9 above shall include a brief statement of:

    10.1 the party's principal arguments of fact and law;
    10.2 in the case of the claim and of any counterclaim, the remedies sought;

and shall be accompanied by copies of all documents on which the party seeks to rely in support of its case and detailed calculations of any sums claimed.

11. Submissions will normally be closed on completion of the procedure set out in Articles 6 - 10. However, the Arbitrator may, in his discretion, permit the parties to make further replies to each other's cases, but shall in every case have to power to determine when the submissions are closed.

12. The Arbitrator may require the parties to submit to him and to each other:

    12.1 on application to the Arbitrator, such documents as are properly discoverable to help the parties in preparing their submissions;

    12.2 in any case, such further submissions, documents or information as he considers to be necessary.

13. Within 14 days of the close of submissions or at such other time as he thinks fit, the Arbitrator may in appropriate cases conduct an inspection of the subject-matter of the arbitration. Either party or both parties shall be entitled to attend, but only for the purpose of identifying for the Arbitrator the subject-matter of the dispute or any relevant part(s).

14. Where, under Article 5, the Arbitrator has directed that a hearing be held, he shall, in consultation with the parties, fix a date and venue for the hearing at the earliest opportunity.

15. Where, under Article 5, the Arbitrator has directed that the arbitration is to proceed on the basis of written submissions and documentary evidence only, the Arbitrator may nevertheless call the parties to an informal hearing solely for the purpose of seeking clarification of any matters arising from the parties' statements and supporting evidence.

16. If during the course of the arbitration, the Arbitrator concludes that the dispute is incapable of proper resolution in accordance with these Rules, or if, having directed otherwise under Article 5, he considers that a full formal hearing is after all required, he shall advise the parties of his alternative proposals for the conduct of the arbitration. The arbitration shall, unless otherwise directed by the Arbitrator, continue from the point already reached.

17. The parties may, by agreement at any time, serve notice on the Arbitrator that the arbitration shall no longer be conducted in accordance with these Rules.

18. The Arbitrator shall have the power to extend or vary any of the time limits stipulated in these Rules.

Costs

19. In making his award under these Rules, the Arbitrator shall, at his discretion, which shall be exercised judicially, order by whom and in what proportion the parties shall pay his fees and expenses. He shall also decide who shall pay the parties' own costs.

20. In determining the parties' liability for their own costs under Article 19, the Arbitrator shall award all costs which have been reasonably incurred, having received representations as to costs from the parties.

Miscellaneous

21. The Appointing Authority reserves the right to appoint a substitute arbitrator if the original appointee dies, is incapacitated or is for any reason unable to deal expeditiously with the dispute following acceptance of the appointment.

22. Awards made under these Rules shall be final and binding on the parties.

23. Neither the Appointing Authority nor the Arbitrator shall be liable to any party for any act or omission in connection with any arbitration conducted under these Rules.

24. The Short Form Arbitration Rules 1990 are hereby revoked.

SCHEDULE — JURISDICTION AND POWERS OF THE ARBITRATOR

Jurisdiction

The Arbitrator shall have jurisdiction to:

1. determine any question as to the existence, validity or termination of any contract between the parties;

2. order the rectification of any contract or the arbitration agreement, but only to the extent required to rectify any manifest error, mistake or omission which he determines to be common to all the parties;

3. determine any question of law arising in the arbitration;
4. determine any question as to his own jurisdiction, including any objections with respect to the existence or validity of the arbitration agreement or to his terms of reference;
5. determine any question of good faith, dishonesty or fraud arising in the dispute, if specifically pleaded by a party.

Powers

6. The Arbitrator shall, without prejudice to any powers conferred by these Rules, have power to:

   (a) allow any party, upon such terms (as to costs and otherwise) as he shall determine, to amend any statement of case, counterclaim, defence to counterclaim and reply, or any other submissions;

   (b) order the parties to produce relevant information, documents, goods or property for inspection, in their presence, by the Arbitrator;

   (c) order any party to produce to the Arbitrator and to the other party, a list of relevant documents for inspection, and to supply copies of any documents or classes of documents in their possession, custody or power which the Arbitrator determines to be relevant;

   (d) allow, limit or refuse to allow the appearance of witnesses, whether witnesses of fact or expert witnesses;

   (e) require, prior to any hearing, the exchange of witnesses' statements and of experts' reports;

   (f) appoint one or more experts to report to the Arbitrator on specific issues and to order a party to produce relevant information, documents, and (so far as is practicable) goods or property or samples thereof for inspection by the expert;

   (g) seek legal advice in such form as he thinks fit;

   (h) direct the parties, in such proportions as he deems just and in any manner he thinks fit, to make one or more deposits to secure the Arbitrator's fees and expenses;

   (i) order any party to provide security for the legal or other costs of any other party by way of deposit or bank guarantee or in any other manner the Arbitrator thinks fit;

    (j) order any party to provide security for all or part of any amount in dispute in the arbitration;

    (k) proceed in the arbitration notwithstanding the failure or refusal of any party to comply with these Rules or with his orders or directions, or to attend any meeting or hearing, but only after giving that party written notice that he intends to do so;

    (l) express awards in any currency;

    (m) issue an order for termination of the reference to arbitration if the parties agree to settle the dispute before an award is made or, if required by both parties, record the settlement in the form of a consent award.

7. If the parties agree, following an explanation by the Arbitrator of the consequences, the Arbitrator may exercise the following additional powers:

    (a) to conduct such enquiries as may appear to him to be necessary or expedient;

    (b) to order the preservation, storage, sale or other disposal of any property or thing under the control of any party;

    (c) to receive oral or written evidence from any party which he considers relevant, whether or not strictly admissible in law. In particular the Arbitrator may, at his discretion, receive secondary evidence and/or draw appropriate inferences from a party's conduct where that party fails to comply with an order made by the Arbitrator;

    (d) to make an award on the basis of fairness and reasonableness, without necessarily being bound by mandatory rules of law.

Practice Directions

PRACTICE NOTE (CIVIL LITIGATION: CASE MANAGEMENT) [1995] 1 ALL ER 385

Lord Taylor of Gosforth CJ gave the following practice direction at the sitting of the court.

1. The paramount importance of reducing the cost and delay of civil litigation makes it necessary for judges sitting at first instance to assert greater control over the preparation for and conduct of hearings than has hitherto been customary. Failure by practitioners to conduct cases economically will be visited by appropriate orders for costs, including wasted costs orders.

2. The court will accordingly exercise its discretion to limit: (a) discovery; (b) the length of oral submissions; (c) the time allowed for the examination and cross-examination of witnesses; (d) the issues on which it wishes to be addressed; and (e) reading aloud from documents and authorities.

3. Unless otherwise ordered, every witness statement shall stand as the evidence-in-chief of the witness concerned.

4. RSC Ord 18, r 7 (facts not evidence, to be pleaded) will be strictly enforced. In advance of trial parties should use their best endeavours to agree which are the issues or the main issues, and it is their duty so far as possible to reduce or eliminate the expert issues.

5. RSC Ord 34, r 10(2)(a) to (c) (the court bundle) will also be strictly enforced. Documents for use in court should be in A4 format where possible, contained in suitably secured bundles, and lodged with the court at least two clear days before the hearing of an application or a trial. Each bundle should be paginated, indexed, wholly legible, and

arranged chronologically and contained in a ring binder or a lever-arch file. Where documents are copied unnecessarily or bundled incompetently the cost will be disallowed.

6. In cases estimated to last for more than ten days a pre-trial review should be applied for or in default may be appointed by the court. It should when practicable be conducted by the trial judge between eight and four weeks before the date of trial and should be attended by the advocates who are to represent the parties at trial.

7. Unless the court otherwise orders, there must be lodged with the listing officer (or equivalent) on behalf of each party no later than two months before the date of trial a completed pre-trial check-list in the form annexed to this practice direction.

8. Not less than three clear days before the hearing of an action or application each party should lodge with the court (with copies to other parties) a skeleton argument concisely summarising that party's submissions in relation to each of the issues, and citing the main authorities relied upon, which may be attached. Skeleton arguments should be as brief as the nature of the issues allows, and should not without leave of the court exceed 20 pages of double-spaced A4 paper.

9. The opening speech should be succinct. At its conclusion other parties may be invited briefly to amplify their skeleton arguments. In a heavy case the court may in conjunction with final speeches require written submissions, including the findings of fact for which each party contends.

10. This discretion applies to all lists in the Queen's Bench and Chancery Divisions, except where other directions specifically apply.

Pre-trial check-list

[Short title of action]
[Folio number]
[Trial date]
[Party lodging check-list]
[Name of solicitor]
[Name(s) of counsel for trial (if known)]

Setting down

1. Has the action been set down?

Pleadings

2. (a) Do you intend to make any amendment to your pleading?
(b) If so, when?

Interrogatories

3. (a) Are any interrogatories outstanding?
(b) If so, when served and upon whom?

Evidence

4. (a) Have all orders in relation to expert, factual and hearsay evidence been complied with? If not, specify what remains outstanding.
(b) Do you intend to serve/seek leave to serve/any further report or statement? If so, when and what report statement?
(c) Have all other orders in relation to oral evidence been complied with?
(d) Do you require any further leave or orders in relation to evidence? If so, please specify and say when will you apply.

5. (a) What witnesses of fact do you intend to call? [Name]
(b) What expert witnesses do you intend to call? [Name]
(c) Will any witness require an interpreter? If so, which?

Documents

6. (a) Have all orders in relation to discovery been complied with?
(b) If not, what orders are outstanding?
(c) Do you intend to apply for any further orders relating to discovery?
(d) If so, what and when?

7. Will you not later than seven days before trial have prepared agreed paginated bundles of fully legible documents for the use of counsel and the court?

Pre-trial review

8. (a) Has a pre-trial review been ordered?
(b) If so, when is it to take place?

(c) If not, would it be useful to have one?

Length of trial

9. What are counsels' estimates of the minimum and maximum lengths of the trial? [The answer to question 9 should ordinarily be supported by an estimate of length signed by the counsel to be instructed.]

Alternative dispute resolution (See Practive Note [1994] 1 ALL ER 34, [1994] 1 WLR 14)

10. Have you or counsel discussed with your client(s) the possibility of attempting to resolve this dispute (or particular issues) by alternative dispute resolution (ADR)?

11. Might some form of ADR procedure assist to resolve or narrow the issues in this case?

12. Have you or your client(s) explored with the other parties the possibility of resolving this dispute (or particular issues) by ADR?

[Signature of the solicitor, date]

Note This check-list must be lodged not later than two months before the date of hearing with copies to the other parties.

PRACTICE NOTE (COMMERCIAL COURT ALTERNATIVE DISPUTE RESOLUTION) [1994] 1 ALL ER 34

Cresswell J made the following statement at the sitting of the court:

'While emphasising the primary role of the Commercial Court as a forum for deciding commercial cases the judges of the court wish to encourage parties to consider the use of alternative dispute resolution (ADR), such as mediation and conciliation, as a possible additional means of resolving particular issues or disputes. The judges will not act as mediators or be involved in any ADR process but will in appropriate cases invite parties to consider whether their case, or certain issues in their case, could be resolved by means of ADR. By way of example only, ADR might be tried where the costs of litigation are likely to be wholly disproportionate to the amount at stake.

The Clerk to the Commercial Court will keep a list of individuals and bodies that offer mediation, conciliation and other ADR services. It would be inappropriate for the Commercial Court to recommend any individual or organisation for this purpose. The list will also include individuals and bodies that offer arbitration services.

This practice statement will be drawn to the attention of all persons commencing proceedings in the Commercial List.

Appendix IV (information for the summons for directions) and App VI (pre-trial check list) to the *Guide to Commercial Court Practice (see The Supreme Court Practice 1993* vol 1, paras 72/A1-72/A31) will be amended to include additional questions to ensure that legal advisers in all cases consider with their clients and other parties concerned the possibility of attempting to resolve the particular dispute or particular issues by mediation, conciliation or otherwise.

While the Commercial Court will remain the appropriate forum for deciding most disputes in its list, legal advisers should ensure that parties are fully informed as to the most cost effective means of resolving the particular dispute.'

Settlement Agreements, Tomlin Order and Consent Award

SETTLEMENT AGREEMENT[1]

Standard Form Only

(This document is intended to serve as a standard form model to help mediators and parties to reduce to writing settlement terms agreed in mediation. In all cases it should be adapted with care to the specific requirements of the situation, and parties should rely on their own legal or other advice in relation to its terms and effect)

THIS AGREEMENT is between

(1) [   ] of [   ] ('   ');

(2) [   ] of [   ] ('   ');

(together 'the Parties'):

DATED [   ]

RECITALS

Whereas:—

(1) The Parties were in dispute regarding various matters:

---

1 This agreement is reproduced by kind permission of the CEDR, Centre for Dispute Resolution, 100 Fetter Lane, London EC4A 1DD, tel: 0171 430 1852, fax: 0171 430 1846.

(2) The Parties have reached agreement as to the terms of settlement of those matters by way of mediation under the auspices of the Centre for Dispute Resolution, 100 Fetter Lane London, EC4A 1DD ('CEDR') pursuant to an agreement between them, CEDR and [   ] ('the Mediator'), dated [   ] ('the Mediation Agreement').

(3) The terms of such agreement are set out below and the Parties intend this document to constitute a binding contract between them in respect of such terms.

[(4) The parties have reached agreement as to the terms of settlement of some, but not all, of the matters in dispute between them. The terms of such agreement are set out below and the Parties intend this document to constitute a binding contract between them in respect of such matters. In respect of the remaining matters upon which no settlement terms have been agreed, the Parties wish to reserve all their rights to take such action as they may think fit.]

OPERATIVE TERMS

1. Warranty of authority

Comment

Although each Party and signatory should attend the Mediation with appropriate authority to bind themselves and their principals a warranty to that effect may be useful to focus their minds and give force to their assertions.

Sample clause

1.1 Each Party warrants and undertakes to the other(s) that it has full right, power and entitlement to enter into this agreement without further reference to any other person(s).

1.2 Each signatory warrants and undertakes to the Parties that he has full right power and entitlement to execute this agreement on behalf of the Party whom he represents.

2. Terms of Settlement

Comment

2.1 Substantive terms of the Settlement (it may well be helpful, for ease of reference, to include these in an Appendix to this Agreement).

2.2 Consider whether any timetable is necessary for the performance of the Agreement, and whether it will take immediate effect.

2.3 Consider how the Agreement will be enforced and how performance will be monitored or assessed (NB CEDR and/or the Mediator can play a very valuable role in this area).

2.4 Consider whether there are any contractual formalities which will be required to give effect to the Agreement (eg, ensure consideration passes between the Parties (it almost always will in practice), if land is involved how will a valid transfer be effected, etc).

2.5 If the Agreement is to be contingent on certain things:-

—What are they?
—Is there a timetable for performance?
—How will performance be assessed?
—What will happen if the contingent events do not happen, or happen late?

3. Future breaches

Comment

The Mediation Agreement sometimes provides that failure to give effect to any of the terms of this Agreement will entitle the other Party(ies) to be released from it. Consider whether this is actually what the Parties want, and if so whether it should apply to a breach of any of the terms of this Agreement or only of the more significant ones (ie, whether a technical breach of a minor term should provide a pretext for rescinding this Agreement).

4. Future disputes

Comment

This Agreement provides a useful opportunity to decide how any future disputes arising out of this Agreement will be dealt with.

Appendix 7

Sample clause

4.1 If any dispute or disagreement arises in relation to any matter which is the subject of this Agreement, the parties will attempt in good faith to resolve it promptly through negotiation between senior executives of the Parties having authority to settle it. If the matter is not resolved, the Parties will refer it to mediation under the auspices of CEDR [and will appoint [the Mediator] as mediator.]

5. Existing proceedings

Comment

In most cases the agreement reached will be in full and final settlement of all claims arising in relation to the matters in dispute and will involve the withdrawal of all court or similar proceedings by all Parties. This should be expressly stated in this Agreement. (Care should be taken where the Mediation has resulted in the settlement of some but not all of the matters in dispute, to ensure that those in each category are clearly identified.) Consider also the position as to costs in existing litigation.

Sample clause

5.1 This Agreement is entered into in full and final settlement of all claims [and counterclaims] arising in relation to any and all disputes the subject of the Mediation Agreement. Any and all court or similar proceedings issued in respect of such matters shall be withdrawn forthwith, [and each Party shall bear its own legal costs incurred in those proceedings].

6. Matters not resolved by mediation

Comment

Where some matters are not resolved in the Mediation, it may be useful to list them (for clarity) and to state expressly that the Parties are free to pursue these matters as they see fit, or alternatively to provide for some other agreed means of dealing with them.

254

Sample clause

6.1 The Parties acknowledge that they have not been able to agree terms of settlement in relation to the matters set out in [Appendix [B]] below and that each reserves its rights in relation thereto.

7. The Mediation Agreement

Comment

Remember that the Parties are still governed by the Mediation Agreement. It may be helpful expressly to terminate the Mediation, and confirm that the Mediation Agreement remains in force following termination of the Mediation.

Sample clause

7.1 The Mediation is hereby terminated pursuant to Clause [7] of the Mediation Agreement.

7.2 Notwithstanding Clause 7.1 above, the Mediation Agreement shall continue to bind the Parties, in particular as regards Clauses 9.1, 10.1, 10.2, 10.3, and 12 thereof.

8. Future agreements

Comment

Where an agreement envisages the execution of further agreements in order to give effect to it, consider whether or not it will be binding on the Parties (an agreement to agree not being enforceable, as a matter of law). If the Parties envisaged, say, the execution of a distribution agreement between them as part of the terms of settlement, consider whether it is possible to agree at least the salient features of such an agreement, so that there is less chance of the settlement subsequently breaking down over such terms.

9. Conflicting agreements

Comment

For clarity, it may be useful to stipulate that this Agreement overrides any existing agreements which have conflicting provisions.

255

Sample clause

9.1 The terms of this Agreement override any previous agreements between the Parties to the extent that there is any inconsistency.

10. Costs of the Mediation

Comment

The Mediation Agreement will (typically) require each Party to bear its own costs in relation to the Mediation. If this is to be altered as part of the final settlement, it should be expressly stated.

11. Governing law

Comment

This is very likely to be the laws of England, but it may be worth saying so for clarity.

12. Execution

Comment

Obviously all the Parties will have to sign the Agreement. If there is concern over whether any of the representatives has authority to bind the Party he represents, it may be possible to get his/her personal signature to the Agreement to give effect to clause 1.2 above. Failing that, Clause 1.2 can be amended to constitute a warranty given by the Parties, rather than the signatories.

APPENDIX A
Main Terms of Settlement

APPENDIX B
Matters not resolved by Mediation

HEADS OF AGREEMENT (SHORT FORM)[1]

THIS AGREEMENT is made between:

(1) [   ]

and

(2) [   ]

following mediation under the auspices of
CENTRE FOR DISPUTE RESOLUTION of 100 Fetter Lane, London
EC4A 1DD.

THIS AGREEMENT is made on:

(4) [   ] day of [   ] 199[   ]

    at [   ]

(5) between the representatives of the Parties (both of whom have full
authority to sign on behalf of the parties)

[   ]

[   ]

(6) in the presence of [   ] (the Mediator)

(8) in the matter of [   ]
referred to in the CEDR Mediation Agreement between the Parties,
CEDR, and [the Mediator], and dated [   ]

1. AGREEMENT

1.1 The following Settlement is binding on both Parties upon signature.
Initialling of each clause confirms that such clause accurately
reflects the settlement terms.

1.2 This Settlement supersedes the terms of all previous agreements
between the Parties in respect of the matters the subject of the mediation.

1.3 The details of this Settlement shall be confidential and not disclosed
to a third party without the express written consent of the other
Party.

1.4 The terms of this Settlement shall have immediate effect.

---

1 This agreement is reproduced by kind permission of the CEDR, Centre for Dispute
Resolution,. 100 Fetter Lane, London, EC4A 1DD, tel: 0171 430 1852, fax: 0171 430
1846.

Appendix 7

2. THE SETTLEMENT

2.1 [   ]

3. CONCLUSION

3.1 Fulfilment of this Agreement will be in full and final settlement of all claims by each Party upon the other.

[3.2 Failure by one party to fulfil [certain provisions] this Agreement will release both parties from the terms of this Agreement.]

3.3 In the event of a dispute arising from the terms of this Agreement, the disputed matter shall immediately be referred to the [Centre for Dispute Resolution]. Such referral shall not prejudice this Agreement.

3.4 It is a condition of this Agreement that the Mediator will not be called by either Party as witness in any proceedings between the parties regarding the subject matter of this mediation.

DATED the [   ] day of [   ] 199[   ]

SIGNED . . . .
for and on behalf of

SIGNED . . . .
for and on behalf of

SIGNED . . . .
Mediator

PRECEDENT TOMLIN ORDER

UPON hearing Counsel/Solicitors for the parties [and upon reading...] AND BY CONSENT

1. IT IS ORDERED that all further proceedings in this action be stayed upon the terms of settlement agreed between the parties set out in the Schedule herein [and that there be no order as to costs]

2. IT IS FURTHER ORDERED that all further proceedings in this action be stayed except for the purpose of carrying this order and the said terms into effect and for this purpose the parties are at liberty to apply

THE SCHEDULE

Dated the   day of   199

PRECEDENT CONSENT AWARD

IN THE MATTER OF THE ARBITRATION ACTS 1950 AND 1979

AND

IN THE MATTER OF THE INSTITUTION OF CIVIL ENGINEERS' ARBITRATION PROCEDURE (1983)/JCT ARBITRATION RULES (1988) / THE CHARTERED INSTITUTE OF ARBITRATORS ARBI-TRATION RULES (1988)

AND

IN THE MATTER OF AN ARBITRATION

BETWEEN:

Claimant

and

Respondent

CONSENT AWARD

WHEREAS:

1. By a contract [under seal] dated   day of   19   the Claimant
    (Limited) undertook for the Respondent (Limited)
2. Clause   of the Contract provides for the settlement of disputes or differences by a Sole Arbitrator whose appointment is to be by mutual agreement of the Parties to the Contract or failing such agreement by appointment by the President of
3. Disputes and differences have arisen between the Parties.

4. By a letter dated   199   the Respondent invited me, ABC of . . . to act as Sole Arbitrator in the dispute the Claimant having previously agreed with the Respondent that I be invited to act.

or

4. On the   day of 199   The President of   appointed me ABC of . . . as sole Arbitrator to determine the dispute between the parties.

5. I accepted the appointment in the disputes on   day of   199   and entered upon the reference.

6. Having heard the parties appearing by their Counsel/Solicitors AND BY CONSENT I HEREBY AWARD AND DIRECT as set out in the attached Schedule

IN WITNESS WHEREOF I have hereunto set my hand this   day of 199

[THE SCHEDULE]

Signed . . . .

Witness . . . .

APPENDIX 8

Case Examples

CEDR MEDIATION RECORD

Some examples

NOTE: The examples listed are given with deliberately generalised and limited information to ensure absolute confidentiality to the parties. They are also a selection only of the mediations arranged by CEDR.

Professional negligence claim valued at £200,000 successfully mediated in one day.

£24m Lloyds insurance market dispute settled in a two-day mediation.

Contractual dispute between a UK company and a Belgian company valued at £150,000 successfully resolved in a one-day mediation conducted in French and English.

Dispute involving a factoring company and an outstanding debt of £5,000 settled in one day.

Pension dispute worth £42,000 between trustees of a pension scheme and an insurance company successfully mediated in one day.

Dispute values at £75,000 arising in connection with a contract to advertise services settled in one day.

£25,000 construction dispute involving a utilities company and private company successfully resolved in one day's mediation.

Professional indemnity dispute between a firm of solicitors and a company settled in one day. The solicitor for the company commented that his client was well satisfied with the process and the result.

£20,000 professional negligence dispute against a firm of accountants successfully mediated in one day.

Motor manufacturing company and machinery supply company involved in £150,000 dispute settled in one day.

Multi-million pound dispute involving a financial services group and a multinational company arising out of alleged breaches of warranty and misrepresentation successfully mediated in three days.

£140,000 professional indemnity dispute involving a design company and a firm of accountants resolved in one day's mediation.

$38 million machinery supplies contract dispute between a Scandinavian trader and an Asian wood pulp processing company settled in three days.

£70,000 insurance dispute involving the lease of machinery to a manufacturing company which subsequently went into receivership resolved in one day.

Three party dispute involving a customer, supplier and contractor arising out of a contract to repair a bridge successfully mediated in one day.

Multi-million pound international utilities dispute successfully resolved in a five-day mediation.

£15,000 construction dispute involving a local authority settled in one day.

£140,000 dispute arising out of various office equipment leasing contracts successfully resolved in one day.

£65,000 dispute arising between a design and marketing company and a local authority over the production of marketing literature successfully mediated in one day.

£17,000 dispute arising between a large supplier and their client over a contract for photocopying services successfully resolved in one day with the preservation of the working business relationship.

Dispute arising over claim for payment for supply of equipment and £82,000 counterclaim for failure of that equipment settled in one day's mediation.

Four-party construction dispute involving a claim for £2.8 million and counterclaim for £365,000 successfully resolved in a four-day mediation.

£51,000 dispute involving major supplier and their client arising out of the supply of photocopying machines successfully mediated in one day.

Five-party dispute concerning various office equipment leasing agreements settled in one day.

Main ADR Providers

COMMERCIAL AND CIVIL DISPUTES

Centre for Dispute Resolution (CEDR)
100 Fetter Lane
London EC4A 1DD
tel: 0171 430 1852
fax: 0171 430 1846

ADR Net
Equity & Law Building
36–38 Baldwin Street
Bristol, BS1 1NR
tel: 0117 925 2090
fax: 0117 929 4429

Academy of Experts
116–118 Chancery Lane
London WC2A 1PP
tel: 0171 637 0333
fax: 0171 637 1893

FAMILY/DIVORCE DISPUTES

Family Mediators Association
The Old House
Rectory Gardens
Henbury
Bristol BS10 7AQ
tel and fax: 01272 500140

National Family Mediation
9 Tavistock Place
London
WC1H 9SN
tel: 0171 383 5993
fax: 0171 383 5994

EMPLOYMENT DISPUTES

Advisory Conciliation and Arbitration Service (ACAS)
Head Office
27 Wilton Street
London SW1X 7AZ
tel: 0171 210 3000
fax: 0171 210 3919

Centre for Dispute Resolution (CEDR)
(details above)

ENVIRONMENTAL DISPUTES

Environment Council
21 Elizabeth Street
London
SW1W 9RP
tel: 0171 824 8411
fax: 0171 730 9941

Centre for Dispute Resolution (CEDR)
(details above)

COMMUNITY/NEIGHBOURHOOD DISPUTES

Mediation UK
82a Gloucester Road
Bishopston
Bristol BS7 8BN
tel: 0117 924 1234
fax: 0117 944 1387

In addition, a number of local community-based schemes exist. Details
are usually available from the local Council, or Citizens Advice Bureau.

APPENDIX 10

Further Reading

Acland, Andrew, *A Sudden Outbreak of Common Sense*, (1990) Hutchinson Business Books

Acland, Andrew, *Resolving Disputes Without Going to Court: A Consumer's Guide to Alternative Dispute Resolution*, (1995) Century Business Books

Bevan, Alex, *Alternative Dispute Resolution*, (1992) Sweet and Maxwell

Brown, Henry and Marriot, Arthur, *ADR: Practice and Principles*, (1993) Sweet and Maxwell

Dauer, Edward, *Manual of Dispute Resolution: ADR Law and Practice*, Shepard's/McGraw-Hill Inc

Doyle, Stephen and Haydock, Roger, *Without the Punches; Resolving Disputes without Litigation*, Equilaw

Goldberg, Stephen, Sander, Frank, and Rogers, Nancy, *Dispute Resolution: Negotiation, Mediation and Other Processes*, Little, Brown and Company

Mackie, Karl J, *A Handbook of Dispute Resolution*, (1991) Routledge.

Wilkinson, John, *Donovan Leisure Newton and Irvine ADR Practice Book*, Wiley Law Publications

Further Reading

Index

Index

Learning Resources
Centre